Cup & Cross

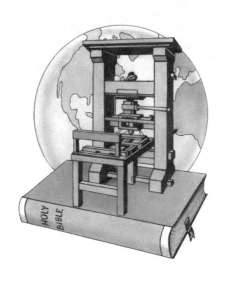

By
Michael S. Martin

Rod and Staff Publishers, Inc.
P.O. Box 3, Hwy. 172
Crockett, Kentucky 41413
Telephone: 606-522-4348

Copyright 2005
Rod and Staff Publishers, Inc.
Crockett, Kentucky 41413

Printed in U.S.A.

Hardcover edition ISBN 0-7399-2366-8
Catalog no. 2316

Paper edition ISBN 0-7399-2425-7
Catalog no. 2318

2   3   4   5   6   —   19   18   07   16   15   14   13   12   11   10

Contents

Introduction

The goal for this book is to tell the story of Anabaptism in a way that the average reader can get an overview of the movement, and to discover what the Anabaptists believed and taught. I have tried to be fair with their strengths and weaknesses, to help us profit practically from this history.

To help the reader gain a clearer, overall picture of Anabaptism, I did not mention unnecessary names, dates, locations, and details.[1] Rather, I emphasized the main points of the Anabaptist story and included material about Anabaptist church life, family life, and economic experiences. The historical material in this book was drawn from over fifty history books, most of which are too specialized to interest the average reader, and some of which are no longer in print. This compilation will keep valuable information available to those who do not have access to these older books.

Most of the available books that interpret Anabaptist teachings are written by authors who do not believe in Bible-based church life. They may accurately portray what the Anabaptists taught but also imply or state that those teachings have little relevance to modern times. It is fine to discover what the Anabaptists taught back in the 1500s, these historians say, but we have no idea what they would say or do in our situation.

---

[1] More in-depth information is available in *Mennonites in Europe* or in the other books listed in the bibliography.

Other historians misinterpret the Bible doctrines the Anabaptists held and capitalize on their mistakes. For example, their Biblical nonresistance is sometimes interpreted as nonviolent resistance. Their unclear teaching on divorce can be used to undermine the clear Bible teaching. The Anabaptists emphasized the priesthood of all believers and the importance of hiding God's Word in the heart. Some interpret this to mean that the Anabaptist church exercised little authority in its members' lives and promoted inner spirituality but gave little attention to correct doctrine. Actually, the Anabaptists saw the priesthood of all believers and the authority of the congregation as mutually indispensable. Likewise, they believed that genuine spirituality and pure doctrine complemented each other in the Christian's life rather than opposing each other.

In this book, the basis of interpreting Anabaptist teachings is threefold. (1) The Anabaptists were a Bible-based church; therefore, their teachings and lives are relevant to Bible-based churches today. (2) The Anabaptists made mistakes, just as all men do. Thus, the Word of God, not Anabaptism, is the authority for our churches. (3) Because the early Anabaptists lived according to the Scriptures, we are not ashamed to embrace the Bible teachings they taught and pattern our lives after their example of Biblical discipleship. Although they made some mistakes, we still appreciate the spiritual heritage of their commitment.

As we study Anabaptism, we face some handicaps. We did not live in Anabaptist times, and the sources from which we draw our information may be prejudiced. Also, we tend to slant the material to suit our own biases. However, through the combined efforts of the editor, reviewers, and other publishing personnel, this work represents not only the author's views but also the understanding of other brethren.

The first part of this book tells the story of Swiss, Dutch, and Hutterite Anabaptism. The second part discusses Anabaptist beliefs on the Scriptures, the church, discipleship, and the civil state. Appendix I tells of various remnants that existed from the 300s through the 1500s and discusses the relationship of these remnants to the rise of Anabaptism. The other three appendixes are Swiss Anabaptist documents referred to in this book.

I am not a historian in the professional sense. I am only a history student and am deeply indebted to the historians of the 1900s who translated many Anabaptist documents into English. Without them, this book would not exist.

Most of all, I thank the Lord, by whom I have obtained mercy and the undeserved privilege of being included in the Remnant. My prayer is that this book will contribute to the growth and maintenance of that Remnant.

Michael S. Martin

Part One

Anabaptist History

Chapter 1

The Background of the Reformation

The Fall of Mainstream Christianity

In the A.D. 60s, the Roman emperor Nero began the first official persecution of the Christian church. During the next centuries, thousands of believers suffered and died for their faith.

Persecution continued in varying degrees until A.D. 313, when Constantine gained control of the western part of the Roman Empire. He publicly recognized Christianity, as represented by the mainstream church, and became its protector.[1] He did not make Christianity the state religion, but he made it a legal religion. (He also protected pagan religions.) Later, Emperor Theodosius I (347–395) made Christianity the state religion and restricted heathen worship.[2]

---

[1] The mainstream church was generally known as the Catholic Church at this time.

[2] Much of the legislation for the "Christian" state came about under Theodosius. However, the concepts that led to the marriage of church and state were largely formed under Constantine.

Constantine's main interest was the unity and moral excellence of the church, which he apparently wanted to use as a political tool.[3] He was not a godly man, and he was not interested in the discipleship of true Christianity.

Before Constantine's time, the church had already lost much of her purity. For example, "Christians" appeared in the Roman military by the end of the second century. Around the same time, the church began to venerate martyrs and believed that faithful martyrs could atone for sins.[4] During the toleration that resulted from the policies of Constantine and his successors, the church grew rapidly but it declined in purity even more rapidly.[5] So-called Christianity became a way to obtain worldly prestige and political power.

The declining purity of the church led to asceticism, a teaching borrowed from Eastern pagan religions. Hermits, monks, and nuns withdrew from decaying "Christian" society, believing that the way to true holiness was to withdraw from worldly cares and possessions and practice strict, physical discipline.

The hierarchy of the church became more complex during this period. The positions of archbishops and patriarchs developed. The archbishops ruled over a number of bishops, and the patriarchs ruled over the archbishops.

Pagan practices, worldliness, religious hierarchy, and ties between church and state gradually caused the downfall of the mainstream church. Some believers remained faithful throughout this period of apostasy, but history

---

[3] Philip Schaff, *History of the Christian Church,* vol. 3, 13–18. Leonard Verduin, *The Anatomy of a Hybrid,* 95–99.

[4] Philip Schaff, *History of the Christian Church,* vol. 2, 82–84.

[5] Lester Bauman, *Wolves in the Flock* (Crockett, Ky.: Rod and Staff Publishers, Inc., 2001) 62–64.

has not recorded many of them. (Some of them are discussed in Appendix I.) The true church has always stood, for Jesus said, "I will build my church; and the gates of hell shall not prevail against it" (Matthew 16:18).

The Growth of the Medieval Catholic Church

What does *medieval* mean? Historians give various titles to the era in Europe lasting from about A.D. 400 to 1500. *Middle Ages* and *Medieval Era* both describe the same period. (The word *medieval* comes from two Latin words meaning "middle age.") *Dark Ages* generally describes only the first five hundred to six hundred years of the Middle Ages. The entire era is a "middle age" in that it spans the gap between ancient culture and the contemporary world.

MEDIEVAL TIMES

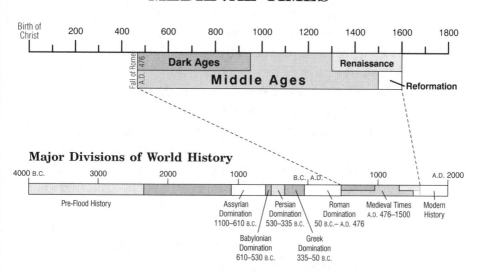

The Age of Faith is another name sometimes used for medieval times because religion was typically at the center of medieval life. Most people did not think for themselves, especially in spiritual matters. Few of them could read, and few had access to the Bible. They simply had faith that they would get to heaven if they submitted to the Catholic Church.

Early in the Middle Ages, the Roman Catholic Church was the one source of stability in politically unsettled Europe. The western part of the Roman Empire had fallen in A.D. 476, and barbarian tribes had taken over some of the empire. Roman trade, education, and civilization declined in the barbarian culture that resulted. The order and stability of the Catholic Church helped to maintain some elements of Roman culture, such as education and care for the poor, sick, and aged.[6] Thus the Catholic Church became the heart of society.

Originally, all the patriarchs had equal authority, but later the patriarch at Rome became the head of all the patriarchs, or the *pope* (a word derived from the Latin word *papa,* meaning "father"). This rise in power and prestige was partly because Rome was the largest and wealthiest city of that time as well as the capital of the Roman Empire. According to the Catholics, Peter was the first bishop of Rome.[7] They believe that Christ made Peter His authoritative representative on earth and that all popes since Peter have held this special authority.

As the church grew in numbers, it also gained power and wealth. Church leaders began to assume political power in addition to their religious roles. If a king did not submit to the pope, the pope could place the offending king or his whole country under the interdict. This was a church censure that prohibited people in question from partaking in most of the sacraments or having a Christian burial. Since the people were taught that

---

[6] Jewish society, scattered in pockets throughout Europe, also provided some of these elements of civilization. Some of the Jewish hospitals, orphanages, and homes for the aged and the poor served "Christian" society as well as the Jews.

[7] History does not confirm this supposition.

these ceremonies were necessary for salvation, they became very agitated against kings who did not submit to the pope. If only the king was under the interdict, the pope said his subjects did not need to obey him. This usually forced the king to accept the pope's demands.

The Catholic Church became the final authority in interpreting the Scriptures and in making practical applications. They believed that the Scriptures were God's Word, but they held that the traditions of the church were of equal or greater importance. Church teachings were authoritative, not because they were Biblical, but because the church taught them.

Worshiping Mary was one false Catholic practice. Another error was worshiping saints. Closely tied to this was the error of attaching importance to relics, or objects such as pieces of clothing that were associated with saints. Relics supposedly associated with Christ, such as straw from the manger or drops of sweat from Gethsemane, were especially important. Of course, many or all of the relics were fakes.

The Catholics also taught many wrong doctrines about baptism, sin, death, and communion. They baptized all the newborn babies into the church and did not require members to be converted. They taught that priests could forgive sins and that certain physical acts of penance were necessary to make amends for sins. In the rite of extreme unction, a priest could supposedly forgive a dying person's sins. In their communion service, known as the mass, they believed that the bread and wine became the actual flesh and blood of Jesus Christ. This was called transubstantiation. Many people also thought that the bread and wine had miraculous healing powers.

The Catholic Church taught that after death people bound for heaven must first suffer in purgatory, a place of temporary punishment for "small" unconfessed sins or for sins without sufficient penance. Another error, somewhat related to this, was the sale of indulgences. According to this teaching, Christ and the saints had a surplus of good works, called merits, which were stored in heaven and could be purchased by people on earth to atone for sin. The official slip of paper sold to the penitent sinner was called an indulgence. Besides buying atonement for personal wrongdoing, the church also taught that people could purchase a shortened stay in purgatory for others by buying indulgences. From this idea came the saying "As soon as a coin in the coffer rings, a soul from purgatory springs."

Superstition and religion often went hand in hand throughout the Middle Ages. Everyone was tied to the church; and they were baptized, married, and buried by the church. However, few people understood the full meaning and blessing of the Christian life. Worship services were a time to adore relics, confess sins to a priest, and hear imaginary tales about the deeds of saints or of the Christ-child.

Though the church pretended to be concerned about the "danger" of the common people interpreting the Scriptures wrongly, it was actually afraid that the common man's interpretation would be inconsistent with Catholic belief and practice. Because it taught that no one could be saved unless he followed Catholic teachings, the Catholic Church had great power over European civilization. To them, salvation was by works, not by faith. The Bible describes the error of this system: "In vain they do worship me, teaching for doctrines the commandments of men" (Matthew 15:9).

The Renaissance

During the Middle Ages, education was confined mostly to church and political leaders. Even among these leaders, education was often poor (some priests could not read). But as towns grew, a middle class emerged, and more common people sought education to help them in business. Also, trade with other countries introduced new ideas into European culture, which stimulated intellectual and cultural study. From the increased interest in education sprang a renewed interest in philosophy, theology, and the meaning of life.

The increased learning, wealth, and international communication brought about the Renaissance. This French word means "rebirth." The Renaissance attitude toward life was a sharp contrast to the outlook of the Middle Ages. In medieval times, men endured life's suffering in hope of the heavenly future that the Catholic Church promised them. But in the Renaissance, men began to glory in the past and present accomplishments of philosophers and "great" men and paid less attention to the hereafter. Renaissance scholars emphasized man's dignity, worth, and individuality.

Many Renaissance scholars believed that ignorance was the source of evil. They considered the Middle Ages a narrow-minded and ignorant time. They cultivated a wide interest in life and a strong quest for knowledge in history, science, and geography. These courses of study were sometimes called the liberal arts or the humanities; thus those who studied them were called Humanists. This was the beginning of the movement called *Humanism*.[8]

Humanism emphasized human abilities and led man to glorify himself. Like modern humanists, some Renaissance Humanists, especially those from Italy, scorned

---

[8] It could be said that Humanism began in the Garden of Eden with Adam and Eve's rebellion. But though rebellion and pride began in the Garden, Humanism as a philosophy only began in the Renaissance, and it is technically improper to refer to the worship of man by man as Humanism before that.

religion and altogether rejected the idea of a supernatural God. However, most Renaissance Humanists were milder than modern humanists. Many of them did not reject the idea of God. Some of them, especially in northern countries, such as the Netherlands, believed that man was the crowning work of God's creation. They emphasized the worth of each individual, as opposed to the degraded, oppressed status of many people in the Middle Ages. They were concerned about the problems that humans faced, and they sought some Bible answers for those problems. Some of them clearly saw that the Catholic Church was far from truth, but they were not willing to support a Biblical church. They favored gradual reform as a result of education rather than a radical revival of Biblical church life. They did not see the seriousness of disobeying God. Though their philosophy made room for God, it did not give God His rightful place.

The Humanists greatly valued the writings of ancient Greeks and Romans. The Renaissance fascination with ancient literature drove them to spend great sums and much time obtaining old manuscripts, including Bible manuscripts. These recovered writings revived the study of the Latin and Greek languages.

The Humanists were independent thinkers. They did not accept others' opinions without critically questioning their accuracy. They carefully examined established ideas to determine whether the ideas were correct according to their personal philosophies. Here lies a great difference between religious humanists and true Christians. Christians test all ideas by the Bible, not by their personal philosophies. And they do not regard their personal opinions in the same sense that humanists do. They simply let truth be their understanding of life.

The Reformation Begins

It seems that God used the Renaissance to help prepare Europe for the Reformation. The revival of interest in the Greek, Latin, and Hebrew languages also revived interest in Bible study. Renaissance scholars could not philosophically reason out everything, and some of them realized that the ancient Greek and Roman literature did not contain life's answers. Because of this, some of them saw the necessity of faith and belief in the Bible. This Bible study was an initial step away from the Catholic errors. As men studied, they began to question the wrong practices of the Catholic Church. In this way, the critical spirit of the Renaissance helped men such as Ulrich Zwingli, Conrad Grebel, and Felix Mantz to turn from the corrupted church and to study the simplicity and purity of the apostolic church.

The emphasis on education and the invention of the printing press also paved the way for church reformation. The common people had more opportunities to learn to read, and the printing press made literature more available than it had ever been. Greater literacy and availability of Bibles placed more people in a position to make sound, spiritual decisions.[9]

The Renaissance emphasis on the individuality of man helped some people to realize their personal accountability to God. Those who believed the Bible doctrine of personal accountability saw the error of submitting to priests and popes. The Bible clearly teaches that Jesus

---

[9] An illiterate person can be saved, but from New Testament times to the present, Christians have recognized that the ability to read and analyze is essential to maintaining the faith. A good understanding of personal accountability and spirituality is strongly enhanced by personally reading and comprehending the Bible. The New Testament emphasizes this many times. "Study to shew thyself approved unto God, a workman that needeth not to be ashamed, rightly dividing the word of truth" (2 Timothy 2:15).

Christ has made all believers "kings and priests unto God" (Revelation 1:6).

Martin Luther's stand against the evils of the Catholic Church (c. 1517) is generally regarded as the beginning of the Reformation. Luther influenced Ulrich Zwingli somewhat, but through following the Bible, Zwingli went further with his reforms than Luther did. Yet Zwingli failed to carry his reforms to their Biblical conclusion when the civil authorities stood against him. The New Testament church was not revived by the power and consent of the state, but rather in humble hearts and hamlets where common men and women placed their all on the altar.

Chapter 2

Church Reform Begins in Switzerland

Zurich was the principal city in the canton of Zurich, Switzerland. The canton was divided into parishes, each of which had a church, a local pastor, and a magistrate. The Zurich city council ruled the entire canton and appointed the magistrates and pastors. The peasants had no voice in the government. As in most of medieval Europe, the Catholic Church and the civil rulers exploited the common people.

Ulrich Zwingli, the Father of the Swiss Reformation

Ulrich Zwingli (1484–1531) served as a priest and preacher in several Swiss towns before the Zurich council offered him a position as head pastor in their main church. He accepted the offer and moved to Zurich in 1519 at the age of thirty-five.

Several years before, Zwingli had become interested in the writings of Desiderius Erasmus (c. 1466–1536).

Erasmus was a northern European scholar, who wrote against the corruption in Renaissance society and the Catholic Church. Although Erasmus' teaching had some deficiencies, he did emphasize studying the Bible and returning to the simple New Testament worship patterns. Through Erasmus' influence, Zwingli read the Scriptures with an open heart and developed a strong interest in spiritual things.

In traditional Catholic worship services, the leaders avoided some Scriptures and misinterpreted many others to support the corrupt church. From 1516 on, Zwingli left this pattern and preached more directly from the Bible. When he arrived in Zurich, he began his sermons in the Gospel of Matthew and preached through many of the New Testament books.

During this time Zwingli heard about Martin Luther's stand against Catholic errors. Initially, Erasmus, Luther, and Zwingli all hoped to reform the Catholic Church through Bible teaching. But when the Catholic Church excommunicated Luther in 1521, these men realized that the church was not interested in their reform efforts.[1] Erasmus remained within the Catholic Church,[2] but Luther and Zwingli were determined to have a Biblical church.

---

[1] Initially, the leaders of the Catholic Church showed little interest in reform. But the Catholic Church soon began to lose ground because of the Reformation. The Reformation also threatened the political stability of Europe, and even Catholic governments started to put pressure on the Catholic Church to eliminate some of the corruptions in the church. As a result, the Catholics began what was called the Counter Reformation, a movement promoting improvements in the Catholic Church, including better morals among the church leaders.

[2] Like most Humanists, Erasmus believed in reformation through education and was bitterly opposed to reformers such as Luther, Zwingli, and the Anabaptists, who divided the church. Although Erasmus stayed within the Catholic Church, he criticized the many abuses of the Scriptures, which the church promoted. Because of that, many dedicated Catholics despised him and accused him of "laying the egg that Luther hatched." Erasmus was tolerated, however, since he aimed his appeals at the scholarly community and did not try to stir up reform among the common people.

Although Erasmus and Luther influenced Zwingli to study the Bible and consider church reform, Zwingli's zeal for church reform came mainly from personal Bible study. And what did he find in the Bible? He found salvation by grace through faith, not by a performance of endless rituals. He also found the Spirit of God ruling in the believer's heart, not simply a conformity to debased, corrupt traditions. This is what he preached, and the simple Gospel message appealed to his listeners.

Zwingli began to zealously attack the corrupt religious authorities. He saw no reason why poor peasants should pay high taxes to support lazy monks and nuns. The Catholic leaders who used the sword to enforce compliance to their system were wolves, he said, not shepherds. For over three years, he preached to large congregations, and his audience clamored for reform.

The older pastors and some of the Zurich council members bitterly opposed Zwingli's unconventional message. The monks saw the potential threat to their status and reacted similarly. However, most of the city councilors sided with Zwingli.

Since the church and the state worked closely together, the religious leaders were very powerful and the church usually had the last word. The leading monks and the city authorities were always vying for the highest power. Quite likely, the majority of the Zurich council members sided with Zwingli for political rather than Scriptural reasons. For example, Zwingli taught that monks had no necessary function in Biblical Christianity, and so people despised the monks. The city council then used the situation as a way to wrest more authority and money for themselves.

The Swiss Reformation Begins

Zwingli's messages began to affect Zurich in practical ways. The council's respect for Zwingli became evident after he preached against mercenary fighting, the practice of sending Swiss soldiers to fight in foreign wars in exchange for money.[3] The Zurich council soon passed a law against this ancient practice. This was a sign that the council was listening to Zwingli instead of the Catholic Church.

A more important event took place on March 5, 1522, when a few of Zurich's citizens broke a very strictly observed Catholic rule. During Lent, Catholics could not eat any meat except fish. About ten men, including Zwingli, were together in a print shop. The shop owner's wife prepared two fried sausages, and each of the men except Zwingli ate a piece.

The news spread swiftly, and the council decided that things had gone too far. They imprisoned several of the men involved. Several neighboring Swiss cantons were Catholic strongholds, and they likely would declare war on Zurich if it moved too far from Catholicism. So, for safety's sake, the council upheld Catholicism by punishing those who had deliberately disobeyed the Catholic rule. They soon released the sausage eaters from prison but required them to make confessions and to stop their radical actions.

Zwingli did not get in trouble because he had not eaten any of the sausage, but he openly supported the offenders. Less than three weeks later, he preached a sermon titled "Concerning the Choice and Freedom of Foods," in which he clearly sided with those who had broken the fast. We need to understand, Zwingli preached, that the

---

[3] Zwingli's teaching against mercenary fighting was not because he believed in non-resistance, but because he, as a patriotic Swiss citizen, opposed the idea that the pope could draw on Swiss soldiers to fight Catholic wars. Some of the Swiss had questioned this idea for a long time. As long as Catholicism maintained an iron grip on the country, the pope had more authority than the Swiss government. But as soon as they saw Catholicism losing ground, many leaders were willing to turn a deaf ear to the pope's demands and assert their own authority.

kingdom of God is not a matter of food and drink. However, we should be careful that we do not offend others if they do not understand Christian liberty. Christians should not have to put up with unscriptural rules, he said, but neither should anyone break the old church rules according to his whims.

When news of this reached the Catholic bishop in charge of Zurich, he sent three delegates to persuade Zwingli and the Zurich council to uphold the Catholic faith more carefully. The delegates planned to threaten the council privately and convince them to squelch the "heresy," but Zwingli demanded and gained entrance into the hearing. He argued convincingly against the delegates, and the council decided to allow Zwingli to preach as he wished. The victory elated Zwingli and his supporters.[4]

Conrad Grebel and Felix Mantz

Among Zwingli's supporters were two young men, Conrad Grebel and Felix Mantz, who later became Anabaptist leaders. Conrad was the son of a respected city councilor, Jacob Grebel. Felix was the illegitimate son of a Zurich clergyman. Conrad was in his middle twenties, and Felix was possibly a bit older. Both had received university training in subjects such as Latin and Greek literature, philosophy, geography, and mathematics.

These two young men admired Zwingli's scholarship and church reform teachings. With a group of local pastors and other young scholars, they met with Zwingli regularly to study literature. They especially studied the Bible and hired a gifted scholar to teach them Hebrew. In these meetings they discussed many Reformation issues. Conrad and Felix heartily supported Zwingli until he began to give way to the Zurich council instead of following the Bible, as discussed later in this chapter.

---

[4] This did not mean that the council supported radical religious reform, but they chose on this particular issue to side with Zwingli rather than with traditional church authority. It was an initial step that eventually led the council to strongly support Zwingli's reformation goals.

The Monks' Opposition to the Gospel

Zwingli kept on preaching and writing in strong language. And the local monks fought back bitterly. There were three local monastic orders, and they all used their pulpits to denounce Reformation ideas. However, this violated an earlier council ruling that preachers could only preach Bible-based messages. As the monks realized that their support from local civil authorities was growing weak, they became increasingly antagonistic and sought additional support from the papal authorities outside the canton.

Several of Zwingli's young adherents, including Conrad Grebel, interrupted the monks' sermons when they taught unscriptural doctrines. Zwingli followed their example. At least once, this resulted in a monk leaving a monastery and supporting Reformation teachings. Notice the following account.

> On Saturday, July 12, a tall erect Barefoot Friar . . .
> Franz Lambert by name, . . . came from Avignon. . . .
> He was given permission to preach four sermons. . . .
> And in the fourth sermon he referred also to the intercession of Mary and the saints; . . . he requested a debate with Master Ulrich Zwingli, for before and during the last sermon he [Zwingli] had interrupted him publicly and said, "Brother, you are in error there."
>
> Thus on Wednesday, July 17, toward ten o'clock, in the barroom of the canons, they began to debate until after lunch around two o'clock. Master Ulrich brought along the Old and New Testaments in Greek and Latin and got the monk to the point of raising both hands, thanking God, and saying that he would in all his needs call only to God and abandon all coronas and rosaries and follow God. The next morning he rode to Basel to see Erasmus of Rotterdam also, and from Basel to Wittenberg to Dr. Martin Luther, who was an

Augustinian monk. There he discarded his robes and married a wife.[5]

The council received complaints against those who had interrupted the sermons, and called them in to account for their behavior. Conrad Grebel and Ulrich Zwingli were among those called. Following heated arguments between the monks and the reformers, the mayor admonished everyone to work together more peacefully.

Zwingli could not stand such a conciliatory attitude toward the monks. Indignantly he burst out, "I am bishop and priest in this town of Zurich, and to me is the care of souls entrusted. I have taken this oath, and not the monks. They should pay attention to me, and not I to them; and however boldly they preach what is untrue, I will counter it even if I have to stand in their own pulpit and contradict it. For we have no use for your begging friars, nor are you so regarded by God that we should have use for you."[6] The council saw that their effort at mediation had failed, and they conceded that Zwingli was right. The mayor then reinforced the previous decision that all preaching must agree with the Scriptures and admonished the monks to heed the ruling.

Rumors of Backsliding Alarm Zurich's Catholic Bishop

When rumors of the wayward Zurich churches continued to reach their Catholic bishop, he sent a letter to the churches and the city council, telling them to suppress the heresy and obey the doctrines and rites of the Catholic Church. In response, Zwingli and ten other reform-minded preachers sent a petition to the bishop. They pled with him to not injure the progress of the Gospel. Among other requests, they asked that he would

---

[5] Georg Finsler, ed., *Die Chronik des Bernhard Wyss 1519–1530* (Basel, 1901). Cited in Leland Harder, ed., *The Sources of Swiss Anabaptism,* 175.

[6] Ibid., 176.

allow church leaders and priests to marry. It seems that Zwingli and his friends were trying to reform their local churches with permission from the Catholic authorities.

Shortly after this, Zwingli wrote a book to the bishop, defending his teachings. He titled the work *Archeteles* (a Latin word meaning "the beginning and the end") because he hoped it would establish his authority to go ahead with church reformation and end his struggle with the bishop. In the book, Zwingli minced no words in telling the bishop how the situation stood.

> I have often said that a fair proportion of the bishops of our time are not real but counterfeit bishops, and I do not think I ought to be blamed for it either, since Isaiah calls them "dumb dogs,"[7] and Christ calls them "thieves and robbers."[8] I am speaking of those who have not entered into the sheepfold by the door. For you will find few who fill the office of bishop to the best of their ability, and do not rather conduct themselves as rulers and satraps and kings. . . .
>
> . . . They defend their own luxury when compared with the gospel simplicity . . . and think it right to regulate even the clearly divine ordinances according to their own sweet will. . . .
>
> . . . So far am I from yielding to you that unless you leave me and mine—that is, the sheep of Christ—in peace and quiet, I shall proceed to deal with you far more roughly, without fear of your words or your frowns. You must deal with me by means of the Holy Scriptures bestowed upon us by God (and do not forget that point), and they must not be twisted.[9]

Zwingli also wrote against Catholic errors such as practicing unscriptural ceremonies, selling indulgences,

---

[7] Isaiah 56:10.

[8] John 10:1.

[9] Ulrich Zwingli, *Apologeticus Archeteles,* published 8/22-23/1522. Jackson, trans., 1912. Cited in Leland Harder, ed., *The Sources of Swiss Anabaptism,* 182–185.

forbidding the clergy to marry, and forbidding laymen to read the Bible. "We ought to obey God rather than men," he declared. "The more unskilled a man is in human devices . . . the more clearly [God's] spirit informs him, as is shown by the apostles and by the foolish things of this world which God has chosen."[10]

The Council or the Gospel?

By 1523, Zwingli's reformation ideas were approaching a crisis. He was ready to radically reform Zurich's churches according to his understanding of the Gospel. However, the city council was still moving slowly toward reform, and Zwingli knew if he pushed things faster, he might endanger his entire reformation program. On the other hand, if he did not act soon on the Bible doctrines he now taught, his supporters would accuse him of fearing men more than God.

After weighing his options, Zwingli decided to persuade the council to let him go ahead with reform. His first step was to introduce a public doctrinal disputation. He appealed to the mayor and the city council for permission to hold a disputation between the Catholic supporters and himself. The council would sit as judges in the disputation and award the victory to the side presenting the best arguments.

The council members readily agreed to the idea and were perhaps flattered by their position in this debate. They invited everyone from the canton of Zurich, their Catholic bishop, and church leaders from surrounding cantons to attend. For discussion at the debate, Zwingli wrote and published sixty-seven articles that he considered to be Scriptural truths opposed by Roman Catholic doctrine and practice.

---

10 Ibid., 185.

On January 29, 1523, six hundred spectators met in the town hall to observe the disputation. The bishop himself did not come, but he sent an able debater as his representative. The debate ended in a decisive victory for Zwingli's side. The council decided that the Catholics had not presented valid arguments against Zwingli's teachings. Once more, they commanded all the priests and preachers within the canton to preach only that which could be proved by the Bible. They decided to deal with anyone who acted contrary to this ruling.

The action pleased Zwingli. The council had reaffirmed their previous decision to make Biblical preaching mandatory and to restrain preachers who disobeyed that order.[11] It was the first step the council had made toward officially approving religious reform.

Zwingli now felt that the council would follow his lead, so he stopped worrying about the Catholic Church authorities and questioned other Catholic traditions. He preached more strongly against the heavy taxes the poor common people paid to support the Catholic Church. Such teaching fell on fertile ground, for much of Europe was suffering under a heavy burden of church-imposed taxes.

Home Bible Studies

Small groups began to gather in homes to study the Bible and discuss the practical changes the Bible called for. Much of the discussion centered on the public's forced support of priests and monks. Many laymen participated in these meetings and spoke out against social injustices. Conrad Grebel and Felix Mantz attended such meetings.

In June 1523, as a result of the home gatherings and

---

[11] Notice that Zwingli never laid aside the idea of a state church, even though some of his statements sounded as if he was ready to reform the church regardless of the council. He continued to believe that men could and should be physically forced to obey the Bible.

Zwingli's preaching, several peasant villages asked the council to relieve them of their heavy tax burden. The council refused. This decision seriously disappointed Zwingli. Thus far, the council had moved with him step by step. Now it refused to take the next step. Either Zwingli would have to give up his confidence in the council as supporters of his reformation, or he would have to slow down the reformation he wanted them to implement. He chose the latter.

Several weeks after the disappointing council decision, Zwingli preached a message titled "On Divine and Human Justice," in which he taught that although the civil authorities could not legislate true faith, they were responsible to implement practical changes in religion. This way, Zwingli left the delicate practical changes for the civil government to implement and held himself responsible only to preach a spiritual message.[12]

This switch in emphasis gained Zwingli the continued favor of the council, but it also firmly established the council as the supreme authority in the church. Zwingli had not wanted that, but he was unwilling to take the consequences of disobeying the council. Previously, he had taught that men should follow truth regardless of anyone else. But now he began to preach more and more in favor of a state church. At this point, the more-committed reformation supporters, later known as Anabaptists, grew disillusioned with their leader.

The Second Doctrinal Disputation

Those who were interested in reform had differing ideas about what constituted the "pure Gospel" that the Zurich council had authorized.

---

[12] Civil issues such as taxation are in the jurisdiction of the state, so Zwingli was right to let the tax matter rest. He erred, however, when he left vital church issues also in the hands of the state.

Small bands of radicals, emerging from the various Bible study groups, wanted to see immediate religious reforms. For several years, Zwingli had preached against the use of images, and now the radicals acted on that teaching. In September 1523, radical groups removed images from churches and destroyed them. The city authorities briefly imprisoned the vandals, and two of them were banished.

Zwingli also regarded the mass as an abomination,[13] but he knew that radical actions could derail his reformation goals. If the council decided that the radical actions were Zwingli's fault, they could turn against him and his reform altogether. So he tried to keep reforms moving along fast enough to satisfy his supporters, but not so fast that he would lose the support of the council. Encouraged by the positive results from the first doctrinal disputation, he asked the council to hold a disputation to consider the validity of the mass and the use of images.

The council agreed, and on October 26–28, 1523, the second doctrinal disputation took place. Over eight hundred people attended the meeting. During the disputation, the participants found that the use of images was unscriptural, and they denounced the mass as an abomination to God.

At the close of the second day, Conrad Grebel, Simon Stumpf (a village pastor), and a few others were ready to see some practical changes. Here is an excerpt from the Zurich court records.

> Then arose Conrad Grebel and expressed the opinion that the priests should be given instructions while they were still together how henceforth to proceed with

---

[13] In the observance of the mass (the Roman Catholic version of Communion), the bread and wine supposedly turned into the actual body and blood of Christ. This was then offered as a sacrifice on an altar. Usually the priest drank the wine on behalf of the people.

the mass; for it would be futile if they did not begin to change the mass. Much has been said about the mass, but there would be no one who would be willing to stop this great abomination to God. . . .

Said Zwingli: "[The council] will discern how the mass should henceforth be properly observed."

Thereupon spoke Simon Stumpf: "Master Huldrych! You have no authority to place the decision in [the council's] hands, for the decision is already made: the Spirit of God decides. If therefore [the council] were to discern and decide anything that is contrary to God's decision, I will ask Christ for his Spirit and will teach and act against it."

Replied Zwingli: "That is right. I shall also preach and act against it if they decide otherwise. I do not give the decision into their hands."[14]

Zwingli then said that the disputation was to consider doctrinal matters. It was the council's duty to decide how to implement changes in religious practice. The doctrinal disputation closed with an exhortation to the pastors to strengthen their preaching against the mass and images. Zwingli strongly emphasized the need for everyone to work together in the reformation efforts.

Zwingli's explanation greatly disappointed Conrad Grebel, Simon Stumpf, and a few others. Where was the Zwingli who had taught that the church depends on the Bible alone for guidance? More than once, he had indicated that the church should initiate reform even if the civil rulers opposed it. But Zwingli decided that he needed the council's protection. He now believed that it was his duty to prepare the people to accept the reforms but that it was the council's duty to implement the changes. He hoped that the council would move fast enough to satisfy all the reform-minded people.

---

[14] *Die Akten der zweiten Disputation vom 26.-28. Oktober 1523*, published 12/8/1523. Cited in Leland Harder, ed., *The Sources of Swiss Anabaptism*, 242.

The Reforms Stall Again

Several days after the disputation, the council reached a conclusion on the issues. They wanted the mass to continue as in the past, and they wanted to keep the images in the churches. Nothing would change until they gave further notice, which they said would be in the near future. The council would have been willing to implement some changes, but they were afraid that to depart so radically from Catholic tradition would cause the Catholic-minded Swiss cantons to declare war on Zurich.

Once again Zwingli's program had suffered a serious setback. Zwingli had hoped that the disputation would bring the same results as the first disputation, and in the discussion he had spoken as strongly as anyone against the mass and the use of images. He had said clearly that no men could make these decisions; the Holy Scriptures must be followed. But when the council failed to do what he wanted them to, he submitted to their decision.

A few weeks after the disputation and the council's decision, Zwingli wrote a small booklet entitled *A Brief Introduction to the Disputation*. He labeled those who wanted to implement reforms in spite of the council's decree as malicious, mischievous people who wanted to do away with the law. He also blamed them for being proud, quarrelsome, and unconcerned about those who were spiritually weak and not ready for religious reform.

About the middle of December, some radicals destroyed some prayer books, made fun of priests who conducted the mass, and demonstrated against torture and capital punishment at Zurich's place of execution. The council soon issued another mandate, saying that all radicals would face severe punishment if they did not cease their agitation. This mandate contained no promise to make new worship regulations. The council also appointed

Zwingli and several other pastors to advise them on how to maintain order.

When Zwingli and his fellow pastors realized that the council was not following through with new worship regulations, they feared that the council would postpone religious reform indefinitely. Zwingli and his fellows drew up an advisory statement that expressed a determination that surpassed anything they had said before. This is evident in the following excerpt.

> It is the sum total of opinion from the Word of God that one should present to the Christian people the body and blood of Christ with both wine and bread as a memorial of Christ's suffering, proclaiming the Lord's death whenever we use this food and drink. . . .
>
> . . . we intend to hold a public observance of this form on Christmas Day [two weeks hence], entirely according to the institution and practice of Christ, for we can no longer withhold the correct practice from the world; and even if they [the council] do not permit us, we must offer both body and blood, bread and wine, to those who desire, or otherwise stand [condemned] as lying by the Word of God.[15]

If Zwingli and his fellows had acted on their word, Protestant church history might be a lot different. But the council rejected the plan, and Zwingli's second proposal showed his compromising nature again.

> The preceding opinion . . . is without doubt the most correct and most conformed to the Word of God. Therefore nothing shall be undertaken in this matter that does not aim toward the point at which, with time, we will come directly to the practice of the pure Word of God.
>
> However, since . . . people are divided at this time— for many are still . . . immature . . . it will be necessary to make some concessions. . . . it has seemed not

---

[15] Staatsarchiv Zurich E.I.1.1. Cited in Leland Harder, ed., *The Sources of Swiss Anabaptism,* 270.

> inappropriate for us to announce an opinion that will
> not be disadvantageous to the mature nor . . . offen-
> sive to the immature.[16]

Zwingli went on with a plea to the council to at least compel no one to observe the mass, nor to prohibit anyone from observing it. But the council rejected this also. They ruled that the mass must continue to be practiced, and Zwingli again bowed to their demands. The description he gave at the end of his first proposition now applied to him. He stood condemned "as lying by the Word of God."

To summarize, in the beginning Zwingli tried to reform religion within the shelter of the Catholic Church, but he soon abandoned that. Next, he endeavored to implement reform within the shelter of the Zurich city council, but again he was brought up short. At this point, he realized that to obey the Bible meant disobeying the civil government. The options were clear: he could follow the Bible and face whatever would come, or he could compromise on truth to stay within the safety of a state-sanctioned reform.

Zwingli chose the "safe" route. He was ready to speak quite strongly about the commands of the Bible in order to persuade the council to make some changes; but if they did not heed him, he tried to back off without losing his dignity. His move was politically convenient, but it cost him a clear conscience, the approval of God, and his most-consistent supporters.

The Anabaptists-to-be Propose an Alternate Plan

Conrad Grebel, Felix Mantz, and their friends were thoroughly disillusioned with the council's administration of the reformation and with the way Zwingli compromised under pressure. On December 18, 1523, the day after

---

[16] Ibid., 271, 272.

the council had rejected Zwingli's second plan, Grebel wrote a short letter to his brother-in-law Vadian. "Not by accident, the cause of the gospel is in a very bad way here (if you can still believe a mistrusted one rather than a liar [Zwingli]). . . . Whoever thinks, believes, or declares that Zwingli acts according to the duty of a shepherd thinks, believes, and declares wickedly."[17]

As the council's unwillingness to institute Biblical reforms became more apparent, the future Anabaptists questioned the whole idea of a state-administered reform. They approached Zwingli with a plan for a separatist church—a church that would obey the Bible on its own without waiting for the consent of the government. Historians have found no documents about this plan written by the Anabaptists-to-be, but Zwingli referred to this plan in a tract that he later wrote against the Anabaptists. In his words,

> They approached us therefore in the following way: "It has not escaped our attention that there will always be those who will resist the gospel, even among those who boast in the name of Christ. It is therefore never to be hoped that all souls will be so established in unity, as Christians should be permitted to live. According to the Acts of the Apostles those who had believed separated from the others, and then as others came to believe, they joined those who were already a new church. That is just what we must do."
>
> They begged us to make a declaration to this effect: Those who want to follow Christ should stand on our side. They promised also that our forces would be far superior to the army of unbelievers.[18]

---

[17] Stadtbibliothek (Vadiana) St. Gallen, VB.II.161. Cited in Leland Harder, ed., *The Sources of Swiss Anabaptism,* 275, 276.

[18] Ulrich Zwingli, *In catabaptistarum strophas elenchus,* published 7/31/1527. Cited in Leland Harder, ed., *The Sources of Swiss Anabaptism,* 278. The "superior forces" probably refer to the side of truth. It could also indicate that the Anabaptists-to-be had hopes of drawing a large following.

Zwingli would not support such a plan. He argued that Christ had commanded to let the tares grow with the grain until the day of harvest, and that this meant that sincere Christians would always live among less-devoted brethren. He pointed out that there were ten virgins awaiting the bridegroom, but only five of them were ready. Applying such Scriptures to the church, Zwingli argued that a separated church would only confuse weak souls.

But the Anabaptists-to-be did not give in easily. They diligently searched the Scriptures in evening meetings. The more they studied God's Word, the more they were convinced that Zwingli's program was not Biblical as long as he insisted on government support for his reforms.[19]

The Rift Widens

Through the end of 1523 and through 1524, the Anabaptists-to-be continued studying the Bible. They formed small groups and prepared curriculum to help new students understand the Scriptures. They continued to develop their vision for a pure New Testament church.

Sometime during 1524, these Bible students obtained

---

[19] Some historians question whether the "radical" church plan was for a church separated from the state. In Zwingli's account of this plan, he noted that the new church proposed to elect its own council. Zwingli interpreted this as a plan for a new city council, and thus he accused the Anabaptists of wanting to do away with the secular government.

From this time on, Zwingli constantly accused the separatists falsely. Nothing in the separatist plan proved that the Anabaptists-to-be wanted to establish a new secular council. In the second doctrinal disputation, Simon Stumpf had firmly maintained that the government had no authority over the church and its application of God's Word. In Grebel's trial in November 1525, he stated that he never taught that people should not obey the government. The question, then, is whether the separatist proposal of a new council was simply a church council or whether it was a replacement for the existing secular council. The testimonies of Grebel and Stumpf support the first idea, and no evidence except Zwingli's polemic can support the latter. In the end, the early Anabaptists did have a proper understanding of church-and-state separation, so the question is not *if* they understood it but *when*.

some writings by Thomas Muntzer[20] and Andreas Carlstadt,[21] dealing with faith, images, and infant baptism. The brethren were overjoyed to find that they were not alone in their beliefs. Immediately Conrad Grebel wrote a letter to Muntzer, commending him on his Bible doctrines, but challenging him on the mass, which Muntzer retained in a modified form. This letter is valuable because it shows us the New Testament beliefs of the Anabaptists-to-be. Their understanding of nonresistance, church discipline, Communion, brotherhood, and backsliding is inspiring when we realize it came from their diligent study of the New Testament.

> Dear Brother Thomas, . . .
>
> . . . Jesus Christ, who offers himself as the only Master and Head to all who are to be saved and commands us to be brethren to all brethren and believers through the one common Word, has moved and impelled us to establish friendship and brotherhood. . . .
>
> Just as our forefathers had fallen away from the true God and knowledge of Jesus Christ and true faith in him, . . . so even today everyone wants to be saved by hypocritical faith, without fruits of faith, without the baptism of trial and testing, without hope and love, without true Christian practices. . . . In respect of persons and all manner of seduction they [Zwingli and his colleagues] are in more serious and harmful error than has ever been the case since the foundation of

---

[20] Thomas Muntzer (1488–1525) had no lasting influence among the Zurich Anabaptists-to-be, although his writings contained some ideas similar to theirs. Conrad Grebel wrote a friendly letter to Muntzer, which never reached its destination, and no contact was established. Muntzer often shifted his position on key issues, such as nonresistance, and he believed that the Bible was secondary to personal visions as a revelation of God's will.

[21] Andreas Carlstadt (1480–1541) supported Martin Luther in many ways. On some issues, such as the authority of the Scriptures and the nonswearing of oaths, he believed like the Anabaptists. However, some of his doctrine did not agree with the mainline reformers or the Anabaptists. He met with the Anabaptists-to-be in Zurich in October 1524, but apparently had no further contact with them.

the world. We were also in the same aberration because we were only hearers and readers of the evangelical preachers who are responsible for all this error. . . . But after we took the Scripture in hand and consulted it on all kinds of issues, we gained some insight and became aware of the great and harmful shortcomings of the shepherds as well as our own in that we do not daily cry earnestly to God with constant sighs to be led out of . . . human abominations and enter into true faith and practices of God. . . .

While we were noting and lamenting these things, your writing against false faith and baptism was brought out here to us and we are even better informed and strengthened and were wonderfully happy to have found someone who is of common Christian mind with us. . . . Therefore we ask and admonish you . . . to preach only God's Word unflinchingly, to establish and defend only divine practices, to esteem as good and right only what can be found in definite clear Scripture, and to reject . . . all the schemes, words, practices, and opinions of all men, even your own.

Grebel went on with a number of exhortations on the proper observance of the Lord's Supper. He seems to have studied this doctrine well, for his conclusions were Biblical. Then he returned to various other concerns.

Pay no attention to the apostasy or to the unchristian forbearance, which the very learned foremost evangelical preachers established. . . . It is far better that a few be correctly instructed through the Word of God and believe and live right in virtues and practices than that many believe deceitfully out of adulterated false doctrine. . . .

March forward with the Word and create a Christian church with the help of Christ and his rule such as we find instituted in Matthew 18 and practiced in the epistles. Press on in earnest with common prayer and fasting. . . . Anyone who will not reform or believe and strives against the Word and acts of God and persists therein, after Christ and his Word and rule have been preached to him, and he has been admonished with the three witnesses before the church, such a man we say on the basis of God's Word shall not be put to death but regarded as a heathen and publican and left alone.

Moreover, the gospel and its adherents are not to be protected by the sword. . . . True believing Christians are sheep among wolves, sheep for the slaughter. They must be baptized in anguish and tribulation, persecution, suffering, and death, tried in fire, and must reach the fatherland of eternal rest not by slaying the physical but the spiritual. They use neither worldly sword nor war.[22]

Before the messenger left from Zurich with Grebel's letter to Muntzer, Grebel and his brethren heard that Muntzer was advocating the use of force. They attached a postscript to the letter, again admonishing Muntzer to desist from all of his own opinions and follow only the Word of God.

The brethren maintained no lasting contact with either Muntzer or Carlstadt because of doctrinal differences. They continued to develop Biblical thought patterns with few outside influences. At this point their group was quite small. In the postscript to Muntzer, Grebel wrote, "Around here there are not even twenty who believe the Word of God."

Infant Baptism Becomes an Issue

Early in 1524, Wilhelm Reublin, a village pastor in Wytikon,[23] preached against infant baptism. At that time, infant baptism was not of major concern to the Anabaptists-to-be in Zurich. As they studied the Bible, however,

---

[22] Stadtbibliothek (Vadiana) St. Gallen, VB.XI.97. Cited in Leland Harder, ed., *The Sources of Swiss Anabaptism,* 285–290.

[23] Wytikon was a small village five miles southeast of Zurich.

they too became increasingly convinced that infant baptism was wrong. In his letter to Muntzer, Grebel wrote strongly against infant baptism, using a number of Scripture passages to back up his teaching.

In December, the issue came to a head. A few parents in Zurich did not baptize their children. The council warned them, but they did not back down. The council then decided that everyone who believed infant baptism was wrong must present his reasons to Zwingli and his fellow pastors, who in turn would discuss the matter with several council members.

Zwingli, who now felt that infant baptism was a good practice, held several private disputations with the dissenters. Neither side changed their views. Felix Mantz wrote a petition to the council, explaining why infant baptism was unscriptural. More parents began to withhold their babies from baptism, especially in the villages of Wytikon and Zollikon. On January 6, a new daughter had been born to Conrad and Barbara Grebel. Conrad had no intentions of baptizing her in the "idolatrous Romish bath," as he called it.

The council decided to settle the question by holding a public disputation on January 17, 1525. Grebel, Mantz, and Reublin argued their case, and Zwingli opposed them strongly. At the end of the disputation, the authorities admonished the dissenters to forget their erring opinions and be peaceful, but the brethren countered, "We must obey God rather than men." The disputation settled nothing.

In reaction to this, on January 18 the council issued a strong decree against the dissenters.

> All those who have hitherto left their children unbaptized shall have them baptized within the next eight days. And anyone who refuses to do this shall, with wife and child and possessions, leave our lords' city,

jurisdiction, and domain, and never return, or await what happens to him. Everyone will know how to conduct himself accordingly.[24]

On January 21, the council issued the following mandate in relation to the Bible study meetings.

> Following the preceding resolution on baptism, etc., it is further decided that the mandate shall be executed, and henceforth the special schools that deal with such matters shall be discontinued and Conrad Grebel and Mantz shall be told henceforth to desist from their arguing and questioning and be satisfied with [the council's] judgments; for no more disputations will be permitted hereafter.[25]

The edict fell on the small Bible-believing group like a sledgehammer. The Word of God was not welcome in Zurich. Zwingli had fallen in line with the city council and had the power to get his way. The Bible believers would have to listen to him and go against their knowledge of truth, or suffer the consequences.

Zwingli—the False Shepherd

During the period leading up to this confrontation, the Catholic cantons of Switzerland became increasingly hostile toward Zurich and seriously considered expelling Zurich from the Swiss confederacy. Rumor had it that zealous Catholics from other cantons might try to murder or arrest Zwingli. However, due to his cooperation with the Zurich council, he had won their confidence and had little to fear from Zurich itself.

Earlier, in December of 1523, a secret council had been organized in Zurich, to which Zwingli belonged. This

---

[24] Staatsarchiv Zurich, EI.7.1 & A.42.1. Cited in Leland Harder, ed., *The Sources of Swiss Anabaptism,* 336.

[25] Staatsarchiv Zurich, V.VI.248.fol.227b. Cited in Leland Harder, ed., *The Sources of Swiss Anabaptism,* 338.

council's role was to plan for Zurich's defense in the event of war with the Catholic cantons. It also dealt with enemies of Zwingli's reformation in the canton of Zurich—both the "extreme reform radicals" and the pro-Catholic persons, including suspected members of the Zurich council.

Early in 1525, war with the Catholic cantons seemed inevitable. Zwingli and the secret council designed a strategy of war to defend Zurich. In light of these developments, the radical reformers seemed to pose an internal danger to Zurich's security. It appears that Zwingli used this as an opportunity to strike against his opponents. Zwingli was rising in power politically, and he was determined to crush those who opposed him. He no longer needed or wanted to reconcile and pacify the dissenters. He was ready to get rid of them completely. The time for strong procedures had come.

Chapter 3

The Rise of the Swiss Brethren

The decrees issued by the Zurich city council made it clear that Zwingli and the Zurich authorities would no longer tolerate dissenters. The "radicals" had to submit to their civil rulers or leave their homeland. The small group of believers gathered to counsel together, almost certainly on the evening of January 21, 1525, the same day that the council had outlawed such meetings. Simon Stumpf was not there; he had been banished earlier. George (Jörg) Blaurock, an ex-priest from Grisons,[1] had recently joined the group. George had left the Catholic Church and come to Zurich to see what Zwingli had to offer. He did not appreciate Zwingli's attitude of compromise and soon zealously identified himself with the little group of future Anabaptists.

---

[1] Grisons, or Graübunden, was a large region in eastern Switzerland. Blaurock's home was about seventy miles southeast of Zurich.

In the early 1530s, an eyewitness wrote an account of this January meeting to German Anabaptists who had wondered how Anabaptism began.

Therefore, dear brethren, since you have asked us about the beginning of the brotherhood of the Swiss Brethren, it was about the time when men wrote the year 1522 that Huldrych Zwingli, Conrad Grebel, a nobleman, and Felix Mantz—all three very learned men, experienced in the German, Latin, Greek, and Hebrew languages, came to discuss matters of faith, and discovered that infant baptism is unnecessary, also not known as a baptism. Thereupon the two, Conrad and Felix, believed and confessed that one must, according to Christian order, be baptized according to the words of Christ: he who believes and is baptized shall be saved. This led to disunity among the three, and Huldrych Zwingli did not wish this and said it would create a disturbance. But the two previously mentioned men held that one could not ignore God's command because of that.

Meanwhile it happened that a priest by the name of Jörg, of the house of Jacob, who was called Jörg Blaurock because he wore a blue coat, also came with a particular zeal which he had toward God's will. He was held to be an ordinary and simple priest but with a godly zeal in matters of faith, who through the grace of God which was given him acted in an extraordinary manner. He came to Zwingli and talked to him about the faith, but achieved nothing. Thereupon he was told that there were others who had more zeal than Zwingli. These he sought out and came to them, namely, to Conrad and Felix, and talked with them; and they became united in these things.

And it happened that they were together. After fear lay greatly upon them, they called upon God in heaven, that he should show mercy to them. Then Jörg arose and asked Conrad for God's sake to baptize him; and this he did. After that, he baptized the others also.

After this, more priests and other people were added who soon sealed it with their blood. . . .

Thus you have the facts about what happened at the beginning. Later many things happened, so that many ran disorderly. But the sure foundation of truth remained. The Lord knows his own. Let those who call upon the name of the Lord forsake unrighteousness. And so you have the account of the beginning concerning which you should have no doubt, for we have most surely experienced it.[2]

This was the birthday of Swiss Anabaptism. The brethren knew they faced certain persecution, but they determined to be faithful to their convictions at any cost. The following week the new movement spread to Zollikon, a village a few miles south of Zurich. There the brethren witnessed, baptized, and held Communion. At least thirty-five people were baptized during the first week.

The Zurich authorities were determined to enforce their new laws against rebaptism and secret meetings. On January 30, nine days after the first rebaptisms, they arrested Mantz, Blaurock, and twenty-five Zollikon villagers. Zwingli and his colleagues imprisoned the villagers and questioned them thoroughly. After nine days, the council fined the prisoners and released them on several conditions: they could not meet in groups of more than three or four and they could not baptize, preach, or hold Communion. The authorities kept Mantz and Blaurock in prison to make sure they would not stir up more trouble.

---

[2] From Klettgau/Cologne letter. Cited in Leland Harder, ed., *The Sources of Swiss Anabaptism,* 341, 342. This letter was sent form Switzerland to Cologne in 1530. A similar account is given in the *Hutterian Chronicle,* on pages 43-47. This account adds some details, such as stating that Blaurock baptized everyone present, which was added to the original letter by a later writer. We do not know whether "he baptized the others also" refers to Blaurock or Grebel.

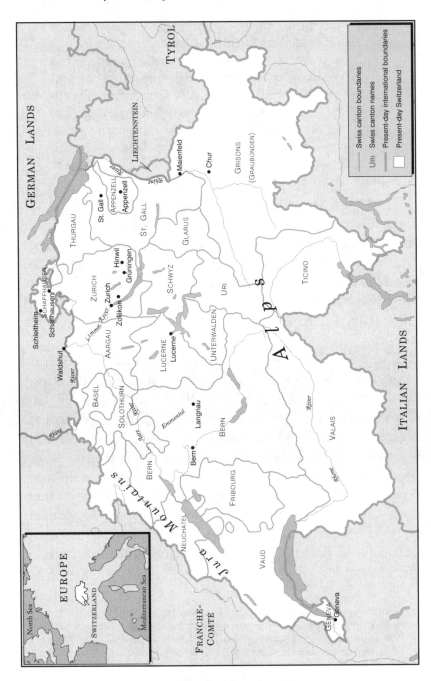

Switzerland

Conrad Grebel's Missionary Labors

Grebel had traveled to Schaffhausen[3] several days after the first baptisms, leaving the work at Zollikon to the other brethren. Hoping to influence the church reform movement in the city, he went directly to the leading pastors. As Grebel discussed the Bible with them, he nearly convinced them of the Scriptural basis for believer's baptism. But then Zwingli sent a letter to Schaffhausen and turned the city council and pastors against Grebel. However, Grebel continued to witness there for about two months, with a number of contacts and at least one baptism.

Meanwhile, back in Zurich, the authorities released Blaurock from prison. He immediately stirred up the Zollikon brethren again. Almost all the Zollikon villagers who had promised to stop their Anabaptist activities broke their promises and became involved in baptisms and meetings again. By March 16, when the Zurich council pounced again, about seventy more people had become Anabaptists. The authorities tried to arrest everyone involved with the movement.

During the court trials, most of the Zollikon Anabaptists recanted and gave up Anabaptism completely. However, George Blaurock and Felix Mantz stood firm. The council banished Blaurock from Zurich, since he was a nonresident. He returned to his native Chur to testify of his new faith. Shortly afterward, Mantz escaped from his prison cell and joined Blaurock. Together the two successfully spread Anabaptist teachings until Mantz was arrested again in July.

Grebel returned from Schaffhausen about the time the Zollikon villagers and Blaurock were released. In April he left Zurich again and joined Wolfgang Ulimann (whom

---

[3] Schaffhausen was a city and a state in northern Switzerland.

Grebel had baptized in Schaffhausen) in preaching the Gospel at St. Gall.[4]

St. Gall supported a large monastery, and the citizens resented the heavy tax burden this imposed on them. They heartily welcomed a Christianity that did not need monks. Grebel preached in a large town building and drew hundreds of listeners. After two weeks of preaching, many of the converts requested baptism, so Grebel baptized several hundred in the Sitter River near the city.

The rapid expansion was short-lived. Two months after Grebel's baptismal service, the St. Gall council outlawed the Anabaptist meetings and banished Ulimann. Many of the Anabaptists in this city turned back under the pressure, and most of those who remained faithful later fled the city.

In July, Grebel traveled to the rural area around the town of Grüningen,[5] where he had lived as a boy. Here he labored for over three months, moving quickly from place to place to avoid capture. The Zurich authorities summoned him to appear in Zurich for trial, on a charge of slander against Zwingli. Grebel was willing to go if the council promised him safe conduct, but they refused to grant it, so he did not go.

Felix Mantz, meanwhile, had been arrested in Chur, a city in Grisons, and sent back to Zurich to be dealt with. He spent several months in prison; then he was released after promising to not disturb the peace. Immediately he went to Grüningen, where Grebel and Blaurock were working with the steadily growing movement.

The day after Mantz left prison, in early October, Blaurock attended the state church in Hinwil, a bit east of Grüningen. The regular pastor was not yet there when

---

[4] St. Gall was about thirty-five miles east of Zurich.

[5] Grüningen lay about eleven miles southeast of Zurich.

Blaurock arrived, so he took to the pulpit and began to preach. When the pastor arrived, much of the congregation supported Blaurock's action, and the pastor soon realized that this situation was out of his control. He summoned the chief magistrate from the Grüningen castle to come and arrest Blaurock.

The magistrate arrived, but no one would help him capture Blaurock. He had to wait until the service was over to arrest the Anabaptist preacher. The magistrate placed Blaurock on a horse and started for the Grüningen castle. As they came near the village of Betzholtz, they found a large crowd gathered around Grebel and Mantz, who were preparing to preach. After recruiting more help, the magistrate also arrested Grebel, but Mantz escaped. The two preachers were imprisoned in the Grüningen castle, once Conrad's boyhood home. The authorities arrested Mantz three weeks later.

Another Debate on Baptism

The Zurich council demanded that the prisoners be brought to the city for a trial, but the Grüningen and Zollikon citizens first wanted another public disputation on baptism. This disputation took place on November 6–8, 1525, before the Anabaptist leaders were tried. According to one report, nine hundred people gathered for this meeting. A number of Anabaptist prisoners were present, including Michael Sattler.[6] The brethren were accused of supporting sedition against the government and of claiming special revelations, which they denied.

Even though this was to be a fair hearing for all, the

---

[6] Michael Sattler had been visiting Anabaptists in the Zurich area and was suspected of heresy. At this point, however, it is not certain that Sattler was a committed Anabaptist. He was released upon paying court costs and promising to permanently leave the Zurich area. (One author adds that he also promised to forsake Anabaptism.) There are no known records of the exact time when Sattler became an Anabaptist, but good evidence points to the summer of 1526.

outcome was predetermined. Zwingli and his supporters claimed the victory and sentenced the Anabaptists to a variety of punishments. Zurich natives received sentences ranging from doing penance to being imprisoned on bread, water, and gruel; and those from other cantons were banished.

Grebel, Mantz, Blaurock, and their fifteen fellow prisoners had a retrial on March 5–7, 1526. They remained steadfast in the truth, so the council sentenced them to prison for life. Their diet was only bread and water, and they received no health care. At the same time, the council decreed that whoever was rebaptized after this would be drowned without mercy.

The "lifelong" imprisonment of the Anabaptists lasted only two weeks. On March 21, the men pried open a high window in their cell. Using the same rope that had let them down into the dungeon, they scaled the wall and lowered themselves one by one to freedom. God provided miraculously for their escape, for the window through which they climbed overlooked a deep moat, which was temporarily drained. The drawbridge over the muddy moat was usually up, closing off the route. However, the city was repairing the bridge, and it was left in the down position overnight.

After crossing the drawbridge, the group discussed where they would go. They "joked among themselves," the account says, "and said they would go to the red Indians across the sea."[7] Little could they realize that in two hundred years their spiritual descendants would do just that. Most of them escaped from Zurich right away, but two men were sick from the imprisonment and decided to stay in Zurich that night. Those two were promptly rearrested, and the account of the escape has

---

[7] Staatsarchiv Zurich, EI.7.1. Cited in Leland Harder, ed., *The Sources of Swiss Anabaptism*, 451.

come down to us through the court record of their subsequent hearing.

After this, Grebel, Mantz, and Blaurock carried on an underground ministry in various areas away from Zurich. Grebel managed to have a pamphlet printed on baptism, to which Zwingli wrote a rebuttal. Grebel preached and worked north of Zurich during this part of his ministry.

During this time, various radical ideas floated among some of the Anabaptists. Grebel and Mantz worked to quell these ideas. A contemporary chronicler (who was against Anabaptism) gives the following account.

> There were also some among them who had earlier learned and heard from Protestant preachers that the New Testament was a matter of the spirit and not of the letter, as Martin Luther also says in his foreword to his translation of the New Testament. Because they now thought themselves more spiritual than anyone else on earth, they threw their Testaments into the stove, burned and tore them up, saying, "The letter is dead, the spirit gives life," and "God says through the prophet: 'I will write my law on their hearts.' ". . . .
> There were some among the first Anabaptists who were not stained with so many opinions but held only to those articles that they had learned from Conrad Grebel.
> . . . The aforementioned Conrad Grebel and Felix Mantz, the arch-Anabaptists, were also deeply distressed by such coarse errors and fantasies; nor was it their intention when they began it. Therefore, they were soon compelled to preach and teach against such error in Appenzell and Gotzhus. But many would listen to them as little as to us; indeed, they regarded them as false prophets and scribes and lashed out at them.[8]

---

[8] Kessler, Sabbata. Cited in Leland Harder, ed., *The Sources of Swiss Anabaptism*, 455, 456.

In the summer of 1526, Grebel traveled to Maienfeld, a city over fifty miles southeast of Zurich, where his sister Barbara lived. The hardships of imprisonment and months of stressful evangelizing had taken their toll on him. Soon after he arrived, he died of the plague, at the age of twenty-eight.

Felix Mantz's Final Labors and Death

Felix Mantz also labored north of Zurich after his escape from prison. Sometimes he and Grebel ministered together. Mantz also evangelized in the St. Gall area and was briefly imprisoned there. Later he joined Blaurock, and the two went back to the Grüningen area. They held secret meetings, successfully strengthening the Anabaptists there, but were captured in the woods with a group of believers in early December.

The prisoners were taken to Zurich, where Zwingli and the council were determined to crush them. Among other charges, Mantz and Blaurock were charged with dividing the Christian church and teaching that a Christian could not serve as a political leader or carry a sword. On January 5, 1527, the council sentenced Mantz to death and Blaurock to be beaten out of the city.[9]

About three o'clock that afternoon, Mantz was taken from his cell to the Limmat River. A crowd had gathered to watch the execution, and Felix testified to them and praised God for the privilege of dying for the truth. His mother and brother stood nearby, encouraging him to remain steadfast. Mantz was taken to a little fishermen's hut in the middle of the river and securely bound. Just before the executioner pushed him into the cold water, he cried, "Into Your hands, Lord, I commend my spirit."

---

[9] The reason for this "leniency" in dealing with Blaurock was probably because he was a nonresident. Also, the council was unable to prove that Blaurock had baptized anyone in the canton after the death penalty for doing so was passed.

The persecutors stripped Blaurock to the waist and beat him with rods to the city gate. There he refused to swear that he would not return to Zurich, so the authorities threw him into prison again. However, he soon gave in and satisfied them with an oath, and they let him go.[10]

After his release, Blaurock labored for two and one-half years more before his death. He evangelized first in northern Switzerland, where he was captured twice. Finally he was outlawed in most parts of German-speaking Switzerland.

Early in 1528, Blaurock headed for the Austrian province of Tyrol to replace a martyred Anabaptist minister. There, persecution raged under the Catholic rule, but Blaurock never considered personal safety at the expense of spreading the Gospel. Through his ministry, the churches flourished and many new converts were baptized. The government seized him in the summer of 1529 and burned him at the stake in early September.

Michael Sattler's Work in Strasbourg

Michael Sattler probably did not join the Swiss Brethren until the summer of 1526, around the time that Grebel died and a few months before Mantz died. Sattler had been a monk, but the immoral monastery life disgusted him. He became exposed to Reformation teachings and began visiting with Anabaptists about a year before he actually joined them. He was a man of talent and deep conviction. Once he made the decision to cast his lot with the suffering Anabaptists, he never wavered.

Late in 1526, Sattler went to Strasbourg, a free city in the Holy Roman Empire, lying on the border between

---

[10] Leland Harder, ed., *The Sources of Swiss Anabaptism,* 474; and John L. Ruth, *Conrad Grebel, Son of Zurich,* 143.

France and Germany. In the early Reformation days, Strasbourg was more tolerant of religious differences than most cities. Sattler discussed Anabaptist doctrines with Wolfgang Capito (in whose home he stayed while in the city) and Martin Bucer, Strasbourg's main Protestant reformers. He also tried (unsuccessfully) to persuade them to release some Anabaptist prisoners in Strasbourg.[11] The reformers thought Sattler should, in Christian charity, give in on his strong doctrinal positions and unite with the mainstream Protestant reform efforts. Though Sattler could not agree to this, the men parted cordially.

After he left Strasbourg, Sattler evangelized in the area of Lahr, about fifteen miles southeast of Strasbourg.[12] Wilhelm Reublin was already evangelizing in this area, and he placed Sattler in charge of the congregation at Horb. Sattler had a successful ministry there, and the congregation grew rapidly, even though strong Catholics ruled the area.

Trials in the Anabaptist Movement

The Swiss Brethren movement was now about two years old, and many dangers faced them. The original leaders had died, persecution kept growing, and false teachers sowed confusion among sincere seekers. The Anabaptists now realized that they could not expect their movement to become an accepted part of the Reformation. They would remain a separate, suffering minority.

Since the Anabaptists suffered so much for practical

---

[11] It is a credit to Sattler's Christian character that he was able to discuss Biblical doctrine with these men, disagreeing with them but retaining their friendship, at a time when other Anabaptists were in prison in the same city.

[12] Some older books say that Sattler was in the Horb and Rottenburg area after he left Strasbourg. Later reasearch shows he was likely at Lahr until the Schleitheim meeting, after which he went to the Horb and Rottenburg area, where he was captured. See C. Arnold Snyder, *The Life and Thought of Michael Sattler,* 95–97.

obedience to Christ's clear commands, some false teachers promoted the idea that a person could hold to
Christ's commands in his heart without actually practicing them. Why could a person not have right intentions and be accepted by God without practicing the
things that got him into trouble with the authorities?
Some people applied this to clear commands of Christ,
such as not swearing, nonresistance, and not being yoked
with unbelievers. They taught that a person could bow
to the demands of the state church and still maintain
true spirituality and worship God in his heart. In other
words, he could be a silent, unobtrusive Christian. He
could avoid bearing his cross and dying for his faith. This
teaching was similar to Pietism, which we shall meet later
in our study of Swiss Anabaptism.

The early Swiss Brethren leaders vigorously denounced
this doctrine. The Christian must put to death self and
the desire for a comfortable existence. The saint must
renounce the world and often his own life if he wants the
heavenly crown. If anyone refuses his cross, he refuses
salvation. This theme runs through all their writings.

The stiff persecution of the state and the false doctrine
of those who claimed to be brethren made life difficult for
the genuine Anabaptists. The crisis was intensified by
the fact that the new church had not yet fully established
its beliefs about the issues it faced. If Anabaptism was
to survive, it needed to find a stable guide to keep it Biblical. This guide could not be only faithful leaders, for
they often passed quickly from the scene. The ultimate
guide, of course, was the Bible. But the Swiss Brethren
realized that unless a faithful church helped its converts
understand how the Bible related to the issues at hand,
the church would be torn by individualism and might
eventually lose out altogether.

The Schleitheim Meeting

The Swiss Brethren leaders realized the importance of gathering their brethren together to discuss the issues and to chart a unified course. They wanted a written statement explaining the Biblical beliefs that made the Anabaptist movement distinct from radical groups, Catholics, and Protestants. Such a statement would also identify false teachers that arose within the Anabaptist church. Also, faithful Anabaptists were being killed in rapid succession. With such a rapid turnover of members and leaders, there was a danger that the movement could lose its Biblical moorings. The Anabaptists wanted to pass on an example of true faith to those coming after them.

On February 24, 1527, some Swiss Brethren met at Schleitheim, about twenty-five miles north of Zurich, in the northern tip of Switzerland. Together, the brethren drew up a document entitled *Brotherly Union of a Number of Children of God Concerning Seven Articles*. The document explained the Anabaptist position on believer's Baptism, excommunication, Communion observance, separation from the world, church leadership, nonresistance, and the oath.[13] Although it was not a complete statement of Christian beliefs, it addressed the issues the Anabaptists were facing at that time.

Copies of the articles spread rapidly among the Anabaptists, uniting their churches and testimony. Evidently, the Protestant reformers considered it an effective document, for Zwingli wrote a refutation of it immediately,

---

[13] The Schleitheim Confession of Faith was significant in the survival of Anabaptism. Sattler wrote it after the meeting and incorporated it into an encouraging letter for his brethren. This document is reproduced in the appendix. Also in the appendix is a short article titled *Congregational Order*, which was circulated with the *Brotherly Union*. Reading these documents will broaden your understanding of the issues faced by the early Anabaptists.

and John Calvin[14] did the same later. Balthasar Hubmaier[15] wrote an argument against the sixth point, concerning nonresistance. Zwingli's refutation accused the Anabaptists of terrible crimes, but it did little to change the effectiveness of the document.

The Schleitheim meeting took place amid increasing persecution from both Catholics and Protestants. Not long after the Schleitheim meeting, the Catholic authorities arrested a group of Anabaptists at Horb, including Sattler and his wife. At the time of his arrest, Sattler was carrying a copy of the Schleitheim Confession and some other notes about the Brethren's activities and plans. To his captors, this marked him immediately as an important Anabaptist leader.

Sattler's Martyrdom

The authorities charged Sattler and his fellow believers with violations of Catholic doctrine and practice. They accused the Anabaptists of not believing in transubstantiation, extreme unction,[16] and infant baptism. And the Anabaptists did not worship saints or Mary, use the

---

[14] John Calvin joined the reform movement in the 1530s. He taught the doctrine we call Calvinism, an unscriptural view of the sovereignty of God, based on the early teachings of Augustine. There are many variations of this view, but basically it teaches that man is predestined to be lost or saved and has no choice in the matter. This view defies the Biblical teaching that man chooses either to give up himself and submit to God's salvation or to rebel against God's mercy and continue on the path to eternal death.

Calvin became a Reformation leader at Geneva, Switzerland, and the rulers of Geneva adopted Calvin's religious views. Many Reformation supporters from areas surrounding Geneva fled to the city to avoid persecution from the Catholics. Because of this influx of people, Calvin's teaching spread rapidly to other parts of Switzerland. The Swiss Brethren did not accept his false views.

[15] See Chapter 8 for more information on Balthasar Hubmaier.

[16] Extreme unction (also called the last rites) was a corrupted form of the Biblical ordinance of anointing with oil. (See James 5:13–16.) Historically, the Catholics anointed both the dangerously ill and those who were about to die. The Anabaptists did not reject the Biblical anointing of the sick, but they taught against the Catholic belief that anointing had power to free one from sin and prepare a soul for death.

oath, or follow the standard practice for Communion. Against Sattler specifically there were two additional charges: he had left the monastery and married, and he had taught nonresistance toward the militant Turks (Muslims).[17]

After one and a half hours of private discussion, the judges read the sentence. Michael Sattler was to be given to the executioner. He was to be taken to the square and have his tongue cut out. After he was fastened to a wagon, flesh was to be torn from his body seven times with glowing metal tongs. After the wagon arrived at the execution site, he was to be burned to powder. The other prisoners received various sentences of lesser cruelty, but most of them recanted.

Sattler told his brethren he would give them a sign that he was remaining steadfast during his execution. On May 20, 1527, the awful sentence was carried out. Even though Sattler's tongue was mutilated, he could still speak. In spite of the pain, he prayed for his persecutors and admonished the people to repent. Just before he was thrown into the fire, he prayed for the grace of God to help him testify to the truth with his blood.

The executioner fastened a sack of powder around his neck to hasten his death. In the fire, Sattler prayed and praised the Lord. When the ropes on his hands burned through, he raised the two forefingers of his hands, giving the promised sign to his brethren. "Father, I commend

---

[17] The warring, expansionist Muslims from the Middle East were a grave threat to "Christian" Europe through much of the Middle Ages. The medieval crusades against the Turks, with great loss of European life and limb, were credited with the survival of Christianity. For Sattler to teach that one should not fight the Turks made him a traitor indeed. Of course, the Swiss Brethren taught nonresistance toward everyone, not just the Turks.

Sattler once made the remark that if fighting was right, he would rather fight against the European "Christians," who persecuted the true Christians, than against the Turks, who did not even pretend to be Christians. This remark was brought up against him in his trial.

my spirit into Thy hands!" he cried as he passed from earthly life.

Sattler's high character was well known. Five months after Sattler's execution, Martin Bucer, one of the Protestant reformers at Strasbourg, wrote, "We do not doubt that Michael Sattler, who was burned at Rottenburg, was a dear friend of God, although he was a leader of the Anabaptists, but much more skilled and honorable than some."[18]

Wilhelm Reublin wrote a booklet narrating the martyrdom. The story seriously embarrassed the Austrian government, which had executed Sattler. His excellent reputation and horrible death caused quite a stir among the people who knew him well.

Zwingli—the "Christian" Politician

Zwingli, afraid that the Anabaptist "radicals" would harm his reform plan, zealously supported, if not instigated, all the harsh measures imposed upon them by the Zurich council. The Anabaptists, however, were not his only opposition during this time. A few staunch Catholics still lived in Zurich, and they worked against Zwingli at every turn. In addition to these two kinds of "radicals," Conrad's father, Jacob Grebel, and several other council members were somewhat tolerant toward the Catholics and the Anabaptists.[19] Zwingli saw Jacob and his colleagues as a threat to his reform movement.

Zwingli's reform faced increasing danger from the Catholic Swiss states. In light of this, Zwingli renewed his efforts to wipe out local opposition and establish his political and religious authority. He carefully built a case

---

[18] *The Mennonite Encyclopedia*, article "Sattler, Michael," 4:433.

[19] This is a possible explanation for the amazing number of times that Anabaptist prisoners escaped from Zurich prison cells.

against Jacob Grebel on the grounds of treason. Evidently Jacob had received foreign pensions for Conrad's education and had kept some of the money himself after a law was made against accepting such pensions. Using this as his primary evidence, Zwingli had Jacob tried and beheaded in late October 1526.

The city of Zurich was shocked at such treatment of the aged senator, but no one dared raise a public protest. Then with the Zurich council completely under his control, Zwingli was able to give his full attention to the Anabaptist problem. Probably at his instigation, the council approved a death penalty for those involved in rebaptizing. In January 1527, Zwingli supported the drowning of Mantz. Zwingli, at this point, had the power to suppress anyone who dared to stand against him, and he was fully prepared to do so.

Although Zwingli disposed of the prominent Zurich Anabaptist leaders, he soon found out that the problem had not disappeared. In the spring of 1527, he received an Anabaptist booklet that contained refutations of his accusations against them. Soon he was given several handwritten copies of the Schleitheim Confession of Faith. He wrote another book against the Anabaptists to refute their teachings and to stir up other cities against them. Soon after the book came off the press, Zwingli held a convention for the Swiss cantons supporting reform, and initiated a joint program of Anabaptist persecution that lasted for years.

But the flame of truth burned on in the hearts of the faithful. Neither Zwingli nor all the persecutors that followed him were able to extinguish the flame. The Anabaptist movement continued to grow and spread under the bitterest opposition.

In May 1529, a Protestant missionary from Zurich tried to evangelize in a Swiss Catholic town and was burned at the stake. Under pressure from Zwingli, the Zurich council declared war on the Catholic states.[20] Zwingli personally accompanied the Zurich troops. Ten miles south of Zurich, at the city of Kappel, the two armies met. Zwingli wanted to attack immediately, but was overruled by other Protestant leaders who favored negotiating. So instead of fighting, the two sides called a truce and negotiated for sixteen days. As a result, in late June, 1529, the opposing parties signed the First Peace of Kappel. Among other demands, the Catholics agreed to refrain from attacking the Protestant Swiss states because of religious differences. The Catholics rejected only one of Zwingli's demands: freedom for Protestant missionaries to evangelize Catholic states. This was considered a victory for the Protestants; yet not all of Zwingli's demands had been realized, and he was uncertain how long the peace would last.

The Swiss Protestants realized that they needed all the help they could find to protect themselves against the Catholics, so they considered uniting with the German Protestants. During a larger meeting that began on September 29, 1529, Luther and Zwingli met together to discuss a union. But they could not agree on the nature of the Communion emblems. Luther insisted that the bread was actually Christ's body, while Zwingli believed that it was only a symbol. The two men parted on unfriendly terms, and they did not achieve the union.

In May of 1531, Zurich and her allies asked the Catholic states to allow Protestant preaching in their jurisdiction. When the Catholics refused, the Protestant cantons formed an economic blockade and would not

---

[20] The terms *Catholic states* and *Protestant states* simply refer to the official religion of each state. Within Catholic states, there were some Protestants and Anabaptists, and within Protestant states, there were some Catholics and Anabaptists. Besides this, a few Jews and other small sects were scattered through many areas of Europe.

export goods to the Catholics. In retaliation, the Catholics declared war on the Protestants, and the two armies again met at Kappel on October 11, 1531. The Catholic army numbered about eight thousand, and the Protestants about fifteen hundred. The Catholics won, and Zwingli and twenty-four other Zurich preachers died in battle.[21] The Catholics mutilated Zwingli's corpse and burned it on a pile of dung. Zwingli's death is a reminder of the words of Christ, which he had rejected: "All they that take the sword shall perish with the sword" (Matthew 26:52).

After the battle, Catholicism regained some of its lost territory in Switzerland, but the Catholics were not able to restore Catholicism everywhere. Zwingli's followers carried on the reform in Zurich after his death. Some Zwinglians joined the Lutherans, and the remaining group merged with John Calvin's followers in 1549. Zwingli is the only major Protestant reformer to whom no denomination today can trace its roots.

---

[21] This time, Zwingli went with the army as a chaplain rather than a military leader. It is not known in what capacity the other twenty-four preachers went.

Chapter 4

The Growth of the Swiss Brethren

The Anabaptists spread out from Zurich and took the Gospel to other areas in Switzerland and Germany. Many small groups of believers formed in the first few years of the movement. Anabaptism took root in Zurich, St. Gall, Basel, Bern, and other areas.

Swiss Anabaptist Leaders

After the first leaders, Swiss Brethren ministers do not stand out prominently in history. Except for those involved in major church strife, the records usually contain only a fleeting mention of their names. There are several reasons for this. Many ministers, especially before 1575, served only briefly before being killed or exiled. Severe persecution hindered surviving ministers from traveling extensively and becoming widely known. And as the number of leaders increased, there was less need to work in other areas besides their own. There seem to have been many Swiss Brethren leaders, especially from the latter 1500s on, but there is little information available about them.[1]

One leader in that time whom we know more about is Pilgram Marpeck. For many years, Mennonite historians assumed that Marpeck was the main leader of the Swiss Brethren from about 1530 to 1556. However, more recently discovered Reformation documents name the Pilgramites and the Swiss Brethren as separate groups. Also, two letters have been found that Marpeck wrote to the Swiss Brethren as a separate group. Although Marpeck traveled among the Swiss Brethren churches and may have lived in Switzerland for a time, it seems that his ministry was concentrated among Anabaptists in southern Germany, not Switzerland.

Marpeck's preaching emphasized freedom in Christ and the Christian's holy life. He combatted what he considered to be a growing legalism among the Swiss Anabaptists. By the 1550s, when Marpeck's ministry drew to a close, the Swiss Anabaptists were becoming the "quiet in the land." Marpeck's preaching opposed this tendency.

Marpeck wrote some books on baptism and church life that give a good picture of early Anabaptist beliefs. Like other Anabaptist writers, Marpeck soundly denounced the idea that a person could serve God acceptably without taking up his cross and showing the world his true loyalties. Doctrinally, there were few differences between the Pilgramites and the Swiss Brethren. Both groups worked together in publishing Marpeck's writings.

After Marpeck's death in 1556, his churches gradually dropped the label *Pilgramites* and were simply known as part of the Swiss Brethren.

---

[1] Often the names of leaders were not revealed in order to shield them from Anabaptist hunters.

The Work at Zurich

Conrad Grebel and Felix Mantz, two original Anabaptist leaders, were sons of Zurich, and the first Swiss Brethren meeting took place there. However, persecution finally exterminated the Anabaptist church there. Persecution also quickly suppressed Anabaptism in the nearby village of Zollikon, where the first Anabaptist congregation had formed.

What caused this decline? By 1529, Zurich laws required its citizens to have their weddings in the state church, to register their children's baptisms, and to attend the state church services. Every citizen was to report at once any known Anabaptist, and the state heavily fined anyone who helped the Swiss Brethren. These restrictions also affected the villages surrounding Zurich, since they were under Zurich's administration.

Some executions took place in Zurich, and some Anabaptists died in prison. But even though Zwingli and the council had decreed death by drowning for every Anabaptist, this sentence was not completely carried out. Imprisonment, loss of property, and banishment from Zurich were the usual punishments. These conditions encouraged the Anabaptists to emigrate. Many Swiss Brethren moved from the Zurich area, as well as from other areas in Switzerland, to Moravia. In Moravia, many of them joined the Hutterites, but some started their own churches. Swiss Brethren churches existed in Moravia until well into the 1600s.

Zurich authorities apprehended a number of Hutterite missionaries who were soliciting immigrants to Moravia during the 1570s and 1580s. So many Swiss Brethren moved to Moravia in the 1580s that the Hutterite communities could scarcely contain them. These emigrations prove the vigor of the Anabaptist movement, even in the

Zurich area. Instead of dying out, the Swiss Brethren were multiplying and moving out.

During this time, the Zurich council tried repeatedly to reform the behavior and morals of the clergy and population in its district in order to offset the influence of the Anabaptists. The councilors realized that the lack of discipline in the state church was causing many God-fearing people to join the Swiss Brethren churches.

Truth was on the Anabaptists' side, and many of the common people expressed strong sympathy for them. In spite of this, Swiss Brethren history in the canton of Zurich basically came to a close in the 1660s, about 140 years after the movement had begun.[2] The suppressive laws were a major factor in forcing them to leave. Also, the canton rulers prevented the Anabaptists from participating in community economic life and fined them heavily for not attending state church services.

Many of the Swiss Brethren from the Zurich area emigrated to the Palatinate, an area in southern Germany, in the 1640s through the 1660s. From the Palatinate, many of them moved on to Pennsylvania. Some historians estimate that nearly 75 percent of the early Mennonites in Lancaster County, Pennsylvania, had roots tracing back to the canton of Zurich.[3]

---

[2] *The Mennonite Encyclopedia,* article "Zurich," 4:1047. J. C. Wenger, in *Glimpses of Mennonite History and Doctrine,* p. 39, notes that "it is claimed that remnants of the Swiss Brethren held out in the Canton of Zurich until about the year 1735." John Horsch, in *Mennonites in Europe,* p. 69, says that "by about the last quarter of the century most of the Mennonites of the canton Zurich had fled, mostly into Alsace and the Palatinate. However, many of the first settlers in the Lancaster, Pennsylvania area, 1710–1727, came from Zurich." These quotes show that, although Swiss Brethren history in Zurich was largely finished by the 1660s, a remnant seems to have persisted in that area for about seventy-five more years.

[3] Most of the remaining 25 percent were of Bernese descent. Delbert L. Gratz discusses this at length in his book *Bernese Anabaptists,* showing that the majority of early Pennsylvania Mennonites trace to the Zurich area, while the majority of early Ohio Mennonites trace to the Bern area.

Anabaptism in St. Gall

Soon after the first baptisms in Zurich, Anabaptism began in the town of St. Gall, nearly forty miles northeast of Zurich. The St. Gall city council did not oppose the movement immediately. In the spring of 1525, Conrad Grebel preached at St. Gall for two weeks and baptized a large group of people there. After his departure, other leaders took up the work.

Originally, some council members appreciated Anabaptism, but the peace was short-lived. Zwingli soon pressured them to stand against the radicals. However, because the councilors found it difficult to refute the brethren from the Scriptures, they were lenient with them for a time. Stiff persecution did not come for several months. In June 1525, however, the council forbade the Swiss Brethren to teach and hold meetings, threatening them with heavy fines and exile.

Because the Anabaptist movement had grown rapidly before the persecution began, St. Gall had a hard time controlling it. But with the stress of persecution, many Anabaptists finally recanted or left the area.

Anabaptists in Bern

Swiss Anabaptism was spreading in Bern, south and west of Zurich, by the fall of 1525. As in the Zurich area, the shallow spiritual life of the state church members and clergy caused many sincere seekers to turn to the Swiss Brethren. The Bernese government passed a number of regulations concerning cursing, drinking, gambling, and other sins. However, these laws did little to improve the morality of the common people. The Anabaptists' righteous lives drew many seekers, and the movement continued to grow. Persecuted Anabaptists from Basel and other areas also came to Bern in hope of finding more toleration.

In August 1527, Bern, Zurich, and St. Gall together passed a mandate against the Anabaptists. Bern held several disputations with the Anabaptists first, to try to convince them they were wrong; but when that failed, they began to persecute them. The Bernese authorities drowned a few Swiss Brethren in July 1529.

Until 1535, however, the persecution in Bern was not severe or widespread. But after this, the government exiled many Anabaptists from Bern. Those who returned were killed or locked in a pillory and exposed to public scorn. Some brethren were sold into galley slavery. Ministers and other Anabaptists who were considered especially dangerous or stubborn were usually beheaded or drowned.

The government hired special police to seek out the brethren. Since the police received payment for each captured Anabaptist, many rogues and criminals joined the police force. These efforts, however, did not exterminate the brethren. One of the Anabaptists testified that in spite of all the persecutions, their numbers continually increased.

The Emmental, an agricultural valley in Bern, became an Anabaptist center during the 1600s. The mountains and dark valleys of this region provided hideaways and secret places for meetings.

Due to the persecution, some Bernese Anabaptists moved to Moravia. In the late 1600s and early 1700s, several hundred Bernese families moved to Alsace, an area in France north of Bern. Hundreds of Bernese Anabaptists also fled to the Palatinate. Many of them were desperately poor when they arrived, so the Dutch Mennonites sent them financial aid. In the 1700s, many of these Bernese Anabaptists emigrated from the Palatinate to America.

Some of the Emmental Anabaptists fled west to the Jura Mountains. The prince of the Jura was Catholic,

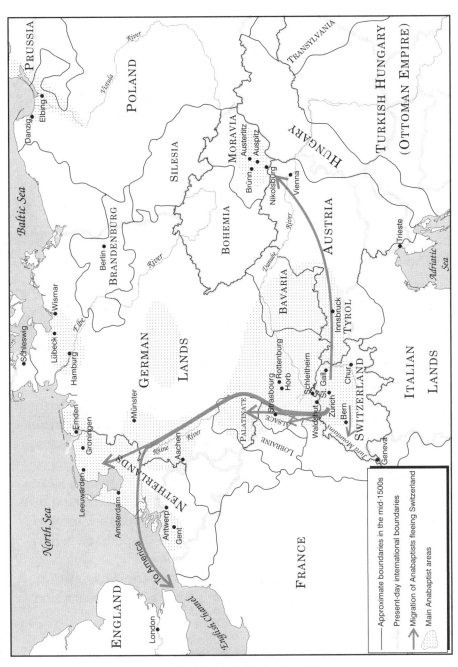

Swiss Anabaptist Emigration

but he tolerated the Anabaptists because they were excellent farmers. The Jura ground was rocky and steep, so the Anabaptists found making a living much more difficult there than in their native Emmental Valley. Nevertheless, so many Emmental Anabaptists went to the Jura that by the middle of the 1700s, very few brethren lived in the Emmental. They did not meet for regular meetings or have a minister of their own.[4]

Throughout the 1800s, many Swiss Brethren emigrated to America. This was largely due to economic pressures, lack of religious toleration, and pressure to serve in the military.

The Halfway Anabaptists

The Halfway Anabaptists were people who sympathized with the Anabaptists, believed much of their doctrine, and tried to shield them from persecution, but they were afraid to actually join the movement. The brethren also called them the "truehearted." It seems that without them the Bernese Anabaptists would have hardly survived, especially during the heavy persecutions. The Halfway Anabaptists often warned the brethren of approaching danger by yelling, blowing horns, or shooting. At times, they gave them food and shelter.

In some Swiss villages, the majority of the people were Halfway Anabaptists. Some state church ministers complained that their congregations were favorable toward Anabaptism. Many people were quite displeased when ministers preached against the Anabaptists.

Many Halfway Anabaptists felt that the Anabaptists were genuine Christians.[5] They felt that their own salvation

---

[4] Delbert L. Gratz, *Bernese Anabaptists*, 95.

[5] According to one book written in 1693, the common people felt that to be an Anabaptist was "by far the surest way of salvation." (John Horsch, *Mennonites in Europe*, 398)

depended on their association with these people of God. Many of them also helped the Anabaptists because they despised the state church, the corrupt clergy, and the government. The oppressed, overtaxed, common man felt a kinship with those who dared to differ with the established system. The Anabaptist persecutions were not popular with the common people. They considered the Swiss Brethren to be better Christians than the persecutors. The state leaders condemned and threatened the activities of the "truehearted," yet they were unable to stop them.

"Great is the number of those who are suspended between heaven and earth, and know not what to do," a Bernese observer noted around 1690. From this testimony, it seems that the Anabaptists did pressure their Halfway friends to join them, or at least that the brethren's faithful Christian lives were a real conviction to their friends. Further, the easier existence of the "truehearted" was a temptation to the Anabaptists as well, for a few left the brethren and became Halfway Anabaptists.

The Swiss Brethren's attitudes toward the Halfway Anabaptists varied, and this became an issue in the 1693 Ammann–Reist division.[6] Reist did not want to say that the "truehearted" could not be saved, but Ammann felt strongly that they could not be saved unless they identified with the suffering church.

The Spiritual, Family, and Economic Life of the Swiss Brethren

Persecution destroys normal life patterns. Nevertheless, the Swiss Brethren did have a distinct lifestyle. A number of early sources give us a picture of their daily lives.

---

[6] See Chapter 5 for more details on this division.

Church leadership and structure. The Swiss Brethren practiced the three-office ministry. The Schleitheim brotherly agreement[7] and a discipline drawn up at a ministers' meeting in Strasbourg in 1568 give us a number of details about the Swiss Brethren's view of church leadership.

The bishop was a minister who led in the observance of the ordinances, in ordinations, and in church discipline, and he had general oversight of a particular church. Bishops who had longer experience instructed the lesser-experienced bishops in pastoral care. The bishops and ministers encouraged and taught the church through preaching and private visitation. They also visited the wives and children of imprisoned brethren to comfort them and see that their needs were met. They occasionally traveled to other churches for preaching appointments. The church supported the ministers financially when their church labors overdrew their financial resources. One state church minister described the Anabaptists as being poor and unlearned workers, with few books besides the Bible, yet they could preach with great earnestness and get more results than the state church ministers.

The Swiss Brethren also ordained deacons, who looked after the material needs of the members. The deacons viewed their work as holy, and they discharged it with great care. In later years, the deacons also had charge of the Anabaptist private schools.

Although the Anabaptists held their church leaders in high respect, they committed themselves to openly address leadership failures. They publicly yet carefully dealt with erring leaders. When members slandered or withstood faithful leaders, the church disciplined them. The 1568 discipline says, "Such gossip and backbiting

---

[7] See Appendix II for a complete translation of this document.

shall not be allowed to anyone, nor shall such slander be accepted by any brother or sister, whether from strangers or from home people, but such matters shall be dealt with."[8]

A new leader was to be ordained immediately when a leader died or was driven away by persecution. However, it does seem that the Swiss Brethren did not carelessly ordain new leaders if a church lacked qualified brethren. Various churches did not have resident leadership for periods of time. Other brethren filled these vacancies by regularly traveling to serve the leaderless group. But the Swiss Brethren specified in the 1568 discipline that bishops should visit the churches that did not have sufficient leadership and ordain ministers and bishops.

The Anabaptists vested church authority in the local congregation and its leadership.[9] They believed that pure, committed churches could only be maintained by vesting the local body with authority to speak to needs and issues. Their church structure was a distinct break from the Romanist system, in which local priests claimed authority through a series of hierarchical positions leading back to the pope in Rome.

The Swiss Brethren made provision for the times when church work was necessary but no bishop was available. In such a situation, the local congregation or ministry had the authority to appoint a brother to lead out. A brother needed to have a good testimony and be in the confidence of the people before he could be appointed. He could take charge of Communion, baptism, weddings, and excommunication as necessary, until a bishop was available. It is not clear whether this included lay members or only ordained ministers.

---

[8] See Appendix IV for the text of this discipline.

[9] Franklin H. Littell, *The Anabaptist View of the Church*, 86–95.

The Swiss Brethren recognized their need for fellowship and counsel among their churches. Their occasional ministers' meetings helped to unite them in the faith. At several of these meetings, the ministers agreed on basic doctrinal and practical positions. These meetings were not regular. Between 1525 and 1568, only six meetings of any size were recorded. These meetings were in 1526, 1527, 1554, 1555, 1557, and 1568. Nearly thirty years passed between the 1527 and the 1554 meeting. Quite likely, smaller meetings occasionally took place throughout this period. By the 1700s, the meetings occurred once a year.

Worship services. In the early stages of the Anabaptist movement, worship services were quite informal. As the movement progressed, however, the Swiss Brethren saw the need for having organized worship patterns. This developed, to an extent, even under bitter persecution, though they were probably less formal than Mennonite church services today. They believed that not everyone in the church had the same gifts and calling, and that therefore the body needed order.

Local rulers often accused the Swiss Brethren of not worshiping on Sundays. Persecution, of course, often made it impossible or unwise to meet during the daytime. They often met secretly at night and frequently changed the place of their meeting. They often met three or four times a week. The meetings would usually last several hours. In the mountainous areas, they met in secluded caves or ravines for preaching, singing, and fellowship. In times of relative peace, the Swiss Brethren gathered in houses or barns for worship. Until 1847, the Swiss Brethren had no church buildings.

The group that gathered was usually small. The members greeted each other with the holy kiss and wished

God's blessing on each other as they met.[10] They greeted nonmembers with the words "The Lord help you," but did not greet them with a kiss.

The Congregational Order document of 1527, possibly written by Michael Sattler, gives an insight into an early Anabaptist church service. The brother with the best understanding of the Scriptures explained a portion of God's Word. Normally this was a minister if one was present; if not, a lay member would teach. The listeners were quiet and paid attention to the one speaking. There was no frivolity in the meeting. If a brother saw anyone erring from truth, he admonished him in a brotherly way. The brethren often observed Communion at these meetings. Early Anabaptist worship services were a warm fellowship of concerned believers, each committed to the truth.

From other documents, we learn that early Anabaptist worship services did not only consist of a preacher teaching the people, but sometimes they included dialogue among the entire congregation. In 1531, an Anabaptist testified that when they met together, they talked about the Word of God and each one asked the other, "How do you understand this passage?" They were committed to perceiving what God was saying to them through His Word. As they left the meeting, they admonished one another to walk steadfastly in truth.[11]

Material aid. In the early 1700s, the church began to build up a relief fund for church members in need. At times, money from this fund was used to help brethren emigrate. The deacons administered the fund. The fund was partly supported by the sale of property of deceased, childless members.

---

[10] Brethren greeted brethren, and sisters greeted sisters.

[11] See also the description of an early Anabaptist service in John Horsch, *Mennonites in Europe,* 128.

There is also record of freewill offerings. A document from 1540 records: "Above all a brother should always have a box or bag nearby with the knowledge of the church members, so that every member knows that a free offering or thanksgiving may be put into it if the Lord so admonishes either during the meeting or after."[12] The poor received the aid according to their need and the amount available. The brother who was in charge of the money, either an ordained man or an appointed older brother, distributed the money carefully. Before a recipient received help, the one in charge made sure that the need was legitimate.

Doctrinal thought. Historical sources give us two main records of Anabaptist beliefs. The Anabaptist writings—confessions of faith, rules, and letters—are an important source. The court records of their trials also help to complete the picture. The sources of the Swiss Brethren's beliefs, whether written by themselves or by their enemies, are in close agreement with each other.[13] The following paragraphs give an overview of their doctrinal positions. Later chapters discuss more thoroughly the Anabaptist view of the Bible, the church, discipleship, and the state.

Outstanding in Anabaptist thought was their attitude toward the Bible. They vigorously pursued studies in the New Testament, building their lives and concepts upon it. Study was not a mental exercise or a calling reserved for church leaders. The entire group pursued doctrine with the intention of being obedient to the whole New Testament. They earnestly sought direction for daily life

---

[12] Leopold Scharnschlager, "Mutual Order," 1540. Cited in Walter Klaassen, ed., *Anabaptism in Outline,* 128.

[13] The Swiss Brethren produced little literature compared with the Dutch Mennonites and the Hutterites.

in the Word and in prayer. The civil and religious authorities of the day were often amazed at the wealth of Bible
knowledge held by the common Anabaptist.

The Anabaptist belief that the Scriptures, rather than
popes and councils, were the final authority was much
like the Protestant position. However, the Anabaptists
carried this further in two ways. First, they were true to
the literal commands of the Scriptures, which many
Protestants took figuratively. Second, they believed that
the Scriptures were a model not only for religious thought
but also for practical Christian living.

The Anabaptists believed that the surest way to test the
truth of anyone's interpretation of the Bible was to check
whether the interpretation promoted a holy life. They also
stressed the need for being satisfied with what the Scriptures said, rather than digging into matters further.

Another hallmark of Anabaptist faith was their commitment to discipleship. The Swiss Brethren were a suffering church. Daily cross bearing was very real to them.
Following Christ, no matter what the cost, always marked
the true disciples. They saw humiliation and pain as vital
to Christian growth. They knew how their Master had
suffered, and they knew that they were no greater than
their Lord; so they endured persecution patiently.

Prayer, fasting, and almsgiving were common among
the Swiss Brethren. They kneeled for prayer. Evidently
some among them questioned this practice, for the 1568
discipline stated that those who had penitent hearts
should be humble and kneel in their hearts, but that this
should not replace actual, physical kneeling.

The later Swiss Brethren used some prayer books. The
first known Swiss prayer books were adopted and
enlarged from the Dutch Mennonites and were first
printed around 1700. In *Mennonites in Europe*, Appendix D, John Horsch has translated parts of prayers from

an Anabaptist prayer book.

The Swiss Brethren obeyed all civil laws that did not require them to violate the Scriptures. Their civil rulers testified that the Anabaptists willingly paid their taxes. They disciplined members who broke civil laws. For example, hunting game was limited to certain areas. The brethren expelled from the church anyone who hunted in forbidden territory.

Persecution played a large part in shaping the Swiss Brethren's thought. It especially affected their view of eschatology. The Swiss Anabaptists had a simple, Biblical view of last things. They felt that the persecution under which they lived was part of the tribulation that would precede Christ's Second Coming. Therefore, the suffering was only temporary. In a short time would come the Final Judgment. A reward awaited the faithful, and condemnation awaited the persecutors. In one undated writing, possibly written by Michael Sattler, the Roman church was considered the beast of Revelation.

Separation from the sinful world was central to the Anabaptist church. The true church was a called-out body of voluntarily submitted and committed believers. This called for separation of the believers from the social life of the world. It also affected their view of worldly fashions and thought patterns.[14]

The Anabaptist congregations held that every member must be personally involved in his brother's spiritual growth. They believed that church membership was voluntary, and held to adult believer's baptism as the only right entrance into the visible church. They also practiced pure Communion.

The Anabaptists believed that the high calling of Christianity precluded service in civil functions. That is why

---

[14] See also J. C. Wenger, *Separated Unto God* (Scottdale, Pa.: Herald Press, 1955), 53–73.

they were not involved in civil government and why they were nonresistant. They lived under a variety of governments, they paid their taxes, and they obeyed civil law as long as it did not conflict with God's law; but they could not give their worship and allegiance to any earthly government. The servants of Christ were servants of love, and love for every man precluded the physical punishment necessary to maintain civil order. Biblical love forbade hatred based on national wrongs, and it forbade the warfare that avenged those wrongs. The true church was maintained only by spiritual appeals to men's hearts, while the civil state was maintained by carnal force. Thus the two could never operate as one.

The Anabaptists often pled with the government to give them freedom to practice their faith. They believed that the true church would never persecute and destroy those who disagreed with it. This concept of "freedom of conscience" was based on the belief that it was every person's personal responsibility and right to choose salvation for himself. The freedom to practice and believe the truth was so important to them that they maintained it even if they were killed for it.

Family life among the Anabaptists was often under the stress of persecution. At times their young children were forcibly taken and baptized.[15] Throughout part of the Swiss Brethren's history, their children were considered illegitimate because the parents had not been married by a Protestant minister.[16] This kept the children from

---

[15] John Horsch says that this was done until about 1812 (*Mennonites in Europe*, p. 113). However, it does not seem to have been done all the time in every Swiss Anabaptist locality.

[16] During the 1800s, in some parts of Switzerland, Anabaptist marriages were considered valid if the planned marriage was announced in the state church pulpit for three consecutive Sundays before the wedding and a state marriage certificate was filed with the local government.

inheriting their parents' property when the parents passed away. The government then confiscated and sold the belongings, using the money to finance the state churches and suppress Anabaptism. During the early 1700s, the Bern officials kept a record of their Anabaptist property seizures. The record indicates that the Anabaptist families of this period had very limited economic resources.[17]

One of the earliest Anabaptist documents, the Congregational Order document (see Appendix III), mentions that the families should read the Psalms daily at home. It does not specify whether this was a family or personal activity, but from other sources, we gather that Anabaptist families did worship at home.

In times of relative peace, the Anabaptists could work and find markets for their products. Often a family all worked together, especially in the winter months, weaving cloth, making baskets, or doing various types of woodworking. During the summer, the Anabaptists who owned or rented land kept their families busy on the farm. Elderly parents lived with their children, passing their old age in work.

A document from 1780 mentions that Anabaptist children married very young, but gives no specific age. The Strasbourg Discipline of 1568 states: "Those who wish to enter the state of matrimony shall do so with the knowledge and counsel of the ministers and bishops, and it shall be undertaken in the fear of God; and since it is fitting they should inform and report to their parents."[18] Marriages were to be only with those of the Anabaptist faith.

A report written by a Swiss in the early 1800s gives us many insights into Anabaptist family and church life in the Jura.

---

[17] Delbert L. Gratz, *Bernese Anabaptists*, 54, 55.

[18] See Appendix IV.

It was as if I were living in the first times of early Christianity, they [Anabaptists] were so content, so pious and without hypocrisy. They live here so hospitable and industrious in patriarchal simplicity and pious customs. Among them are no drunkards, gamblers, no night revelers, no liars, no jealous neighbors. If a quarrel or dispute arises among them, which is very seldom, it is adjusted in a friendly manner by one of their elders. One helps the other at hay and corn harvest and whenever necessary without pay. Their temperance and customary cleanliness preserves their good health to a ripe old age. An old man of more than 70 years who was one of their teachers (they do not have preachers)[19] led me vigorously over mountains and valleys like a youth, to his church brothers' homes. What genuine love of married people, what tenderness among the brothers, sisters, what heedfulness of children toward their parents did I witness here! Practically their entire system of education rests simply upon the examples of the adults for the children and in a few words, "Have God before your eyes." And still they enjoy a rearing which is often nobler than the best given in the large world. What a people, what a Christianity that needs no lawyers, no preacher, no judge, and seldom a doctor!

On Sunday they come to this or that teacher . . . to be instructed in the open or in the barn or in a large room in a home. The teacher speaks as it lies nearest to his heart on what the people need or reads out of an old book of edification. He baptizes, gives communion, marries, but is a farmer like the others. Baptism precedes first communion and often the marriage of an engaged couple.[20] Their devotional, prayer, and song books including their martyr songs smack of

---

[19] The Anabaptists did not have *professional* pastors, but rather lay pastors as we do today. To the state church, this meant that they had *no* pastors.

[20] This sentence probably means that when several ordinances were observed in one church service, they were in this order—baptism, then Communion, and then weddings.

ancient times. When the services are finished those families living at a distance are served meals as these had been at their home at some former time.

Their implements and clothing are clean and unadorned like their modest homes. Like all other church groups of the Christian world, the Anabaptists have their fancies and peculiarities. That married men let their beards grow as a mark of distinctive manhood would not be so bad if only their dress were of the middle ages or Old Testament fashion. But the short gray coat, short trousers and stockings drawn up over the knees do not harmonize majestically with the beard. Buttons on their clothes are also forbidden. They are replaced with hooks and eyes and lacing. The women appear just as plain. No gold, no velvet nor silk, not even a bright or many-colored silk ribbon dare flutter from their straw hat. But in spite of all this the girls know how to find a means to adorn themselves without bringing their religion into danger.[21]

The brethren provided for the orphans among them. Due to the persecution of the parents, there were more orphans in the church than is the case today. The Swiss Brethren took orphans into their homes and raised them as their own children. The orphans whose parents had some economic means were cared for with their parents' money, and those whose parents had no means were cared for with church funds.

It seems that the Swiss Anabaptists homeschooled their children until the 1800s. The parents taught the children the essentials of reading, writing, and math as well as they could. At that time, only the most basic skills were necessary to function in society. Probably few of the Anabaptists were skilled scholars, but they did not need to be. In the 1800s, they developed church schools,

---

[21] Heinrich Zschokke, *Novellen und Dichtungen* (Philadelphia, 1854). Cited in Delbert L. Gratz, *Bernese Anabaptists*, 113, 114.

supporting them financially and often providing teachers from among the brethren. As time went on, these schools developed a nine-year program. Ministers often taught the schools, but occasionally persons of non-Anabaptist faith filled the need.

Economic life. In the 1600s and up to 1743, the state often confiscated the Anabaptists' personal goods. During the 1700s, however, persecution slowly wound down. The Anabaptists' peaceful testimony, the esteem in which most of their neighbors held them, and their loss of active evangelism finally brought a measure of toleration. In 1743, the Anabaptist Commission was disbanded.[22] When it ended, persecution largely ceased. However, the Anabaptists were still subject to fines for not serving in the military. The fines ranged from three hundred to four hundred fifty dollars, in modern values.

Information about Anabaptist economics and work ethics during the 1600s can be gleaned from the writings of a state church minister in the Emmental. This writer told his readers to follow the Anabaptists' example of good conduct but to avoid their erring doctrine. The Anabaptists of this period did not wear expensive clothing or drink and eat intemperately. They spent little time in play. Most of them were manual laborers.

By the close of the 1600s, heavy persecution had forced most Anabaptists out of the villages into the steep valleys leading away from the Emmental. In these regions, making a living was difficult. They farmed by hand on the steep slopes.

During the 1700s, many of them moved into the Jura Mountains in western Switzerland. Here most of them

---

[22] This state committee had been set up in 1659 to administrate persecuting and fining the Anabaptists.

raised cattle and grew vegetables. Some of them wove cloth as well. However, the government did not let them own land. They usually could not rent the best land or the land close to the villages.

Landowners who rented out their estates preferred the Anabaptists over other renters. The Anabaptists paid their rent promptly, paid more rent than anyone else would, and were willing to work on difficult land that others would not rent. They were a great asset to local communities.

Though the estate owners were glad for the brethren, not all the local people were. The local residents of Jura complained several times to their authorities, urging them to rid various areas of the Anabaptists. A main complaint was that the Anabaptists paid higher rents than the local residents could pay, thus forcing the local residents to seek other jobs or suffer unemployment. They also complained that food prices were higher since the Anabaptists moved in. The local cattle markets were hurt, they said, because the brethren imported cattle from other areas. Whether all these accusations were true is unknown, but it is known that the brethren were careful with their finances, were diligent, and put their families to work, so they could pay higher land rent than others were willing to pay.

Another side to the picture is the letter of an officer in a district where many Anabaptists lived. He supported them wholeheartedly, saying that they brought money to the area, worked land that no one else would use, and were a quiet, careful people who caused no trouble for the community.

In the early 1730s, the local citizens of Jura complained so much about the Anabaptists that the prince finally did order the Swiss Brethren to leave. The Anabaptists were very sorry at this turn of events. However, a high official appealed to the prince to revoke his order.

He told the prince that the Anabaptists did not harm the land but that they were a real benefit to it. He also reminded the prince that the government received one-tenth of their produce. Because of the pleas for toleration, and because the prince had not wanted to expel the brethren anyway, he did not enforce his order, and the Anabaptists did not leave. In appreciation, the brethren sent him a fine piece of linen.[23]

The stony, dry soil of the Jura Mountains and plateaus did not support a great variety of crops. The Anabaptists grew flax, which they worked into linen cloth. Oats, barley, and potatoes grew well and provided food for man and beast. The farmers made cheese and butter, which they usually sold to pay their rent. Woodworking also provided an income for some families. In many ways, these Anabaptists were self-sufficient. Since they usually lived far from the villages and marketplaces, they did not travel there unnecessarily.

A professor who visited the Jura Anabaptists in the 1780s wrote a description of their economic and church life, as follows:

> We took courage and after an hour and a half climb came to the home of old Benz . . . a clever Anabaptist. He lives on this part of the Jura called the Biel mountain. As he had to leave his place of birth in Canton Bern because of his religious beliefs, he built a home here. He leased his present location, which was formerly a waste, with a loan from the city of Biel of 50 crowns [approximately $600] and built a comfortable and roomy house. He planted a variety of fruit trees, laid out a garden, cultivated fruitful meadows and fields and together with his children plies his old handicraft of weaving in the remaining hours. As we came to his house we found him with his children sitting at the

---

[23] Delbert L. Gratz, *Bernese Anabaptists*, 74, 75.

table where they were eating breakfast. The breakfast consisted of mashed potatoes and the syrup from dried pears. Both of these were in special dishes and very tasty and clean. Although the industrious Benz is already well over 60 years old and has grey hair and beard, he is nevertheless still so robust that he can go down to Biel every day one or more times. He is one of the most esteemed ministers of the approximate 1,000 Anabaptists who are scattered over the plateaus and valleys of the Jura which belong to the city of Biel and the bishop of Basel. As both of these powers have not taken part in war for many years and as it appears they will not take part in any in the predictable future, it is possible for them to permit such a sect who considers it a sin of death to go to war and shed man's blood. Besides old Benz the Anabaptists have 25 ministers. The old prophet who received us in such a friendly way preaches nearly every Sunday and goes every third or fourth Sunday several hours distant to proclaim the word of God to his brethren. The more difficult the journey he must make, the more rich are his spiritual treasures. Ordinarily he preaches three or four hours. He told me himself that a minister (Reformed) from Zurich heard him and thought that he must have studied in his youth. He has an unbelievable knowledge of the holy scriptures and there is no scripture passage of value that is not always present for him and that he can't immediately say. Some of our party started in a high manner to discuss with him the particular tenets of his faith and we all marveled at what he said, for they had seldom heard the ideas of his sect, and especially how he knew how to use the favourable passage of the Bible. The conversation of this old, vigorous and ingenious man was for us a main source of conversation and I am convinced that this old man who has with his own hands built up and beautified a formerly unused piece of earth, and through his piousness has comforted many souls and held them back from corruption, that much more will be his heavenly reward than many of the renowned conquerors who have destroyed whole civilizations and laid waste flourishing lands.[24]

A son of a Swiss Brethren immigrant to Ohio wrote another account that depicts well the economy and lifestyle of the brethren in the Jura during the early 1800s.

The occupation of our fathers in Switzerland was principally that of farming and cattle raising. However, nearly everyone had a trade besides in order to earn something during the long winter. A deep snow falls upon the mountains deep enough to cover the fences, and at that time there is no work in the fields nor in the forest. Among them were joiners, turners, and shoemakers who made both wooden and leather shoes. But in our fathers' time the principal occupation in winter was weaving. The flax grew well so the women were able to spin a long yarn. In the narrow mountain valleys the winter evenings were long as the sun shone only a few hours during the shortest days, and in some places it did not shine at all for 16 to 18 weeks. The spinning wheels hummed by the light of the pine branches and the weaver's shuttle rushed back and forth until late at night. Because there is so much snow which drifts high, the house and barn are under one roof. There are some wooden buildings chinked with a mixture of clay and straw which is placed about the pieces of wood and between the logs. Many of the homes were constructed of limestone and plastered on the outside as well as the inside. The shingles were cut by means of a broadax and were kept in place with stones so that they would not be blown off by the wind.

Even though raising cattle is a part of their industry, most of them were not able to raise many. They each raised a cow and a few goats or a goat and several cows according to their means. The rich people kept a horse to help haul in hay. The cow was often

---

[24] C. Meiners, *Briefe über die Schweiz. Erster Theil* (Berlin, 1790). Cited in Delbert L. Gratz, *Bernese Anabaptists,* 83, 84.

hitched beside the horse to plow. Two men were always necessary, one to plow and the other to drive. From four to six persons followed the plow to hoe the furrow. Their plows looked like old prairie plows of our own country. They had two wheels under the beam to regulate the depth of plowing. One drove continuously back and forth along the side of the hill and all the furrows were made toward the bottom of the hill and then the ground from the last furrow was transported to the top of the hill in order to fill the last furrow.[25]

Very little wheat was sown as it did not ripen in the high altitudes. A type of spelt[26] was raised but generally oats, barley, and peas. These three, mixed, ground, and baked, composed the bread that the mountaineers ate. It was black and heavy yet it contained more food value than bread made from the finest white flour. Their principal product was the potato which found its way from America to the remotest mountain districts of Europe.

All work of the field like haying and harvesting was done with simple tools as the scythe, hand rake, and sickle. Threshing was done with flails. Both men and women worked during the busy season from four in the morning until ten at night.

Their food was simple and had little variety. It consisted generally of black bread, potatoes, milk, vegetables, and some meat. The latter was seldom served, perhaps on Sunday or holidays, for there was generally only one or two hogs killed for a family. Meat was therefore considered a rare dainty by many and when it was placed on the table the father cut it into pieces so that everyone received his right portion.

There was little luxury in setting the table. The potatoes boiled with the jackets were poured out on the

---

[25] I think this means that they would carry the dirt from the last furrow at the bottom of the hill to the first furrow at the top of the hill. Otherwise, the topsoil would have moved farther down the hill each year.

[26] Spelt is a hardy wheat grown mostly in Europe.

table. A bowl of milk or soup was given to each. Everyone carried a long pocket knife which was used in cutting bread if the father had not already cut it into the proper size.

Butter and molasses did not burden the table of our parents, and they did not spoil their stomachs with all kinds of unnecessary tidbits. The good things like butter had to be taken into the village in order to purchase necessary articles from the proceeds and also to pay the annual tax. Generally, a man was considered fortunate who could support his family in an ordinary manner and pay his rent. There were some who could make their livelihood very well and could lay aside a small capital for old age. But there were also many who had to rely on the church for support.

On account of these difficulties they became accustomed to laboring hard and learned to become very thrifty. Profuse idleness was not customary among them.[27]

The hard toil and handwork of the Anabaptists in Switzerland continued to be a part of their life well into the nineteenth century. These conditions prepared them for similar experiences on the American frontier.

By the 1800s, the Jura area became quite crowded with Anabaptists, and over half of them moved to America. Then it was much easier for those who stayed in Switzerland to make a living with the available land.

---

[27] Abraham J. Moser, "Aus dem Leben der Schweizer-Mennoniten," *Christlicher Bundesbote,* August 15, 1885. Cited in Delbert L. Gratz, *Bernese Anabaptists,* 109, 110.

Chapter 5

Difficulties in Swiss Brethren Church Life

Persecution

Some Christians think that persecution is a healthy experience for the church. That is true in some respects. Tertullian was partly right when he observed that the blood of the martyrs is the seed of the church. Persecution emphasizes the high cost of discipleship, which can result in a more committed membership. In times of persecution, the church may become the center of attention of society. God can use this to show the world an example of true Christianity and to draw sincere seekers to it.

However, Tertullian's statement does not portray the entire impact that persecution has had on the church. God commands us to pray that we may lead a peaceable life (1 Timothy 2:1, 2) for good reason.[1] The history of the Anabaptists illustrates this clearly.

---

[1] Satan, not God, spills the blood of the martyrs. Although God at times *allows* persecution, He does not *instigate* it. Satan is at the head of all opposition to the church.

Persecution played a large part in stifling the Biblical development of the Anabaptist church. It tore apart normal family life. It often restricted their evangelistic activities. It left some groups without leaders and severely strained the surviving leaders. Sometimes persecution wiped out entire churches. It finally wore down most Anabaptists until they were willing to accept unscriptural mandates in exchange for being unmolested.

A long time of religious freedom, however, can also wear down the spiritual vigor of the true church until Christians become willing to accept unscriptural terms to maintain that freedom. Whether the church remains faithful in any period does not depend on her setting but on how she relates to that setting. God's power can help her to always relate rightly. There is no excuse for failure.

Many people who desired to follow Christ did not join the Anabaptists, because of the suffering. Also, many who did join them turned back later under persecution. Those were only dross in the church anyway, we could argue, but that is not realistic. A few may have been hypocrites. Many, however, were weak or young persons who could have become strong Christians if they had been able to mature before facing a physical life-or-death choice. Many of us can look back and see weak times in our own spiritual experience when persecution would have likely caused us to leave the faith. This does not excuse failure, because God's grace is sufficient for any trial that He allows at any moment in the Christian's life. But it does show that physical circumstances affect people who are struggling with truth and who are weak in the faith. In some cases, favorable physical circumstances have probably allowed some weak Christians to mature and become more firmly grounded in truth. Physical suffering causes great fear, and the devil uses that fear to cause some to squelch the Holy Spirit's voice.

Sometimes people feel that persecution deters church divisions and disagreements among brethren. However, this was not always the experience of the Anabaptists. Men who were intensely loyal to truth and willing to die for their faith were at times unwilling to let their personal view of truth be tempered by their brethren.

Daniel 7:25 speaks of evil forces wearing out the saints of the Most High. This was certainly the case with the Anabaptists. In the early years of the movement, they would have emphatically rejected the idea of purchasing peace by keeping their faith to themselves. They willingly suffered death rather than accept terms that were contrary to God's commands. But persecution finally altered that firm conviction.

The Anabaptist settlements in the Palatinate are an example of this. The Thirty Years' War (1618–48) had devastated the Palatinate, and very few people lived there. Hoping to rebuild his economy and land, the ruler of the Palatinate opened the area for settlement by Protestants, Catholics, and Anabaptists. However, the Reformed Church was the state church. The Reformed people tried to suppress Anabaptism and succeeded in having Anabaptist meetings outlawed in 1661. After much pleading from the Anabaptists, however, the ruler changed that law in 1664. The Anabaptists could have meetings, but they could not admit non-Anabaptists to their meetings. Apparently, many of the Anabaptists accepted the new ruling gladly.

Similarly, in Switzerland, in 1823, after a period of relative peace, the Swiss government ruled that the Anabaptists were not allowed to evangelize. Again, the regulations were apparently not of great concern to many of the brethren. The stiff persecution and intolerance they had faced had almost completely extinguished the original evangelistic vision.

The early fervent Anabaptist evangelization we so much appreciate seems to have largely died out by the early 1600s. Throughout the years of persecution, almost all Anabaptists gradually withdrew themselves into a secret church. Most of their growth was from their own children joining the church. When at last they experienced freedom, it seems their original missionary spirit had burned out. They were content to be the quiet in the land.

Even though almost all of the Swiss Anabaptists lost their missionary zeal early in their history, they were still concerned about keeping the other aspects of their faith. Those who were most deeply concerned about maintaining their faith emigrated. Most of these found their way to America, where they maintained the faith more carefully for a time than their kin who remained in Europe. Most of the able leaders also emigrated, which further weakened the European churches.

Although the Swiss Anabaptists maintained much right doctrine and practice, their spiritual life lost much of its early vigor. The new birth lost its Biblical importance among some of the brethren. They began to view their faith as a culture to preserve instead of a living message that could meet the needs of all men. Eventually most Swiss Anabaptists fell to Pietism and other deceptive influences.

Discord

There are two main divisions in European Swiss Brethren history. The most significant is the Amish division of 1693. The other one is the Fröhlich division of 1834.

The Amish division of 1693. In the late 1600s, the Swiss government placed increasing pressure on the Anabaptists—fining them heavily, threatening them with execution, and confiscating their personal property. During this persecution, many Anabaptists fled north to Alsace and to the Palatinate. During this time, some Swiss Brethren attended the state church services, took Communion there, and even allowed the state church to baptize their babies, in order to avoid the persecution. They felt that these actions did no spiritual harm, and they continued to be Anabaptists, attending the secret services and identifying with the movement. Some of them even felt that the Halfway Anabaptists in the state church were saved, even if they never joined the Anabaptist church at all. These departures from the earlier Anabaptist positions became issues in the Amish division.

Earlier, in 1660, a group of ministers from Alsace had adopted the Dutch Dordrecht Confession of Faith as their own. The Dordrecht Confession upheld the ordinance of Feet Washing and took a strict position on social avoidance of excommunicated persons. The Swiss Brethren had never held these positions up to this point. Both of these positions played a part in the Amish division.

A little before the trouble erupted, Jacob Ammann, a bishop in the Alsatian churches, became concerned about the laxness of some of his brethren. He felt that many of the Swiss churches did not exercise church discipline properly. He took issue with the Anabaptist brethren who attended the state church services and with those who felt that the Halfway Anabaptists could be saved without uniting with the Anabaptist church. He wanted to introduce feet washing to the Swiss churches. The Swiss Brethren observed Communion once a year, and Ammann wished to change that to twice a year. Ammann also believed that the churches should maintain a stricter dress code and have untrimmed beards. But his greatest contention was with the Swiss Brethren's interpretation of excommunication. Ammann felt that the ban should eliminate social interchange with the banned person, even to the point of not eating, sleeping, or living with a banned person.

The Dordrecht Confession of Faith supported several of Ammann's concerns, so he and his supporters appealed to it as a basis for their contentions. They were not trying to introduce anything new, they said. They were simply trying to make the church consistent with its confession of faith. However, the Swiss Brethren in Switzerland had never adopted the Dordrecht Confession and did not feel bound by it.

After Ammann introduced some of these changes in the Alsatian churches, he traveled around to some of the Swiss Brethren churches in Switzerland, trying to get them to consent to a strict practice of the ban. However, he met stiff opposition from Hans Reist, a Swiss bishop. Most of the Swiss and the Palatinate churches refused to support Ammann's views, even though some of the ministers from both sides met several times to discuss the matter. Most of Ammann's brethren in Alsace sided with him, and whoever did not was promptly excommunicated. In the end, Ammann excommunicated Reist and his supporters and many of the Palatinate ministers, including some brethren whom he had never seen. Not content with dealing with the ministry, Ammann sent out a letter to all the Swiss church members, asking them to agree with him on the controversial issues. If not, he would ban them in a little over two weeks. No one except Ammann's group recognized these excommunications. These actions divided Ammann and his followers from mainstream Swiss Anabaptism.

Many brethren tried to persuade Ammann to stop his hasty excommunicating, but these pleas did little good. At one point, the Swiss Brethren agreed to yield to Ammann on all but the radical teaching of the ban, yet

Ammann and his followers would not agree to make peace. Wrong attitudes on both sides hindered the efforts at reconciliation.

By 1698, the Amish wanted to reconcile themselves with the Swiss Brethren. They admitted that they had done wrong in their rash use of excommunication. Some of the Amish leaders even excommunicated themselves to show their sincerity. But they still insisted that the Swiss Brethren needed to agree with the Amish view of shunning and with other controversial points. The Swiss Brethren were willing to accept everything but the extreme aspects of shunning, so the reconciliation effort failed. The division became permanent and continues to the present day.

Jacob Ammann had some valid concerns. If he had handled them Scripturally, he might have sparked a revival of conviction among his brethren. However, his insistence on certain details that were not backed by the Scriptures (regarding the ordinances, dress, and excommunication) discredited his valid concerns. Also, some of the details he insisted on had never been practiced among the Swiss Brethren. The Anabaptists of Ammann's time needed help, but his rashness hindered his efforts to give that help. Each group became more firmly set in their own imbalances and weaknesses, and both declined spiritually.

The division of 1834. Continual emigration, lack of solid leadership, and spiritual apathy hindered the spiritual growth of the Swiss Anabaptists. The Anabaptist churches in the Emmental, which had firmly resisted the Amish division, became severely divided in 1834.

Samuel Fröhlich, an ex-minister of the state Reformed Church, started the trouble. Fröhlich was educated in Reformed theology, but he came to believe in conversion through repentance and faith and in baptism upon confession of faith. These beliefs were contrary to Reformed doctrine, and Fröhlich soon lost his Reformed ministerial position.

After being baptized by another expelled Reformed minister, Fröhlich began to hold private meetings and preach his understanding of the Gospel. In 1832, he met Christian Gerber, an Anabaptist leader. Through Gerber, Fröhlich had an opportunity to preach to a group of Anabaptist church leaders. His energetic preaching created a sensation and a following in the Anabaptist churches.

Christian Gerber and another Anabaptist minister, Christian Baumgartner, were already dissatisfied with the spiritual apathy of their fellow ministers and members before they met Fröhlich, and he readily attracted both ministers. They supported his teachings and innovations. For the most part, Fröhlich's teaching was Scriptural, and it revived conviction in the churches, but he discredited some of the Anabaptist customs and teachings. He also stressed that Communion should be held every Sunday. One report states that "at a public meeting he gave the admonition like a preacher and in the evening often taught, so that the old simple doctrines now seem to some as foolishness."[2]

By 1834, Fröhlich had a large following. However, the Swiss government forced him to leave the area. This did not stop the controversy. The Anabaptist churches tried to correct the situation, but disunity increased until Gerber and Baumgartner met and held Communion separately with some of their followers. Several ministers from the Jura came to help unify the Emmental churches, but to no avail. The division rapidly spread into surrounding areas of Switzerland.

---

[2] *The Mennonite Encyclopedia*, article "Neutäufer," 3:858.

The division deepened when Fröhlich sent a young disciple of his, George Steiger, to the Emmental. Steiger claimed that everyone who stayed in the Anabaptist or Reformed churches was spiritually dead until they received baptism by immersion and joined his church. He drew more people away from the Anabaptists. He immersed Gerber and Baumgartner and organized a church of about 120 members. Half of these were former Anabaptists, and half were former Reformed church members. Before anyone could be a member of this group, he had to confess that until then he had been the devil's child. The Fröhlich group stressed emotional conversions and immersion and placed less emphasis on doctrine than their Anabaptist counterparts. The Anabaptist church soon excommunicated their two erring ministers and their followers.

The Fröhlich division has continued to the present day, and their group consists of far more former Reformed members than former Anabaptists. However, their doctrine has remained Anabaptist in many ways, and they have held to nonresistance better than the European Swiss Anabaptists. In America, their group is called the Apostolic Christian Church.

Like the Amish division, the Fröhlich division was augmented by spiritual laxity in some of the Anabaptist churches. Again, those who had concerns for the church handled them in a wrong way and thus were not able to spark a Biblical revival. In the end, the Fröhlich group underemphasized doctrine and overemphasized emotions, while the Anabaptists remained firmly entrenched in their "doctrinal correctness" and spiritual apathy.

However, not all spirituality was lost in the Swiss Anabaptist churches. Bishop Ulrich Steiner was a bright note after the 1834 division. Steiner was a gentle yet earnest and edifying preacher. He devoted himself to God and was ordained bishop soon after the division.

He traveled widely among the Swiss churches. He also stayed in contact with the Swiss Mennonites in America, especially with the Sonnenberg church in Ohio, to which some of his brethren had emigrated.

According to an 1823 law, the Anabaptists could not evangelize their Reformed neighbors. But some Reformed members attended the baptismal instruction classes that Steiner conducted, which aroused the local Reformed pastor. Through his efforts, the state placed Steiner in prison for several days on the charge of "proselyting." On another occasion, they fined him because of his mission activity. He was actively involved in evangelistic work, which was uncommon for Anabaptists of his day. His ministry brought new life to some of the churches and was appreciated by many of his brethren.

Pietism

Pietism[3] began in the Lutheran and Reformed state churches in the late 1600s. Some of the members were not satisfied with the spiritual deadness of the state church. They wanted a deeper experience of heartfelt religion. They emphasized emotional conversions, good works, and some aspects of nonconformity to the world. In general, the advocates of this movement did not withdraw from the state churches, but lived out their personal beliefs in a quiet and unobtrusive way, occasionally meeting with other like-minded persons for Bible study.[4]

---

[3] *Pietism,* as a common noun, simply means "stressing the emotional and personal aspects of religion, piety, or piousness." As a proper noun, it refers to a particular historical movement.

[4] A few Pietistic groups began new churches, but these were the exception, not the rule. The very essence of pietism militates against the basis on which the true church operates. Pietism in its purest form could never establish a true church. Such a group would lack the commitment to rise any higher than a friendly, religious association of similarly minded persons. Their commitment would simply be "I'll let everyone else enjoy his experience as long as he lets me enjoy mine."

Their concern focused on having the right feelings and experiences in their own hearts. Some of them emphasized Bible study, but they gave little attention to Biblical unity with fellow believers or to evangelism. The Pietist believed that his own conviction was his only standard of right and wrong.

The quiet, inner, personal emphasis of the Pietists was welcomed by many people, especially to those who were uncomfortable with the spiritually dead state church but were afraid to leave it because of persecution. Pietism gave them a way to silence their consciences without bearing the cross of Anabaptism. Pietism did not require a commitment to discipleship. Rather, it was emotional and experience-oriented, focusing heavily upon the sensation of personal contact with the Spirit and personal enjoyment of the redemption experience. And although the Pietists were willing to be nonconformed to the world in some areas, they were not willing to follow through with a Biblical separation that the world would reject them for. Pietism was a way to be "Christian" without giving up the self-life.

Let us compare Anabaptism and Pietism. The early Anabaptists insisted on true conversion and a deep spiritual experience. Their attitude toward martyrdom is evidence of a powerful, personal relationship with Jesus Christ. Both Anabaptists and Pietists believed that the Christian should experience a deep, satisfying relationship with God. They both emphasized inner piety. Neither group sought a religion built on creeds and traditions.

What then was the difference between the two? The Anabaptists believed that a sanctified heart produced a sanctified life. They believed that true Christians obey the Bible regardless of the persecution such obedience brings. The Pietists, however, wanted to enjoy a good relationship with God without conforming their lives to the Gospel.

The Anabaptists practiced New Testament church life, while the Pietists were simply a friendly association who gathered to talk about their personal union with God. The Anabaptists submitted to the body of Christ and supported Scriptural discipline in that body. They ordained leaders and gave them Scriptural authority to lead the church. The Pietists did none of those things.

The Anabaptists sacrificed their personal wills, thoughts, and desires so that God's work could be accomplished. The Anabaptists wanted the true church to prosper and wanted lost souls to find salvation. They believed that personal deprivation and hardship were essential to Christian discipleship and were a normal part of the conflict between truth and falsehood. The Pietists, however, allowed their personal thinking and comfort to take priority over the call to discipleship. They did not want to suffer hardship. They did not want to face the world's rejection. They based their joy on happy, emotional sensations instead of a deep-rooted faith in God's promises. Anabaptism in its early, powerful form was much different from Pietism.

As long as the Anabaptists maintained their commitment to Christian discipleship, they were a strong religious force. But during the 1600s, their commitment began to weaken. They partially lost their vision of true faith as an active discipleship based on a living relationship with God and His people. Consequently, the Anabaptist movement lost much of its power and willingness to suffer. There were still many Anabaptists; but they largely held their faith in secret, and they evangelized little. They accepted restrictions on proselytizing. They placed more stress on personal salvation, while quietly maintaining the faith and reproducing the faith in their families, instead of openly proclaiming the Gospel and completely committing themselves to discipleship. This quiet, inner emphasis came very close to the Pietist's attitude, and thus Pietism sounded good to many Anabaptists.

As time went on, this quietness affected more than just their relationship toward the hostile outside world. Although the Anabaptists maintained many traditional customs, their understanding of Biblical conversion became very weak. For example, by the 1760s many of the Palatinate Anabaptists regarded baptism as a mere form to be administered at a certain age. A genuine change of heart was not required for joining the church. For the Anabaptists who saw the need to revive spirituality and genuine conversion, Pietism appeared to be the answer.

Although having a spiritual heart is necessary and has at times been underemphasized in Anabaptism, pietism has not been able to answer that need. The overall pietistic influence on the Anabaptists led them to sacrifice Bible doctrines in order to recover a so-called deep spiritual life. True spiritual life is built on true conversion and true doctrine. If either one is missing, the spiritual life is not genuine.

Overall, the effect of pietism on the Swiss Anabaptists was a quiet, pervasive influence rather than divisions and great conflicts. When the Anabaptists attended Bible schools during the 1800s in preparation for preaching, or simply for religious education, they attended pietistic institutions. In the 1800s, they also associated more freely with other religious groups, including some of pietistic background. This propelled the nineteenth-century Swiss Anabaptists on a course of apostasy. The temptation to avoid conflict with the world, to leave Bible obedience for a so-called inner Christianity, and to reduce the authority of the church in the believer's life made tremendous inroads into the Anabaptist faith.

There also seems to be a connection between the Halfway Anabaptists and Pietism. In areas where Halfway Anabaptists were common in the 1600s, there were many Pietists in the 1700s. Halfway Anabaptists believed Anabaptist doctrine but did not join the Anabaptists, because of persecution. They lived with a guilty conscience. Pietism provided a theological escape route for such people.

Conclusion

From the 1800s on, the course of Swiss Anabaptism in Europe was increasingly apostate. The more-committed Anabaptists emigrated to America before the nineteenth century, and those who stayed behind succumbed to worldly pressures. This also happened in America, although not as soon. Faithful remnants in America separated from the mainline, apostatizing group, but this was not the case among the Swiss Brethren in Europe.

In 1850, the Swiss government made a new army conscription law, which did not exempt the Anabaptists from military service. (For a number of years, the government had made a special exemption for the brethren.) Stirred to action, the Jura Anabaptists appointed five leaders to investigate the problem. They requested the former exemption and signed the request with 126 names. The Emmental Anabaptists also made a similar request. Although the law was not changed, the Anabaptists were not forced to serve in the military at this time.

In 1874, however, the Swiss adopted a new federal constitution that exempted no one from military service. The government enforced the new law, though the Anabaptists tried in many ways to have it changed. Many of the young men went to Alsace, in France, until they were no longer liable for military service. Some of them employed other means to avoid military service. One young man cut off his trigger finger. Another sent a cripple in his stead; though the cripple did not have to serve, the government discovered the deception and punished the dishonest young man.

The Swiss government would not give in. The Anabaptists finally succumbed to the pressure and entered army service. They usually did their service in the hospital corps, although as time went on, some chose other areas of army service. Today the Anabaptist church in Switzerland does not censure these young men, but in general the church frowns upon any service other than the hospital corps.

Army service was not the only change among the Swiss Anabaptists. Beginning in the late 1800s, a steady decline eroded their separation from worldly clothing patterns. Their relationship to the state church was one of growing toleration. Since the 1930s, the Anabaptists of Switzerland have successfully competed for political offices.

As the Anabaptists moved toward the world, the friction between them and their Reformed neighbors slowly disappeared and was replaced by a friendly cooperation and appreciation. Around 1938, the Anabaptists of the Emmental stated that they did not consider infant baptism, as practiced by the state church, to be wrong. In 1947, the Emmental Anabaptists agreed to work with the state church without altering their doctrine or organization. The Jura Anabaptists, however, opposed this union and considered cutting off fellowship with their tolerant brethren.

Apostasy has taken a heavy toll on European Anabaptism. The cradle of Anabaptism is now a mission field, which should deeply concern us.

Chapter 6

The Rise and Growth of Dutch Anabaptism

In Germany and Switzerland, the official Reformation worked its way down through the government to the common people, as we saw in the second chapter.[1] Many common people in Germany and Switzerland also became involved in the religious upheaval, but the majority of them were willing to comply with whatever religion their government placed over them. In the Netherlands, however, the Reformation affected almost everyone in society. It was a movement that, especially in its early days, came from deep feelings within the Dutch people. As a whole, the Dutch manifested a greater tenacity and conviction

---

[1] The Reformation movement in southern Germany, Switzerland, and surrounding areas was also a grassroots movement, to a certain extent. But most of those in the grassroots movement became Anabaptists. As a whole, the official Reformers, Luther, Zwingli, and Calvin, supported a movement that came down from the top instead of up from the bottom. But in the Netherlands, the Protestant Reformation was a work carried on quietly and in hidden ways by lay people, much as Swiss Anabaptism had formed.

than the Swiss and Germans in clinging to Protestant beliefs in the face of strong Catholic pressure.

Pre-Reformation Religious Conditions in the Netherlands

The Catholic Church. The Catholic Church in the Netherlands was less organized and efficient than in other western European countries. In the early 1500s, there were only five bishoprics in the Netherlands, serving approximately three million people. In countries where the church had developed its system better, nearly twenty bishoprics served that number of people.

The lack of adequate organization was equaled by the apathy of high church officers in the Netherlands. Some of the bishops had little interest in their responsibilities

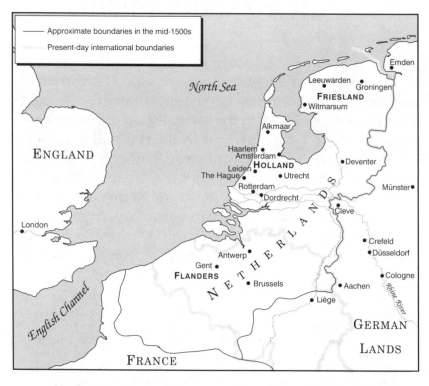

Netherlands and Surrounding Area, Circa 1540

and were usually absent from their bishoprics. Many church offices under the bishops were filled by nobles with political or financial motives. These nobles had no genuine interest in furthering Catholicism.

The lack of Catholic control showed up especially in the undisciplined and poorly trained clergy. There was no lack of priests, monks, and other lower officers. Church officers made up between 1 and 2 percent of the total population in the early 1500s. But many members of the clergy were morally corrupt and failed to live up to their vows. Drunkenness and concubinage were rife everywhere.

Despite these serious shortcomings, the Catholic Church held tremendous sway over the Dutch until the late 1400s. Monasticism flourished, and many people held a strong belief in the saints. Many people went on pilgrimages to Rome and Jerusalem to see historical Christian sites. The church was rich; and throughout the 1400s, it took on large building projects. The common people donated money to help finance these extravagant projects.

The rise of "Christian" Humanism. As we noticed in Chapter 1, much of European Humanism was secular and godless. Italian Humanism, especially, represented little more than a return to paganism. In northern Europe, however, Humanism developed a Christian flavor. The birth of "Christian" Humanism in the Netherlands laid the groundwork for the Dutch Reformation and indirectly for the Dutch Anabaptists.

In the late 1300s, a Catholic named Geert Groote led a religious and educational movement called the *Devotio Moderna,* or "Modern Devotion." Groote's followers were also called the Brethren of the Common Life or the Brothers of the New Devotion. The *Devotio Moderna* did not question Catholic doctrine. Rather, it emphasized the improvement and spread of schools, teachers, and libraries. It stressed inner, spiritual development and personal devotion to Christ. The movement grew in Deventer and the surrounding cities of the northeast Netherlands, attracting both common people and monastic orders. Many people in the northeast Netherlands learned to read in the schools run by the *Devotio Moderna*. These schools were a seedbed for Renaissance ideas and cultivated the idea that men should think for themselves.[2]

The *Devotio Moderna* directed men's attention from outward religion to inner devotion and gave them the tools to learn and be influenced by books. Thus it broke the ground for Dutch Humanism, which arose in the same northeast area of the Netherlands about one hundred years after the *Devotio Moderna* began. Dutch Humanism was a marriage of the man-centered Italian scholarship with the spiritual ideals of the *Devotio Moderna*. In general, it produced a more God-conscious scholarship than was practiced in southern Europe.[3]

Erasmus was an example of this fusion. He was born in 1466 and was educated by the Brethren of the Common Life. He became a prominent "Christian" Humanist scholar and wrote some books supporting Bible truths. He called attention to some Catholic practices and beliefs that were not Biblical. He pointed out some of the follies of Renaissance society. These things were good, but Erasmus did not see the need for Biblical repentance. He

---

[2] *The Devotio Moderna* did not reject Catholic forms of worship. It remained loyal to Catholic theology and institutions. It promoted a piety and an education that developed individuals beyond the normal religious experience of the day, but it did so entirely within the context of the Catholic Church. As such, it was not a Biblical reform movement, although it did promote some good goals and helped prepare the ground from which the Reformation sprang.

[3] This does not mean that northern scholarship was Bible based, but that it recognized and reckoned with God's truth much more than the southern scholarship did.

believed instead in changing society by the means of education. He held up certain Bible truths as good human ideals, but he taught that man can live up to those ideals by human effort. Erasmus did not recognize the place of the Biblical church in the believer's life. One of the main themes in his philosophy was that every individual has the responsibility to shape the content or form of his own Christian life.

Erasmus also had a tremendous fear of church schism and revolution because he was afraid of the social and civil uproar that usually accompanied such changes. He was afraid that the church or government might blame Humanist studies for creating religious strife, and repress scholars. Because of this fear, Erasmus railed bitterly against the Anabaptists[4] and refused to support Zwingli or Luther.[5]

In the thirty-year period between 1490 and 1520, "Christian" Humanism grew rapidly in the Netherlands. A growing number of schoolteachers and civil leaders supported the movement. The intellectual freedom and individuality promoted by Humanism made deep and lasting impressions on the Dutch religious mind. While the more liberal sector of Humanism concentrated on a revolution in education and secular culture, the "Christian" form of Humanism also emphasized a revolutionary idea of piety and religious thought. It distanced its adherents from the fixed patterns of devotion and worship that the Catholic Church taught.

---

[4] In 1534 Erasmus wrote: "The Anabaptists have flooded the Low Countries just as the frogs and locusts flooded Egypt, a mad generation, doomed to die. They slipped in under the appearance of piety, but their end will be public robbery. And what is like a miracle, although they teach absurdities, not to say impossibilities, and although they spread unlovely things, the populace is attracted as if by a fateful mood or rather the impulse of an evil spirit in this sect." Cited in *The Mennonite Encyclopedia*, article "Erasmus," 2:240.

[5] He supported Luther at first but soon withdrew.

This did not go unnoticed by the church. Although Humanism had exerted a strong influence over Dutch society, the defenders of the traditional church and religious philosophy remained both stubborn and powerful. The corrupt Catholic Church, fortified with both power and privilege, was too strong to be simply swept aside.

Dutch society becomes estranged from the Catholic Church. Both the influence of "Christian" Humanism and the corruptness of the church served to erode public confidence. Despite its impressive structure, the prestige of Catholicism in the Netherlands declined after the 1400s. Monasteries and nunneries emptied rapidly. Respect for the clergy declined radically. Several leading church officers noted that in some parts of the Netherlands, the clergy was universally hated.

The Dutch also largely lost faith in the worship practices and philosophies that the old church had carefully nurtured for centuries. Pilgrimages to the Holy Land lost their appeal. The traditional Catholic processions still took place, but there were many signs that these were no longer respected as they once were. The Netherlands was on the eve of the Reformation.

The Dutch Reformation Begins

The influence of Martin Luther. The Dutch people's gradual loss of confidence in the church was well under way by 1517, when Luther nailed his ninety-five theses to the Castle Church door in Wittenberg, Germany. Within several years, Luther's early writings circulated everywhere in the Netherlands. The high literacy rate and the large number of booksellers and printers in the Netherlands contributed to this circulation.

Luther's zealous protest against the decadence of the Catholic Church and his insistent focus on the Gospels touched a harmonious chord in the Dutch heart. Luther gave the Gospel to the people in the common vernacular and used it heartily in condemning the Roman Church. By the early 1520s, several political leaders in the Netherlands were open supporters of Luther, and Luther's ideas had strongly influenced the Dutch religious mind.

Emperor Charles V resists the Reformation. Charles V, the so-called[6] Holy Roman Emperor, ruled a vast territory in Europe, including the Netherlands. A staunch Catholic, in 1521 he declared Luther a criminal, banned his writings, and demanded that he be seized and put to death. The Catholic leaders in the Netherlands lost little time in putting the decree against Luther's writings into effect. They burned hundreds of Lutheran books in the next few years.

In 1522, Charles set up the Inquisition in the Netherlands. In 1523, the Inquisition burned to death the first Protestant martyrs in western Europe. The Inquisition's efforts, however, were hampered by the fact that it had arrived on the scene too late. Its officers soon became aware that support for the church was at an extremely low ebb in the Netherlands. But this did not keep the Inquisition from having an impact on the Dutch Reformation. It targeted men of influence, such as booksellers, schoolmasters, and other officials, and made it impossible for such men to openly support the Reformation without losing their positions and lives.

The persecution could not completely silence Protestantism in the Netherlands, but it did temporarily break the back of the movement. It became nearly impossible to set up any Protestant organization there.

---

[6] The title *Holy Roman Emperor,* which the popes conferred on powerful kings who were protectors of papal interests, was a misnomer. None of these men ruled an actual empire, none were Roman, and certainly none of them were holy.

Differences between the Dutch and the German Reformation. In parts of Germany and Switzerland, the Reformation was implemented by powerful civil leaders who dared to defy the pope and the emperor. But even while Luther and Zwingli were developing their positions and creeds and strongly influencing their religious settings, the hope of setting up a Protestant church in the Netherlands was fast disappearing. The only separatist church in the Netherlands during this persecution was the Anabaptist church. The Reformation of the countries south of them did influence the Dutch people, but since there was no opportunity for Protestant church groups to develop, structured Protestant doctrine and creeds did not become a part of Dutch thinking. A form of Protestantism existed in the minds of many people, but it was simply a spiritual outlook, not a powerful church organization.

The Reformation in the Netherlands was more of a grassroots effort than the German Reformation. In Switzerland and Germany, many people were willing to be a part of whatever church their government placed over them. In some areas, Swiss and German people passively changed their religion from Catholic to Protestant and back again several times, depending on who controlled their area at the moment.[7] But the Dutch held to Protestantism with great tenacity under the surface, even though they were forced to retain an outward form of Catholicism under the rule of Charles V. In 1568, when Philip II (Charles V's son and successor) began to lose his hold on the Netherlands, Protestantism burst forth again with a warring vigor.

The Rise of Dutch Anabaptism

One group of people—the Dutch Anabaptists—refused

---

[7] John Horsch, *Mennonites in Europe*, 25.

to give in to government demands. Before 1530, there were no known Anabaptists in the Netherlands. After that, however, their numbers grew rapidly.

Dutch Anabaptism arose with much more confusion than did Swiss Anabaptism. Dutch Anabaptism was born amid a religious chaos that spawned some unbiblical movements. Although many of these bore the name Anabaptist, and many historians have attached their sins to Anabaptism, a careful evaluation of history vindicates the faithful Anabaptists. The militant "Anabaptists" soon passed off the scene, but they brought lasting infamy on the faithful Anabaptists. On the other hand, the faithful, Biblical Anabaptists, by the blessing of God, have continued until the present day.

Melchior Hofmann introduces Anabaptism to the Dutch. Melchior Hofmann (c. 1495–1543) had an interest in the Bible and religious literature, and acquired an extensive knowledge of both through diligent study. He became an early follower of Luther and his reformation efforts. Hofmann became a Protestant minister in Germany and labored there until he fled persecution in the early 1520s.

Throughout the following years, Hofmann moved from city to city more than ten times, seeking acceptance as a preacher. Wherever he went, he emphasized a radical interpretation of prophecy and typology. Invariably, he lost favor with religious and political leaders and was forced to move on. Even Luther, who had once befriended him, turned cold and denounced Hofmann strongly.

In 1529, Hofmann came to Strasbourg, Germany, where again the local reformers did not accept him. Nevertheless, he continued in the city. He managed to publish some of his writings, which contained a detailed account of the end times. He also met the Anabaptists, apparently for the first time, and became interested in their teachings. Hofmann may have joined the Swiss Anabaptists in Strasbourg early in 1530. There is no clear evidence for this, but it is certain that he learned some Anabaptist doctrines during his stay there. Soon Hofmann, however, had to leave the city. His prophetic writings had circulated to the city authorities, who felt that his views presented an intolerable challenge to their religious authority.

Hofmann then found his way to East Friesland. In the town of Emden, he gathered a group of people who were dissatisfied with the other churches, and began holding services with them. The group he founded seems to have held a basically Anabaptist doctrine, except for their chiliastic end-time beliefs. At this point, he was teaching baptism upon confession of faith, holiness of life, nonswearing of oaths, and nonresistance. These teachings were good, but to support his ideas and visions about the end times, he often twisted the Scriptures. The group grew rapidly, but the growth caught the attention of the city authorities, who forced Hofmann to move on. He left Jan Volkerts (Trijpmaker) in charge of the church and returned to Strasbourg.

Hofmann returned to the Netherlands twice, and was active in evangelizing and baptizing. He also became increasingly fanatical in his views of the end times. Soon he believed that he would take a leading part in the return of Christ, after which he would lead the Anabaptists to armed victory over other religious groups. Hofmann set dates for Christ's return and predicted that Christ would come to Strasbourg, where he would meet Him at the head of 144,000 saints. First, however, Hofmann believed he would be imprisoned for a short time. He turned himself over to the authorities at Strasbourg in May 1533 and was thrown into prison. Hofmann lay there for just over ten years. He gave up his position on believer's baptism and revised his end-time dates several times. He finally died in prison in 1543, his health and spirit broken.

In his later years, Hofmann advocated that his followers should remain quietly in the state church until the Lord returned to deliver them. The Swiss Brethren and many of the Dutch Anabaptists emphatically rejected such teaching. Hofmann's fanatical end-time beliefs, his encouragement to "stand still" and wait for less persecution, and his wavering on swearing and believer's baptism finally made the Swiss Brethren state that they had nothing to do with the teachings of Melchior Hofmann. If he had ever joined the Swiss Anabaptists in Strasbourg, of which there is no certain proof, he was no longer a part of them in his later years.

Melchiorite converts introduce Anabaptist teachings to the Netherlands. While Hofmann was in Strasbourg, Jan Volkerts and Sicke Freerks, as well as other converts, spread Anabaptist teachings in cities of the Netherlands. Many of these missionaries soon became martyrs. Freerks was beheaded at Leeuwarden, Obbe Philips's hometown. Freerks's martyrdom caused Menno Simons, a priest in the neighboring town of Pingjum, to study the Scriptures, the church fathers, and the Reformers on the doctrine of baptism. At this point, however, Menno was still almost five years from renouncing his priesthood and the Catholic Church.

Despite the executions, Anabaptism in its Melchiorite form grew rapidly in the Netherlands. Jan Matthysz, Bartholomew Bookbinder, Dirk Cooper, and Peter Woodsawer were among the foremost leaders. Near the end of 1533, Obbe and Dirk Philips were converted to this group. At this point, many of the Melchiorites continued as members of the Catholic Church to avoid persecution, but

inwardly gave assent to Anabaptist beliefs. They emphasized visions and dreams and the interpretation of prophe-
cies of end-time events. These deviations from Biblical
Anabaptism seem to have come from Melchior Hofmann's
influence. This misuse of the Scriptures was soon taken
to even more radical extremes by Hofmann's followers in
the earthly "city of God"—Münster.

The Münster Tragedy

The growing Catholic repression in the Netherlands
generated frustration and pent-up anger among the common people. Since the Protestant church had stopped
visibly resisting the Catholics, people too aroused to keep
quiet had nowhere to turn but to the Anabaptists. Absorb-
ing this element gave early Dutch Anabaptism a character quite different from the Swiss Anabaptists. Early
Dutch Anabaptism was certainly fervent, but also chaotic
and prone to fragment.[8]

It was not long before the Dutch Anabaptists divided
into two main factions. By 1534, the Philips brothers led
one group. They taught nonresistance and separation
from the state church, and they did not trust radical,
prophetic notions. Jan Matthysz and Jan of Leiden led
the other faction. These carnal men became increasingly
obsessed with the idea that God would set up a kingdom
on earth and that they were central figures in this plan.
They decided that they needed to forcibly help Christ usher
in His new kingdom. When they heard that the common
people of Münster, a city in northwest Germany, had over-
thrown their upper classes and their Catholic bishop, the
two Jans contacted the preachers of Münster. After win-
ning the preachers to their views, the Jans came to Münster early in 1534 and took control of the city.

---

[8] Jonathan Israel, *The Dutch Republic—Its Rise, Greatness, and Fall, 1477–1806.*

From Münster, they sent out prophets to call all "Anabaptists" together to the "New Jerusalem." Hundreds of misguided souls streamed to the city, under the impression of being on the verge of a great, violent, apocalyptic change. The Catholic bishop of Münster, who did not reside there, soon besieged the city, and fanatical Anabaptists could no longer enter it. For eighteen months, the siege dragged on. Jan Matthysz was killed in a brief skirmish with the Catholic army, and Jan of Leiden took his place as the king of the city. Terrible famine and disease swept the city. During the chaos, Jan introduced polygamy, defending it from the example of the Old Testament.[9] The Catholic forces finally overcame the city in June of 1535. Heavy slaughter ensued, and Catholics caught the main Münsterite leaders. The authorities tortured these leaders to death and then placed their bodies in iron cages and suspended them from the tower of St. Lambert's Church, where they remained for four hundred years. While awaiting death, Jan of Leiden confessed his wrongdoing and admitted that he was being punished justly for it.

When the Münsterite rebellion was crushed, Jan van Batenburg, another revolutionary "Anabaptist," gathered more radicals and traveled around the Netherlands, plundering churches and murdering innocent people who would not adhere to his doctrine. His wild career ended with his capture in 1537, and he was executed the following year.

These radicals brought tremendous suffering to all Anabaptists, both the peaceful and the militant. It seems that the Dutch authorities realized that there was a difference between the two groups, at least at times, but trusted neither of them. Consequently, the authorities

---

[9] This was too much for some of his followers. They rebelled, but their rebellion was violently quelled.

condemned approximately twenty-five hundred to a martyr's death.[10] The nonresistant brethren who completely rejected the Münsterites and Batenburgers often suffered the same punishments as the worst radicals.

The Obbenites

The growing differences in the Dutch Anabaptist movement had forced Obbe and Dirk Philips to separate from the other fanatical sects even before the culmination of the Münsterite tragedy. Obbe testified of his sorrow that none of the other teachers lived according to the Word of God. The world persecuted them, and their supposed brethren misled them with notions and dreams. The Obbenites soon entirely rejected the idea of new revelations that superseded the written Word. They also rejected the false teaching that one could be a member of the Catholic Church and secretly be an Anabaptist.

The Batenburgers, when rebuked by the Obbenites for their militancy, took an oath to persecute and kill the Obbenites. Under these circumstances, Obbe and Dirk separated from all other groups and gathered the faithful Anabaptists, who refused resistance and oaths and had separated themselves from the Catholic Church.

The Obbenites' doctrine was very similar to the Swiss Brethren teachings. Though Melchior Hofmann transmitted a few basic Anabaptist beliefs from Strasbourg to the Netherlands, the Obbenites had no known contact with the Swiss Brethren. They had only the Scriptures to guide them as they cut the Melchiorite and Münsterite connections. In most of their doctrine and practical beliefs, they were identical to the Swiss Brethren, even though they apparently arrived at many of their conclusions independently. This attests to the careful,

---

[10] *The Mennonite Encyclopedia*, article "Netherlands," 3:827.

Scriptural approach they each took as they reformed their views of God, salvation, and the church.

Menno Simons Joins the Obbenites

Menno Simons was alerted to the errors of infant baptism by the martyrdom of Sicke Freerks, an early Anabaptist evangelist in the Netherlands. Menno's awakening took place in 1531. For two years, he had doubted the Catholic teaching of the mass. Now the question of baptism came up.[11]

Menno carefully searched the Scriptures for evidence of infant baptism and found no mention of the practice. On that basis, he rejected the Catholic doctrine, the teaching of the church fathers, and the Lutheran and Zwinglian teaching on infant baptism. Yet he continued in the Catholic Church. He loved the ease and financial security his church positions brought him.

About the beginning of 1534, some Münsterite prophets came to Witmarsum, where Menno was priest. Here they led some of Menno's parishioners into their perverted beliefs, which was a great grief to Menno. He immediately taught against the Münsterite errors and became very adept at defeating them. He also wrote a tract against them.

But Menno's conscience did not let him rest. Though he now knew that the Catholic mass and infant baptism were wrong, he continued to observe these sacraments. He endeavored to keep seeking souls from going astray after the Münsterites, but realized that he was only calling them back to the Catholic Church, which he did not believe was a Biblical church either. It took one more tragedy, however, to break Menno loose from the Catholic Church.

---

[11] Detailed accounts of Menno's spiritual search and conversion can be found in *Menno Simons' Life and Writings, The Complete Writings of Menno Simons,* and *Mennonites in Europe.* These books are available from Rod and Staff Publishers, Inc.

Early in 1535, a band of rebels, under the leadership of Jan van Batenburg and others, seized and held the Old Cloister near Bolsward.[12] The government immediately besieged the monastery and soon overcame the fanatical occupants. About half of those not slain in the battle were executed afterward. This event tremendously burdened Menno. Here was a group of misguided radicals who were willing to give their lives for their faith, while he was not willing to break with the Catholic Church, even though he knew it was clearly unbiblical. Would he have been able to help some of these misled fanatics if he had broken with the errors of the Catholic Church and taught the whole truth? He did not know, but neither could he shrug off the feeling of condemnation. He had a knowledge of the truth which he was unwilling to proclaim, and it did not let him rest. In his agony, Menno sought and found rest in repentance and in giving his life to the Lord. In his own words:

> My heart trembled within me. I prayed to God with sighs and tears that He would give to me, a sorrowing sinner, the gift of His grace, create within me a clean heart, and graciously through the merits of the crimson blood of Christ forgive my unclean walk and frivolous easy life and bestow upon me wisdom, Spirit, courage, and a manly spirit so that I might preach His exalted and adorable name and holy Word in purity, and make known His truth to His glory.[13]

Soon after this, Menno left the Catholic Church. For a time, he lived quietly, studying the Word, writing, and communicating with the few Anabaptists around him who were firmly committed to truth. There is evidence

---

[12] Some sources say that Menno's brother was killed in the Old Cloister battle. Historians disagree about that. It appears that if a Simons was killed there, he probably was not Menno's brother.

[13] *The Complete Writings of Menno Simons,* 671.

also that he was involved in some evangelistic work at this time. An Anabaptist who was executed in 1540 testified that Menno Simons had baptized him 1536.

About a year after his conversion, Menno, who was probably now residing in the Groningen area, was asked to consider becoming a leader among the Anabaptists. Several brethren came and presented the request to him, in the name of other brethren in the area. The request greatly troubled Menno. He knew what dangers accompanied leaders in the persecuted church. Yet he also saw the great need of many seeking souls who were wandering as sheep without a shepherd. After considering the matter and spending much time in prayer, Menno yielded to the entreaties of his brethren. The exact date of his ordination is unknown, but it was near the end of the 1530s and performed by Obbe Philips.

Trials Face the Fledgling Church

When Menno joined Obbe and Dirk Philips in leading the Dutch Anabaptists, the church was facing a number of obstacles. There were, at this point, about five different groups of Anabaptists in the Netherlands, some of which did not deserve the name. There were still some Münsterites, who continued to cling to the program of their slain leaders. Secondly, there were the Batenburgers, who continued their murderous raiding for some years after Batenburg himself had been executed. These were the only two groups that advocated the use of physical force. There were three nonresistant groups—the original Melchiorites, the followers of David Joris (the Davidites), and the followers of Obbe Philips (the Obbenites).

David Joris joined the Anabaptists in 1534, before Menno Simons cast his lot with them. Subsequently, the church ordained him to the ministry. Soon, however, through fanatical visions, he began to consider himself a special, anointed prophet. Rejected by the Obbenites, he established a group of his own. He emphasized a so-called spiritual relationship with God at the expense of a holy life, which led to sinfulness among his followers. Joris did not believe that the Bible was the sole authority for true Christianity. He interpreted all Bible doctrine by what the "Spirit" told the believers personally. The visible church, the ordinances, and even the Scriptures finally lost all meaning in Joris's mind. He thought his own heart and mind taught him all he needed to know.

From 1539 on, Menno attacked Joris's teaching. Nevertheless, Joris had many followers and exerted a great influence for a time. Under pressure of persecution, he finally fled to Basel and became an honored member of the Reformed Church there, under the name Jan van Brugge. He lived a double life, communicating with his Dutch followers in secret until his death. The Basel authorities did not discover his true identity until nearly three years after he died. When they realized that their late citizen was David Joris, they dug up his body and burned it along with many of his books.

Another obstacle arose from within the Anabaptist brotherhood: Obbe Philips decided to leave the church. In a list of Dutch Anabaptist elders in 1540, a note mentions that Obbe Philips had left the faith. Obbe wrote a confession that outlined his reasons for leaving. He thought that since the true church is invisible, it is wrong to establish an organized, visible body of believers unless one has received a direct command from God to do so. Since Jan Matthysz had taught and ordained him, Obbe felt that God had not commissioned him. He believed that he had been personally deceived and had led others into deception as well.

But Obbe had not always believed this way. He failed

to realize that the Scriptures do contain many teachings relating to the establishing of a visible church, and that to do so was not only sanctioned but also directly commanded by God. The Obbenites recognized his errors. There is no record of a division or of a group that followed Obbe; indeed, his principal reason for leaving the church would have prohibited any such organization. Concerning religion, from his defection until his death, he seems to have led a solitary life. Some conjecture that he related to the Lutheran Church.

Until 1540, David Joris's followers seem to have been a larger group than the Obbenites. However, despite Obbe's departure, after 1540 the Obbenites gradually became the mainstream of Dutch Anabaptism. The other groups faded into the background and became extinct.

The Faithful Anabaptists Unite and Grow

Menno Simons seems to have been the Dutch Anabaptists' main leader after Obbe left. Together, he and Dirk stabilized and invigorated the Obbenites, helping the young church to form out of the ashes of previous "Anabaptist" ruins. They did not build a great system of theology, but their writings greatly influenced the church and world of their day. Their main contribution to the growth of the church was their strong emphasis on practical holiness, the believer's separation from the world, and the necessity of personal submission to the church. Such a base gave the church an important place in the lives of those who committed themselves to it. Dirk seems to have placed a greater emphasis on the authority of the church and elders than Menno did.

This emphasis on order and discipline stabilized the Dutch Anabaptist church and made it capable of expanding. Within thirty years after Menno joined the church, it had grown tremendously, in spite of the severe persecution. The movement reached south from the northern provinces of the Netherlands to present-day Belgium. The concentration of Anabaptists in Friesland, where persecution was not as heavy as in other areas of the Netherlands, may have been as much as 25 percent of the entire population around 1586.

This growth was due to not only Menno and Dirk. They ordained Adam Pastor, Gillis of Aachen, Leenaert Bouwens, and other leaders to help build the church. However, Menno was undoubtedly the foremost leader among the Dutch Anabaptists until his death. By 1545, the Dutch Anabaptists were known as "Mennists," which later changed to "Mennonites."

Menno ordained Adam Pastor around 1542, but by 1547 Adam was banned for denying the Trinity. Gillis of Aachen was ordained at the same time as Pastor. He worked in Flanders, the southern part of the Netherlands. The Flemish Anabaptist martyrs frequently named him as the one who had baptized them. In 1557, Gillis was captured. He recanted but was still beheaded. Because of his unfaithfulness, *Martyrs Mirror* does not mention him. Some sources say he repented of his recantation before his death.[14]

Leenaert Bouwens was ordained a minister around 1546, and Menno ordained him bishop in 1551. Leenaert was a strong leader, perhaps too strong, in some ways, for the good of the church, as we will see in Chapter 7. Nevertheless, he did a tremendous amount of evangelizing and baptizing in his thirty years as a leader. Leenaert kept a list of those whom he baptized, which records at least 10,252 baptisms between 1551 and 1582.

All of these leaders lived in extreme danger, constantly

---

[14] John Horsch, *Mennonites in Europe*, 218.

being sought by the authorities. Because of this, Menno and Dirk lived in Germany but often traveled into the Netherlands to strengthen the churches.

Persecution Spreads the Church

Charles V ruled the Spanish Hapsburg Empire, which included the Netherlands, during most of the early Reformation years. Brussels, a city in Flanders, was the headquarters of the Spanish empire in the Netherlands. Flanders also contained the Inquisition headquarters for the Netherlands, begun by Charles V to root out the Dutch Reformation efforts. Because of the strong Spanish presence in Flanders, the edicts against the Anabaptists and all other dissenters there were enforced strictly and successfully.

In the northern Netherlands, however, Charles's hold was noticeably weaker. Spain had less direct control of the nobles in the north, and many of those nobles were supportive of reform efforts. They appreciated the ideals of the *Devotio Moderna* and refused to enforce a strict application of Catholicism. Charles was still able to cause persecution in the north, and many died there, especially because of the evil name the militant "Anabaptists" brought upon their peaceful counterparts. But in the south, the persecution was stronger, and the number of martyrs much higher. Our look at the persecution and the subsequent dispersal of Anabaptists will largely involve Flanders, since, for the most part, the Anabaptists of the northern Netherlands were not forced to emigrate.

Both peaceful and militant Anabaptists were present in Flanders from the first years of the Dutch Anabaptist movement. As in the north, the militant groups faded away and the nonresistant Anabaptists flourished. One historian has estimated that there were fifty-four hundred

Flemish Anabaptists at the peak of the movement. Though other historians consider that an overestimation, it is evident that the movement was popular.

Leenaert Bouwens baptized 592 believers in Flanders during his three visits there. Gillis of Aachen worked extensively in Flanders. Hans Buschaert was a leading Flemish bishop whom Menno Simons ordained, but not much is known about his work. Hans van Overdam was another outstanding Flemish leader. There were periods when some Anabaptists in Flanders did not have enough leadership, as they indicated in distressed letters to their brethren in the north.

The extremely severe persecution in Flanders from the 1540s on caused over sixty thousand Anabaptist and Protestant refugees to flee north. This made a problem for northern cities, such as Antwerp, where many refugees went. At times, mandates were made that did not allow more refugees to come to the cities. Nevertheless, whether in town or country, many of the Flemish Anabaptists did

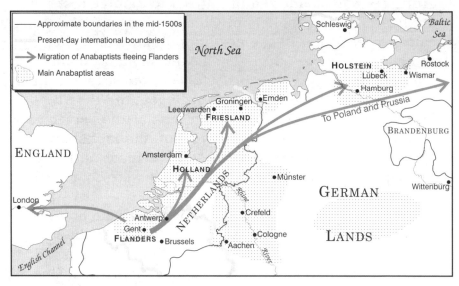

The Dispersal of Flemish Anabaptists

find permanent homes in the northern part of the Netherlands.

London, England, also became a haven for Anabaptist refugees. The English government issued a warning against them in 1538. Some of these Anabaptists faced martyrdom on English soil, and the Anabaptist church did not continue on the island. However, the religious ideas the Anabaptists deposited there may have been one of the influences that led to the rise of English separatist churches, which contained the seeds of the Baptist churches.[15]

Many refugees fled northeast to Poland and Prussia. Danzig, a city on the Baltic Sea, was a popular center for Anabaptists. Danzig (modern Gdańsk) is situated where the Vistula River empties into the sea. The Mennonites first settled the delta area, for it provided conditions and occupations similar to what many of them had experienced in the Netherlands. The Lutheran or Catholic authorities generally tolerated them because of the great contributions they made in draining the wetlands and improving the value of the land. Many of them also contributed to the economy through weaving. They paid a price, though, for this toleration. Many of the initial settlers died from fever and diseases before the swamps were drained.

As the delta area filled with Mennonites, other refugees settled farther up along the river, gradually establishing settlements almost as far south as Warsaw. The flow of refugees continued until the end of the sixteenth century. One historian has estimated that about half of all Mennonites today have roots leading back to the Vistula

---

[15] One separatist church was led by John Smyth. He and part of his church applied for membership in the Mennonite Church in Amsterdam. The other part, not agreeing with the Mennonite views on war and the oath, began the General Arminian Baptist Church in London around 1610. The Calvinistic Baptists began several years after this.

River area, either directly or by way of Russia. Many of the Vistula River Mennonites settled in Russia in the 1700s and 1800s.

Not all the refugees traveled as far as the Vistula River area, however. Some of them settled in the areas of Hamburg, Lübeck, Wismar, Rostock, and Schleswig, cities in modern northern Germany.

Chapter 7

Dutch Anabaptist Church Life

In this chapter we will explore the Dutch Anabaptist divisions, influences that led them into apostasy, their doctrinal writings, and some doctrinal struggles they faced. Some of this is not pleasant reading, but hopefully it will help us to avoid making similar mistakes today.

Divisions Rock the Brotherhood

By the middle of the 1550s, about twenty years after Menno's and Dirk's ordinations, there were two groups within the Dutch Anabaptist church. On the one hand, some held the position of the ministry very high. They gave the church great authority in their lives. They wanted a system of firm, doctrinal beliefs by which the church could separate between believers and unbelievers. They supported a strict application of the ban (excommunication) against those members who did not measure up to the church's expectations.

On the other hand, others felt that in order to keep the authority and power of the Word of God as high as it should be, there should be no place in the church for dominant leaders. They did not want the local church to assume much authority in the lives of the members. They felt that firm, doctrinal systems could be dangerous because they might gain more authority than the Bible. They supported only a mild use of the ban. They considered their spiritual life to be largely a private matter that should attract little interference from the church.

The Waterlander Division. In 1556, the two sides came into open conflict over the use of the ban. The husband of a certain Swaen Rutgers had been excommunicated from the church. Leenaert Bouwens demanded that Swaen shun her husband, which meant that she could not live or eat with him, but she refused to do this. Dirk Philips supported Leenaert's stand. Menno Simons, however, was inclined to be lenient in such cases.

Because of Bouwen's insistence on the issue, a group of the more lenient members left the church and formed their own church. The two groups did not ban each other, but they had little contact for many years. The dissidents were known as the Waterlanders because many of them lived in the district of Waterland in North Holland. They were the first Dutch Mennonites to drop the name Mennonite, and called themselves the *Doopsgezinden* (baptism-minded). They did not want to be named after a man.[1] The Waterlanders became one of the major Mennonite groups in the Netherlands. They were less traditional in dress and lifestyle than the original group.

---

[1] Eventually, all Dutch Mennonites dropped the name Mennonite in favor of the term *Doopsgezinden.*

The Flemish and Frisian Division. Around ten years after the Waterlander division, another major upheaval took place in the original group. Menno Simons was now dead, and Dirk and Leenaert were the principal leaders. We have already noted that many Flemish Anabaptists emigrated to the northern Netherlands and settled there among the native Frisians. These two groups were somewhat different culturally. The Frisians accused the Flemish of being worldly in their dress, while the Flemish accused the Frisians of being worldly in their homes and household goods.

However, the cultural differences were not the immediate cause of the division. Four congregations in Friesland had agreed to work together in a sort of conference. A minister ordained in one congregation would serve the other three as well. The congregations administrated the care of the poor centrally, and church problems were solved by the ministry of all four congregations.

The problem came when one congregation ordained a Flemish minister, and one of the other congregations questioned the choice. Finally they called in several ministers, who settled the question in favor of the new minister, but the sting of rejection remained. Feeling that the union of the four congregations was the cause of his problems, the new minister pulled his congregation out of the group. Part of his own congregation rejected this action. The two groups began to meet separately, and the names Frisian and Flemish were attached to them.

Despite several attempts to rectify the situation, the division spread. The deep-rooted Frisian and Flemish cultural differences fueled the dispute. Tensions between Dirk and Leenaert, who took opposite sides in the issues, were also divisive. The names Frisian and Flemish were soon nothing but party labels. There were Frisian Flemish and Flemish Frisians. Dirk Philips, for example, was a native Frisian who joined the Flemish side. Many Mennonites who were finally involved in this division had no idea of the original issues. The two sides banned and shunned each other for many years.

The High Germans were a smaller group that came out of this shuffle. These Mennonites were from southern Germany and had moved to several cities in the Netherlands to pursue their trades. The High Germans opposed extending the ban to such matters as marital shunning. They did not agree with any of the Dutch Mennonite branches. Through the time of the Frisian–Flemish division, the High Germans stood for a moderate application of excommunication and shunning.[2]

An Attempt to Bring Unity

Early in February 1567, two ministers from Hoorn attempted to heal the Frisian–Flemish problem. Both the Frisians and the Flemish agreed to submit to this committee's decision. After careful consideration of the matter, the two ministers called a meeting to reconcile the division.

Many people from both sides attended the meeting. After introducing the plan, the ministers asked the Frisians to kneel and pray for forgiveness for their part in the split. When the Frisians arose, the Flemish were asked to do likewise. But when the Flemish were ready to rise, the ministers told them that the Frisians would need to help them up, since they (the Flemish) carried a greater share of the blame for the problem. Some of the Flemish agreed to this, but most of them were deeply insulted and refused to make any such concession. The reconciliation effort accomplished little except to more deeply entrench the problem.

---

[2] The High Germans had been part of the Swiss Brethren before they emigrated to the Netherlands. Their moderate position on shunning came from this Swiss background. Most Swiss Brethren in Switzerland never accepted the radical Dutch view of shunning.

The Old Flemish and Mild Flemish Division. After the Flemish divided from the Frisians, they still did not agree among themselves on how conservative to be in lifestyle or how strictly to apply banning and shunning. In 1586, twenty years after the Frisian–Flemish division, these matters again became divisive issues in the Flemish church.

The immediate cause of this division took place when a Flemish bishop bought a house. To some of his brethren, his dealings appeared dishonest. In the quarrel following the purchase, two sides emerged, aptly called the *Huiskoopers* (house buyers) and the *Contra-Huiskoopers.* These names soon disappeared, however, and the two parties were labeled the Old Flemish and the Mild, or Soft, Flemish, which more accurately reflected the real cause of the division. This division spread rapidly in the Flemish church.

The Old Frisian and the Young Frisian Division. Among the Frisians, there were also many different ideas on how conservative the church should be and how to apply the ban. Especially strong among the Frisians was the question of whether or not any church could be a true church if it was not a Frisian Mennonite church. Some of the leaders felt that their Mennonite church was the only true church, and they strictly practiced banning and shunning. Other Frisian leaders, however, did not feel this way. Some of them felt that marriage outside the Frisians was allowable, that the true church could also be found in other groups, and that shunning of marriage companions was not necessary.

In 1589, the more-conservative, strict leaders banned one of the more moderate ones. This began a division that split the Frisian churches into the Old Frisians and the Young (also called Moderate and Weak) Frisians.

These four divisions were the most far-reaching of the Dutch divisions, but they were not the only ones. In both the Frisian and the Flemish churches, numerous small splits took place over the same basic issues that had caused the large divisions.

Reunification of the Divided Churches

Among the various groups of Mennonites, there were always a few brethren that supported unity and working together. Many of these were scarcely heard in the clamor of quarrel and division, but they finally did succeed in bringing about some agreements between the estranged parties. It is questionable whether these unions were always good for the spiritual health of those who were faithful and desired to remain so. Many of these unions took place only after apostasy had set in among almost all parties of the Dutch Mennonites. Later in this chapter, we will look closer at this apostasy.

The Concept of Cologne. In 1591, about twenty-five years after the Frisian–Flemish division, representatives of the Young Frisians, High Germans, and Palatinate Mennonites (of a Swiss Anabaptist background) met in Cologne, a city in northwest Germany. They discussed their differences and worked toward a platform of agreement. They discussed many doctrinal and practical aspects of the church, such as the Trinity, Baptism, Communion, ordination, Feet Washing, and Marriage. Also included in the discussion was how strictly to apply the ban. In these discussions, the brethren felt that it was a mistake to make members shun their banned marriage companions. On the basis of these discussions, these groups united.

The Satisfied Brotherhood. Hans de Ries, a prominent leader among the Waterlanders, strongly desired to make peace with the other Mennonite groups. He urged the Waterlanders to unite with the churches who had joined on the basis of the Concept of Cologne. Many Waterlanders did join that union around 1601. This group then became known as the Satisfied Brotherhood, also called the Reconciled, or Pacified, Brotherhood.

In 1603, the Satisfied Brotherhood sent a request to the Old Frisians and both branches of the Flemish, asking them to join the union. These groups did not heed the request.

The Satisfied Brotherhood suffered a setback in 1613, when a large number of the High Germans and Young Frisians left the union. Leenaerdt Clock, a leader who had been very active in bringing the union together, led out in this division. He felt that the Satisfied Brotherhood did not apply the ban and shunning strictly enough. His group became known as the Separated Brotherhood.

Other unions. About 1610, just before the Satisfied Brotherhood divided, some of the Young Frisians and Soft Flemish united. In 1632, on the basis of the Dordrecht Confession, most of the Old Flemish united with the Soft Flemish. In 1639, these united Flemish also reached an agreement with the Satisfied Brotherhood. By 1640, the only groups that had not united with others were the Old Frisians, a few Old Flemish, and the Waterlanders who had not joined the Satisfied Brotherhood. These Waterlanders, in 1647, tried to unify themselves with the other groups. The other Mennonites did not accept their efforts because they still felt that these Waterlanders were too liberal. The general unification of all Dutch Mennonites was not accomplished until 1801, after apostasy had taken a heavy toll among all of them.

Main Dutch Anabaptist Divisions and Reunifications (1534 – 1670)

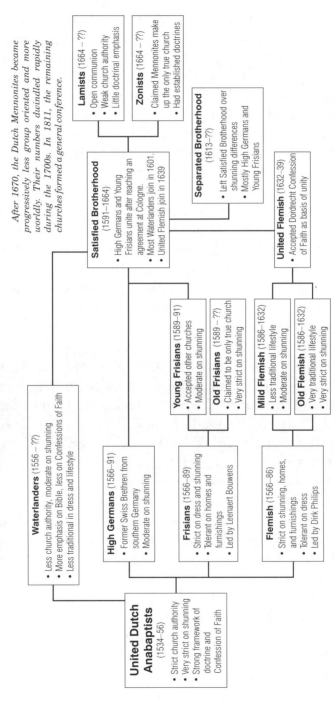

After 1670, the Dutch Mennonites became progressively less group oriented and more worldly. Their numbers dwindled rapidly during the 1700s. In 1811, the remaining churches formed a general conference.

United Dutch Anabaptists (1534–56)
- Strict church authority
- Very strict on shunning
- Strong framework of doctrine and Confession of Faith

Waterlanders (1556 – ??)
- Less church authority, moderate on shunning
- More emphasis on Bible, less on Confessions of Faith
- Less traditional in dress and lifestyle

High Germans (1566–91)
- Former Swiss Brethren from southern Germany
- Moderate on shunning

Frisians (1566–89)
- Strict on dress and shunning
- Tolerant on homes and furnishings
- Led by Leenaert Bouwens

Flemish (1566–86)
- Strict on shunning, homes, and furnishings
- Tolerant on dress
- Led by Dirk Philips

Young Frisians (1589–91)
- Accepted other churches
- Moderate on shunning

Old Frisians (1589 – ??)
- Claimed to be only true church
- Very strict on shunning

Mild Flemish (1586–1632)
- Less traditional lifestyle
- Moderate on shunning

Old Flemish (1586–1632)
- Very traditional lifestyle
- Very strict on shunning

Satisfied Brotherhood (1591–1664)
- High Germans and Young Frisians unite after reaching an agreement at Cologne.
- Most Waterlanders join in 1601.
- United Flemish join in 1639

Lamists (1664 – ??)
- Open communion
- Weak church authority
- Little doctrinal emphasis

Zonists (1664 – ??)
- Claimed Mennonites make up the only true church
- Had established doctrines

Separated Brotherhood (1613–??)
- Left Satisfied Brotherhood over shunning differences
- Mostly High Germans and Young Frisians

United Flemish (1632–39)
- Accepted Dordrecht Confession of Faith as basis of unity

This is an overview of the main divisions and reunifications. Not everyone in each group held all the positions listed.

148

The Lamist and Zonist Division

The new partial unity only survived until 1664, when a major division again split the entire Mennonite Church of the Netherlands. The quarrel began in Amsterdam, at the Church of the Lamb. Two of the ministers at this church held different views regarding the nature of the church. Samuel Apostool, who was of a conservative Flemish background, felt that the Mennonite Church was the only true church, and placed much importance on the necessity of fixed, doctrinal systems. The other minister, Galenus Abrahamsz de Haan, was much more liberal in his view of the importance of the church. He was strongly influenced by an informal Dutch group known as the Collegiants. To help us to better understand what took place here, we will digress a moment to consider the Collegiant movement.

The Collegiant movement came into being because of a division in the Reformed (Calvinist) Church of the Netherlands. Jacobus Arminius started a group called the Remonstrants, which disagreed with some of the doctrines of strict Calvinism, such as predestination and eternal security. When the Dutch Reformed Church met for its synod in 1618–1619, the strict Calvinists dismissed the Remonstrant ministers from their duties in the church. This left some of the Dutch Reformed churches without leaders. The church near Leiden, which now had no leader, decided to gather occasionally in an informal way to read the Bible, pray, and exhort each other.

These meetings soon grew beyond the church that started them. Others began gathering in this way in many areas of the Netherlands. These groups owned no church buildings and had no ministers. They denied having established a church, although for some of their constituents, these meetings essentially replaced the church.

They believed that no established churches followed the New Testament pattern; and through their influence, they wanted to improve the churches.

The Collegiants baptized those who desired it, and they held Communion occasionally. They expressly taught that their baptism was not a required initiation into their group. Anyone could be a Collegiant without being baptized. Lay persons, at the request of the one who desired baptism, performed this ordinance. Ministers could attend Collegiant meetings and be a part of them just like anyone else, but they could not exercise ministerial authority.

The Collegiants believed that everyone should interpret the Bible for himself; no one should have to believe something with which he did not personally agree. Such a pietistic, informal group was attractive to elements in the existing churches who wanted freedom from orthodoxy. Reformed Calvinists, Arminian Remonstrants, and Mennonites attended the Collegiant meetings. The Collegiant meetings were frequently held in Mennonite churches. Most of the Collegiants continued attending their own church meetings as well.

It is not hard to see how such influences caused a major division among the Mennonites. Many of them appreciated the relaxed religious ideas of the Collegiants, but on the other hand, a sizable portion of them wanted nothing to do with the mixture this informality created. As already mentioned, the original upheaval took place in the Mennonite Church of the Lamb, with Apostool and de Haan as the leaders of the opposing factions. This conflict became ironically known as "the war of the lambs." The unfolding struggle shows how far the church had drifted from a Biblical approach to their problems. The side that was against de Haan went as far as to ask the civil government to ban him from the country! They even asked the burgomaster to help restore peace.

No attempts at restoration were successful. De Haan finally clinched the disagreements by insisting that anyone could be admitted to Communion regardless of his beliefs, as long as he lived a righteous life. He believed and taught that God judged men only by their deeds, not by their beliefs. In 1664, Apostool left the Church of the Lamb, taking about five hundred members with him.[3] De Haan kept fifteen hundred members in the original building. The building that Apostool and his followers met in had a sign on the front that represented the sun (Dutch *zon*), and his church soon became known as the Zonists. De Haan's group became known as the Lamists. The division eventually affected all the Mennonite churches in the Netherlands as well as some related churches outside Dutch borders.

After this division, the Frisian and Flemish labels disappeared, for the most part. Most of the Waterlanders who had never joined any previous reunions now joined the Lamists. A few of them joined the Zonists. The remnant of Old Flemish that did not join either of the new groups finally died out. In the next twenty-seven years, four attempts were made to heal the Lamist–Zonist division, but these failed.

Negative Influences

Quite early in their history, the Dutch Mennonites began to drift away from the Biblical characteristics of the true church. During the 1600s, more principles of truth were lost among them, and later centuries saw a continued drift toward apostasy. The divisions were sources of bitterness that sapped the spiritual life of the churches. Most of the divisions were caused by radical

---

[3] Historians vary on the exact number of members that left with Apostool.

reactions to disagreements over issues that the Scriptures did not speak to directly. The refusal to allow some latitude where the Scriptures are not specific resulted in lifting up the reasoning of men instead of the Bible. In most of the Dutch Mennonite divisions, no side was entirely Scriptural in its actions and attitudes. These attitudes set the stage for further drift from truth, and finally for apostasy.

Besides the negative influences of the divisions, there were other influences that affected the Dutch Mennonites. We will examine some of these.

Material prosperity. In the latter half of the 1500s, the Netherlands gained independence from Spain and persecution of the Mennonites officially ceased. They did not, however, immediately have the same privileges as the Reformed Church. Well into the 1600s, they faced acts of intolerance, such as obstructing their efforts to build churches and temporarily closing their shops. Most of this pressure came from the Reformed Church leaders, who wanted the Netherlands to establish the Reformed Church as the state church and reject all others. The government refused to do this, although for many years, it did favor the Reformed faith.

For the Dutch Mennonites, this freedom produced an experience entirely different from what the Swiss Brethren faced. The Swiss Brethren were not economically free until much later. They had to live separate from general society, they often could not freely take part in the economy, and they had to pay heavy taxes at various times. In contrast, the Dutch Mennonites were able to participate in the economic life of the Netherlands. They were able to move to areas of opportunity, which they frequently did, to take advantage of expanding markets and new economic frontiers. So marked were their achievements in commerce and culture that the period between approximately 1580 and the middle of the 1600s is often called their Golden Age.

Besides agricultural pursuits, the Dutch Mennonites had many businesses. Some Mennonites were ship-builders. Some Mennonite businessmen owned fleets with up to seventy vessels involved in fishing, whaling, and shipping between major commerce centers. Some led the Dutch lumber business from 1650 through the 1700s. Some owned and operated flour mills, vegetable oil presses, dye factories, flower export industries, grocery stores, and a starch and sugar factory. The von der Leyen family's silk firm, established in the 1600s, became known around the world for its fine products. Based in Crefeld, Germany, this company employed about three thousand workers, almost half the population of the town. The company made such an economic contribution to the country that the family was eventually knighted and became a part of the German nobility.

Others took up many various trades on a smaller scale, including clothing manufacturing, metalworking, build-ing, inn-keeping, printing, dentistry, and optometry. There were many Mennonite doctors. Also of note is the Men-nonite contribution to the banking and insurance indus-tries.

This prosperity did not bring gain in the spiritual life of the church. Instead, a loss of faith closely paralleled the rising affluence. One hundred years before the prosper-ity, many of the Dutch Mennonites faced persecution and death. When that ceased and time brought increasing worldly security, many of them no longer held as strongly to Biblical beliefs. Hans de Ries, a Waterlander leader, summed up their condition: "The goods are enriched but the soul is impoverished. Clothing has become precious but the internal decorations have perished. Love has diminished and quarreling has increased."[4]

Galenus Abrahamsz de Haan, the leading minister at the Church of the Lamb, believed that the devil had found a more successful method than persecution to deal with the Mennonites. Instead of making them suffer, he led them into material interests and the accompanying worldly snares. If Galenus would be given the privilege of looking back on his own era from over three hundred years later, he would realize more than ever the truth of his statement.

Relaxed attitude toward the state, culture, and arts. Closely associated with Dutch Mennonite prosperity was their rise in worldly status and culture. Famous poets, painters, and artists were among their ranks. The Mennonites, as a whole, relaxed their idea that the world and its achievements represented a threat to spiritual life. Love for the worldly, social culture around them led many away from the church and sapped the spiritual vigor of many who stayed in the church. There was also a strong desire to erase the differences between the Mennonite Church and other churches. These pressures came upon the Mennonites because their wealth and active social contributions gave them a place of prominence in the world. Instead of shunning this prominence, many of them cultivated it and enjoyed it.

Though all the Mennonites held to nonresistance for a time, they eventually lost it. The government excused them from army service until 1799, but when this privilege was lost, only a few Mennonites complained.

The Mennonite separation from functions of civil government also faded rapidly.[5] The Waterlanders held

---

[4] Cornelius J. Dyck, *An Introduction to Mennonite History,* 131.

[5] *The Mennonite Encyclopedia,* article "Anabaptist-Mennonite Attitude Toward State," 4:614.

government offices from the late 1500s on. At first, the Mennonites held only acceptable offices such as inspectors or trustees of a polder. From the 1680s on, they served as city council members and mayors. Later they became sheriffs, ministers of finance and reclamation, burgomasters, governors, judges, and even generals of the army. According to *The Mennonite Encyclopedia,* Mennonites in the Netherlands have served in every level of state office except prime minister.

The influence of the Collegiants. The influence of the Collegiant movement on the Mennonites has already been shown. Several outstanding emphases of the Collegiants made a deep impression on most of the Mennonites. The most devastating to a Biblical view of the church was the pietistic idea that personal feeling and understanding of the truth should be the primary direction of a person's life. There was, in Collegiant thinking, no place for the church to require its members to submit to something with which they did not personally agree.

Since many of the Mennonites, especially the Waterlanders, freely participated in Collegiant meetings, these influences soon made their way into the Mennonite Church. All Dutch Mennonites practiced close Communion up to this time, but Collegiant influence called this into question. If the church cannot ask for submission to the New Testament, how can it refuse Communion privileges to anyone? Open Communion became a growing trend in the churches.

The forms of baptism and even the necessity of baptism were questioned as a result of Collegiant influence. In some Mennonite churches, people who had never been baptized and those only baptized as infants could take part in Communion.

A few congregations strongly opposed this open-ended

toleration and firmly insisted on submission to the Scriptures and the proper observance of the ordinances. But even among these churches, the forces of apostasy were at work. Although these congregations endeavored to preserve some Scriptural teachings, they were too far from the Bible in practice to remain faithful. All of them finally either succumbed to Collegiant thinking, emigrated, or died out.

The influence of the Remonstrants. The rise of the Remonstrants, the part of the Calvinist Reformed Church that followed Jacobus Arminius, has been noted in the discussion of the Lamist–Zonist division. When the Reformed Church expelled the "Arminian" ministers, most of them left that church with their followers and began the Remonstrant Reformed Brotherhood.

Since the Reformed majority tried to oppress both the Mennonites and the Remonstrants, a natural sympathy formed between the two minority groups. The Remonstrants actually used a Mennonite confession of faith, and members of the two groups met each other regularly in the Collegiant meetings. The Remonstrants practiced infant baptism and placed a greater emphasis on theology than the Mennonites did. The Remonstrants had a theological seminary in which some Mennonites received ministerial training. This seminary influenced the Mennonites to relax their stand against infant baptism. Also, the idea that ministers needed professional training to properly serve their churches arose partly through this seminary influence. Many Mennonites became dissatisfied with simple sermons. They demanded more philosophically and theologically oriented leaders, such as the Remonstrant and Reformed Churches had.

The Remonstrants and Mennonites had a few joint publishing efforts through the years, and at various times the idea of a union between the two groups was promoted. This took place between the two churches in Dokkum, Friesland, but never happened on a larger scale.

A gradual decline in numbers took place among the Dutch Mennonites from the 1650s on. Although the Collegiants claimed to not have established a new church, their services did replace other churches for some people, including some Mennonites. Some Mennonites also joined the Remonstrant Church for greater freedom and trained leaders. Even the Reformed Church attracted some from the Mennonite fold. Most of these had long lost the faith for which their fathers died, and they joined the Reformed Church only for social prestige and the opportunity to pass their government positions on to their families.

The gradual loss of Scriptural ordinances and other principles. We have already noted that under Collegiant and Remonstrant influences, baptism in the Mennonite Church came under question.

The Dutch Mennonites practiced the mode of pouring from the beginning.[6] The Collegiants practiced immersion as well as pouring, depending on what the individual wanted. As a result of the Mennonites' close fellowship with the Collegiants, a number of them desired immersion. One Mennonite congregation actually installed a stone immersion font, but there was resistance to the practice, and they soon restored pouring. One division occurred over the matter when a small group in Hamburg, Germany, separated themselves and practiced only immersion.

Much more serious than the deviation in the mode of baptism was that some congregations made baptism

---

[6] All the Anabaptists practiced pouring as the mode of baptism. The only known exception to this took place when Wolfgang Ulimann, an Anabaptist in St. Gall, Switzerland, asked Conrad Grebel to immerse him in the Rhine.

optional. At least one congregation even abolished baptism for a number of years. The Mennonites also began to feel that infant baptism was valid. Though they did not practice it, they recognized it as sufficient for someone joining their church or taking part in Communion. In some cases, during baptismal services, the leaders made it clear that the baptized individuals were not being baptized and received into any particular congregation or denomination, but rather into the general Christian church. Collegiant influences were clearly having an effect on the Mennonites.

There were voices of caution and dissent, however. In 1866, one minister wanted the church to require candidates for the ministry to preach a sermon defending adult baptism. But too many of the ministers rejected the proposal, and it never became a requirement. Later meetings were held as well to discuss the matter, with some participants willing to do away with baptism, and some insisting that this command of Christ had to be obeyed. The two sides never reached an agreement.

In the matter of Communion, similar carelessness was manifest. Most of the churches became increasingly lax in practicing pure Communion. From the 1650s on, open Communion with "Christians" of many beliefs gradually became standard. Even people who had never been baptized could take part in Communion. As the significance of Communion was lost, so was the conviction for its observance. The churches also gradually laid feet washing aside. In the latter 1800s, some of the Mennonite churches entirely did away with Communion. A number of them still practice it today, but it does not hold the significance it once did.

From the late 1600s on, the Scriptural command to marry "only in the Lord" was also disregarded more and more. This was simply another result of the growing feeling that all Protestant groups were Christians and that there could be few restrictions on socializing with them. Church discipline was set aside. As already noted, Communion in some Mennonite churches was open to all "Christians," so it is no surprise that the church gradually ceased to exercise discipline. After the mid-1750s, the ban was hardly ever used, although at times the more-conservative churches kept back members from Communion for various errors.[7]

Another principle that received insufficient attention was nonresistance. Some Mennonite sailors began sailing on armed vessels; and from the latter 1700s on, many of them joined the army.

Rationalism, the theological seminary, and the Réveil movement. The Collegiant movement was fading by the middle of the 1700s, but other influences continued to ravage the Mennonite faith.

In the 1700s, a movement known as the Enlightenment spread across Europe. This movement, born out of the liberal humanism that rejected the Word of God, became a major steppingstone toward the unprecedented rejection of the Bible in present Western culture. In many ways, the Enlightenment was a darkness instead of a light. The philosophers of the Enlightenment concerned themselves with questioning traditions, the Bible, and all established values. They rejected everything that they could not reason out in their own minds. They rejected the supernatural nature of God and Christianity. Many "enlightened" philosophers considered themselves to be above the need for faith, yet failed to realize that they had only transferred their faith from traditions and the Bible

---

[7] Note how the Dutch Mennonites went from an extreme position on excommunication to *no* position. Satan has often used an extreme application of a Bible truth as the first step in eliminating that truth.

to their own human reasoning. Another word for this influence is *rationalism*.[8]

The Enlightenment strongly affected the Reformed, Remonstrant, and Mennonite Churches in the Netherlands. As the inner, spiritual emphasis of the Collegiants faded away, its influence in the Mennonite Church was replaced with a rationalistic attitude that led men to place more faith in their own intellect than in God. To a large degree, this led them directly away from the Mennonite Church. Between the early 1700s and the early 1800s, the number of Dutch Mennonites dropped by over 130,000. Over one hundred churches closed.

Many Mennonites who stayed with their church believed in a modified view of salvation. They had a theological, or rational, knowledge of God but knew little about true regeneration. They saw Jesus as a good, moral teacher rather than the divine One who died to purchase eternal redemption for mankind. The aim of the Dutch Mennonite Church in this period was to preserve good morals among its people and to promote a mental knowledge of God.

Some Mennonites joined the Reformed or Remonstrant churches through this period. But this step was no longer such a hurdle as it had been at one time. The Dutch Mennonites had drifted so far from Biblical faith that there were few real differences between them and the other churches.

When Galenus Abrahamsz de Haan retired in 1703 from the Church of the Lamb in Amsterdam, no replacement minister could be found for him. The practice of ordaining uneducated ministers from the local church was becoming very unpopular. The Remonstrant professors

---

[8] Rationalism is the belief that human reasoning, instead of Bible truth, is the basis for actions and beliefs and that man can answer all his problems.

were training Mennonite ministers, but the Mennonites were still not entirely in agreement with the Remonstrants and disliked that graduates of the Remonstrant school filled their pulpits. To address this supposed need, the Amsterdam Mennonite Church began its own seminary in 1735.

The seminary received little help from other Dutch Mennonites until the Doopsgezinde General Conference formed in 1811, which almost all Dutch Mennonites joined. The conference then administrated the seminary. Much of the influence that this seminary exerted on the church was toward the world. Rationalism and modified rationalism spread through the churches from the central influence of the seminary.

All down through the years of rationalism, there were those who disagreed with the direction the church was heading. Part of this disagreement found expression in the Réveil movement, which arose around 1820. The Réveil was a renewal of the older Pietistic movement and was felt in much of western Europe. In the Netherlands, it arose first in the Reformed Church and then among the Mennonites as a reaction against the liberal, "enlightened" ideas that had taken root. Personal conversion was stressed, and much emphasis placed upon knowing Jesus Christ as Redeemer, not just as a theological topic. The sermons preached at Réveil meetings were warm and evangelical instead of the dry, rational lectures that Reformed and Mennonite ministers gave. Some Mennonites engaged in the movement without leaving their church, and some tried to stir up their Mennonite churches with Réveil ideas, but many others left completely. The message of the Réveil movement had an understandable appeal to any spiritually inclined members left in the largely dead Mennonite Church of that day. Despite its shortcomings, it probably had a more

Scriptural message than what the Mennonites taught at that time.

Looking back over the course of the Dutch Mennonites, a pattern becomes evident. With growing freedom and prosperity, the church lost its first love by the beginning of the 1600s. Many of the people, however, still held to outward separation, nonresistance, and church discipline. Because of the growing coldness in the Mennonite Church, the Collegiant movement appealed to members looking for more spirituality. The Mennonites regained a level of spirituality through the influence of the Collegiants, but it was a spirituality with a strong pietistic emphasis on individual thinking. This did not lead the church back to Biblical Anabaptism, but rather left it open for a greater loss of Scriptural principles. Around one hundred thirty years later, when the Collegiant movement had faded away, the church was firmly set in individualism, church discipline was basically gone, and men believed and practiced what was right in their own eyes. When the influences of the Enlightenment began to shake people's faith in God and the Bible, there was nothing to keep those influences from entering directly into the Mennonite Church.

The lessons are clear. A careless relationship to freedom and prosperity leads to spiritual decay. Drifting churches can easily become hotbeds for pietism. But pietism fails to restore the Biblical vision. Instead, it dilutes and rechannels the Biblical vision into a warm, personal fervor that places experience over holiness. When pietistic ideals saturate a group, it can seldom be recovered to a Biblical stand. Such a course finally allows anything—rejection of God's Word, rejection of Christ's divinity, and rejection of the body of Christ.

Doctrinal Writings and Confessions of Faith

Some of the early Dutch Anabaptist writings were

apologetics,[9] but most of them were doctrinal essays written to warn and encourage the church. Most of these writings are in print today.

Dirk Philips's first tract was an apologetic written in 1534 to Bernhard Rothmann, a supporter of the Münster "kingdom." Rothmann had written a book, calling people to Münster and recommending the use of force to aid Christ in ushering in His kingdom. Dirk strongly opposed the use of force and wrote in support of the peaceful, suffering Obbenites.

Menno Simons also directed his first known writing against the Münsterites. He wrote this in 1535, before he left the Catholic Church. At least five more of Menno's writings were also directed to those outside the church. These writings were rich in doctrinal and practical teaching, however, and served as stabilizers and reference points for the church.

Dirk's and Menno's writings were born out of burdens for needs in the church. Though these men were not the best writers, their efforts served their people well. Even though many of these writings seem heavy and redundant to the modern eye, they were read much by the common Dutch people who managed to secretly obtain them.

Although the exact dates for some of these writings are unknown, both Dirk and Menno seem to have done more writing in the first part of their ministries than in the latter. The extensive workload that accompanied the burgeoning movement, as well as dealing with conflicts within the church, took much of the leaders' time. Besides this, it was at times difficult to find someone to print their literature.

The Mennonite confessions of faith were produced after Dirk and Menno were gone. The Waterlanders published

---

[9] An apologetic is a writing that justifies or defends a cause, principle, or person.

the first Dutch Mennonite confession in 1577. This confession was not a complete doctrinal statement but a brief explanation of where the Waterlanders stood on issues under question (such as the ban).

From 1591 to 1665, many confessions were published. The Concept of Cologne (1591) was an important confession produced by discussions of several Mennonite groups who desired to unite. Around 1600, Pieter Jans Twisck wrote the first fully developed confession with thirty-three articles. The 1660 *Martyrs Mirror* contained this confession. Fully developed confessions, however, were not generally produced throughout this period. Most of them were smaller statements pertaining to issues under question. They served as bases for the groups that wished to find their way back together. In that sense, they were conclusions on disputed points rather than confessions of faith. However, since they became documents that stated the position of the holders, they were also confessions of faith.

Later the church wanted more complete statements, so they grouped previous ones together, added points, and published the whole collection. The Mennonite Church generally supported these confessions and considered them to be clear, brief discussions of the tenets of their faith. However, these confessions were not creeds in the sense that the Catholics and Protestants held creeds. The Anabaptists held that confessions were subject to improvement, as the church saw fit, and were not a higher authority than the Bible. Creeds held by other religious groups were usually considered the final authority on questions of church policy. For the Anabaptists, the Bible remained the absolute authority, while their confessions were simple explanations of their understanding of Biblical truth. Because many Dutch Mennonites saw the danger of Catholic and Protestant creeds, they at first resisted publishing confessions in their churches. This receded gradually as it became clear that the writers of the confessions did not aim to create creeds.

Among the Dutch Anabaptists, the confessions of faith lost importance as individualism and Pietism took over the churches. Today, American Mennonite confessions contain many elements from the Dutch confessions. Many Mennonites in America especially appreciate the Dordrecht Confession (1632).

The martyr history books produced by the Dutch are also a valuable contribution to Mennonites everywhere. They are the product of concerned men who desired to challenge and awaken their drifting churches. A number of small martyr booklets were printed and went through many editions before the Waterlanders published a larger martyr book in 1615. But the crowning work in martyr histories is the *Martyrs Mirror,* collected by Thieleman Jansz van Braght. First published in 1660, his work was built on the previous editions but also included much new material. The last Dutch edition was published in 1685. *Martyrs Mirror* was used by some of the Swiss Brethren as well. Mennonites in America desired to strengthen their faith, especially in the doctrine of nonresistance, by making the book available to their people. In 1749, the first American edition was printed in the German language. The *Martyrs Mirror* is still in print, now in the English language too, but it finds little use except among the conservative Mennonites and Amish.[10]

---

[10] Sometimes people question the reliability of the *Martyrs Mirror*. The work is not entirely complete, nor is it without occasional error. A few names and dates are wrong, and some martyrs are named twice. A number of the accounts of the apostles' martyrdoms seem to be founded on tradition. On this basis, a few historians, even as early as 1671, felt that the book was largely compiled from erroneous sources. However, at least eight notable historians, Mennonite and Protestant, have verified that *Martyrs Mirror* is reliable, with the exception of minor mistakes.

Early Doctrinal Struggles

A number of doctrinal issues troubled the Dutch Mennonites in their early years. This was partly due to Dutch
Anabaptism's turbulent beginning under radical leaders.
Discussions about these issues resulted in numerous
meetings and many divisions. Later, many of the issues
lost importance as the church drifted.

The nature of the church. The radical environment in
which Dutch Anabaptism began was largely due to wrong
views of the church. Melchior Hofmann taught that the
church was to be peaceful until the return of Christ, when
they would then take up arms and aid the Lord in destroying the wicked and bringing a new order to earth. Under
this influence from Melchior, men such as Jan Matthysz
and Jan of Leiden went to even greater extremes, trying
by force to realize a "kingdom of God" immediately.

Obbe and Dirk Philips then faced an important question: "Of what nature is the church?" Distrusting their
self-appointed leaders more and more, they turned to the
New Testament. They began to realize that peacefulness,
purity, discipline, and suffering marked true believers.
Very shortly, they separated from the radical groups and
began building a Biblical church on the New Testament
ideal. Menno Simons came to similar conclusions. After
he joined their ranks, these three leaders labored diligently to build a church, "not having spot or wrinkle."

But what is "not having spot or wrinkle"? The Dutch
Anabaptists grappled with this over and over. The leaders knew from the Münster experience that unbridled
individuality could lead to terrible ends. This influenced
some of them, especially Dirk Philips and Leenaert
Bouwens, to hold very strictly to their personal idea of
what constituted a pure church. They excommunicated

those who did not agree with them, even when other leaders and a large portion of the church were not in agreement with their interpretation of purity. It was largely from this type of action that the Dutch Mennonite divisions arose. The church continued splitting into smaller factions, each committed to its own view of maintaining the faith. It is evident from the beginning of the divisions that much carnality and bitterness were displayed on both sides of all the divisions. The root question remained unanswered.

Finally, under the influence of the Collegiants, the issue took a new turn. Instead of asking what "not having spot or wrinkle" means, the question became, "Of what value is the church to me?" Different factions within the churches answered this question differently. As discussed previously, some felt that strong doctrinal positions were important and that a high view of the church was necessary. Others felt that individual interpretations and desires should be the most important factor, while the church took second place. The latter position finally won the day, although vestiges of the older view survived for many years.

The pietistic influence hastened Dutch Mennonite apostasy. Today, the Dutch Doopsgezinde Church has a high view of individual freedom and a correspondingly low view of church authority. Their churches basically serve social interests.

The Incarnation. Dirk Philips and Menno Simons held that Christ's physical flesh was divinely created. They received this view from Melchior Hofmann. Dirk and Menno felt that Protestant preachers in the Netherlands stressed the humanity of Christ too much and did not place enough emphasis on His divinity. To counteract that weakness, they developed strong teachings on this subject. However, Dirk and Menno were somewhat imbalanced in the opposite direction. They tended to emphasize Christ's divinity at the expense of His humanity. Early in his writings, Dirk Philips asserted the following:

> Jesus Christ . . . became man in Mary. . . .
> But if the body of Christ had been formed by Mary, . . . then there would be no difference between the body of Christ and that of Adam. . . .
> Now, if Christ is the bread of heaven, and if the bread of heaven moreover is the flesh of Christ, it is impossible for the flesh of Christ to be formed by Mary; for neither the seed of Mary, nor that of any earthly creature can by any means be the true living bread that came down from heaven, or be so called.[11]

Dirk taught that Christ became man, but he denied that Christ took upon Himself human flesh and blood from a human source. He believed that if Christ had received His human flesh and blood from Mary, he would have necessarily assumed man's fallen nature and could not have served as "the living bread which came down from heaven" (John 6:51).[12] Thus Dirk believed that while Christ was formed *in* Mary, He was not *of* Mary.[13]

When Menno Simons became an Anabaptist, he studied the matter thoroughly himself. In tremendous fear of being deceived, he fasted and prayed much before finally coming to the same conclusions.

Menno studied the Incarnation primarily to satisfy his personal questions about this doctrine. He directed his

---

[11] Dietrich Philip, *Enchiridion or Hand Book,* 99, 100.

[12] Ibid., 100.

[13] The Book of Galatians states that "God sent forth his Son, made *of* a woman, made under the law" (Galatians 4:4). The angel Gabriel told Mary, "That holy thing which shall be born *of* thee shall be called the Son of God" (Luke 1:35). The emphasis is clearer in the English King James Bible than in some other languages. For instance, Luther's German Bible (for Galatians 4:4) states that Christ was "born from a woman" rather than "made of a woman." This German rendering would have made Dirk and Menno's interpretation easier to defend.

writings concerning this issue to his accusers outside the Mennonite Church. He did not delve deeply into the Incarnation when instructing his fellow brethren. In his own churches, Menno's teaching on the Incarnation was almost exactly the teaching that Conservative Mennonites hold today—a simple, basic view that Jesus' earthly life and body had both human and divine aspects, and that it is not possible to understand this mystery completely.

What effect did these views have on the church? From all appearances, and from Menno's own testimony, the Dutch Anabaptists did not debate this issue. Menno seems to have questioned whether his view was sound, and he shrank from discussing it unless forced to do so. In a letter to a Protestant reformer, Menno explained his view of the Incarnation and then added:

> I repeat, this is my confession to those who demand to hear my belief and feeling in regard to this matter. However, I never teach it so profoundly in my common admonitions to the friends and brethren. . . . But I simply teach that the blessed Christ Jesus is truly God and man, a Son of God, and a son of man, conceived of the Holy Ghost, born of the Virgin Mary, a poor, despised man, like unto us in all things, sin excepted. . . . For I know full well that there are few who can understand this intricate matter, even after it is explained to them.
>
> Therefore, I say, I think there is nothing better for me and for all teachers than in a simple apostolic fashion to teach the incarnation of Christ for the simple congregation, with a view to its edification, love, comfort, and sanctification, and to follow Him in His holy doctrine and life.[14]

In 1555, the Swiss Brethren agreed that they did not approve of Menno and Dirk's teaching on the Incarnation.

---

[14] *The Complete Writings of Menno Simons,* 430, 431.

They considered it sufficient to understand that the Bible teaches the two aspects of Christ and that one should not probe into the mystery beyond the plain statements of the Bible. Eventually, the entire Mennonite Church held the Swiss view. Even in Holland, this controversy did not long outlast Menno and Dirk, except for isolated instances. Most of the Dutch Anabaptists of Menno's day considered the controversy nonessential.

Shunning. The radical forms of shunning, or avoidance of an excommunicated (banned) person, originated with the Dutch Anabaptists. The term *ban,* as used by some Amish and Mennonite churches today, does not refer to *shunning. Banning* is excommunication. *Shunning* is the social and religious avoidance that follows banning in most Amish and a few Mennonite churches. In a setting where shunning automatically follows banning, such a person is often referred to as being "under the ban."

In Chapter 6, we noticed that Obbe Philips completely separated from the radical, militant, visionary pseudo-Anabaptists. His group was extremely small in the beginning. Obbe was firmly convinced that the other groups were terrible deceivers. In order to protect his little flock from deception, he felt that they must shun all social contacts with the radicals. In this, Obbe seems to have been correct. The faithful Anabaptists were, at that point, few and weak at best. Jan Matthysz and his accomplices were deceiving many well-meaning people every day. Many people whom Obbe had baptized were soon drawn into the Münsterite web, even though Obbe himself was separated completely.

The great peril of deception seems to justify Obbe's strong teaching on avoiding the radicals. Marital avoidance does not seem to have been an issue in this early stage. If Biblical churches today faced a similar situation, they would probably follow Obbe's example.

The Dutch Anabaptists grew in numbers and strength, and the radical visionaries gradually subsided, but strong avoidance did not subside with them. Dirk Philips, Menno Simons, Leenaert Bouwens, and almost all other Dutch leaders ordained in the following century held to the teaching of avoidance to a greater or lesser degree. That "greater or lesser degree" caused countless problems for many, many years. A strong teaching on avoidance had been a necessary safeguard against deceptive, radical influences. When this teaching was applied to fellow brethren who felt differently about a few issues, trouble resulted.

Obbe's position, and the later teachings of Dirk Philips, Menno Simons, and Leenaert Bouwens, were based largely on the following Scripture verses.

> "Now I beseech you, brethren, mark them which cause divisions and offences contrary to the doctrine which ye have learned; and avoid them" (Romans 16:17).
>
> "But now I have written unto you not to keep company, if any man that is called a brother be a fornicator, or covetous, or an idolater, or a railer, or a drunkard, or an extortioner; with such an one no not to eat" (1 Corinthians 5:11).
>
> "And if any man obey not our word by this epistle, note that man, and have no company with him, that he may be ashamed" (2 Thessalonians 3:14).
>
> "If there come any unto you, and bring not this doctrine, receive him not into your house, neither bid him God speed" (2 John 10).

These verses clearly teach avoidance. Every Biblical Anabaptist group of the Reformation era practiced some form of this teaching. Even today, every Biblical church practices avoidance in one form or another, and this generally includes more than exclusion from Communion.[15] The controversy that arose over this issue was not whether the Bible taught avoidance, but how it should be exercised. Should it extend, as Menno and Dirk taught, to children and marriage partners whose spouses or parents had left the faith? Should it apply, as Leenaert Bouwens demanded, to faithful members of the church who did not shun banned persons quite as much as you thought they should? Should it also extend, as happened among the Dutch Mennonites many times, to banning and shunning almost every person and group who disagreed with you on how severely these doctrines should be implemented?

The Swiss Brethren said that avoidance did not apply to marriage, and they did not extend it to exclude all social contact. Sometimes Menno also answered these questions negatively, contradicting himself as he did so. In his tract writings, he held that shunning extended to banned marriage partners and parents, yet in his private

---

[15] Most conservative Mennonite churches today do not spell out the ways they practice avoidance. To spell out small details on avoidance seems to cloud the spiritual purpose for avoidance. Nevertheless, common practices on avoidance do exist in conservative Mennonite circles. For example, when a person is excommunicated, the close friendships his brethren had with him are broken, and they begin to relate to him with the same reserve they use when relating to any other sinner. Their communication with him will relate largely to business or his spiritual need. Regular social visits are not considered Biblical, even by the excommunicated person's close family members. The tension that always exists between the godly and ungodly has rightly been placed upon their relationship.

Scriptural avoidance involves more than relationships with members that leave our local church. Scriptural avoidance applies to some degree to everyone outside Christ, but does not relieve the church of her duty to warn the sinner with compassion and love. When this avoidance is consistent, charitable, and accompanied with Biblical testifying, God uses it to make sinners ashamed of their deeds (2 Thessalonians 3:14).

Since the Bible does not spell out exactly how to observe avoidance, some variation is allowable. But when avoidance becomes a complete shunning of those who leave the church, yet the church members socialize rather freely with their neighbors without a sense of evangelistic obligation, it is not being Scripturally observed. Scriptural admonitions about backsliders indicate that a greater or more-concentrated effort is in order to rescue such individuals.

letters and conversations, he constantly urged charity. As far as we know, he never insisted on the shunning of banned marriage partners in his actual church administration. In spite of Menno's milder, actual application, the Swiss Brethren strongly challenged him on the basis of his writings. Strained relationships existed between Menno and some of the Swiss ministers for the rest of his life.

Dirk and Leenaert answered positively to every one of the questions above and enforced their radical application in their church work. Menno pleaded with them to be more lenient, but they felt they could not safely do so. They were working to preserve a pure church, but their strong application of shunning caused some of the first divisions among the Dutch Anabaptists. The emphasis on a pure church was vital, but too often it was defined by the ideas of a few leaders and not by the consensus of most of the leaders and churches. At various times in the Dutch churches, a prominent leader arose with a strong view of what constituted purity, gathered a following, and banned those who would not agree with him. Yet both sides of all the documented divisions contained actions and attitudes that the Bible clearly forbids. It seems clear that there was some misuse of excommunication in the Dutch Anabaptist churches.

In summary, Menno, Dirk, and other early leaders defended strict shunning until their deaths. In 1556, the Waterlanders left the mainstream Mennonite Church largely because of Leenaert Bouwens's strict application of the ban. (Leenaert was the main leader in the area where the Waterlanders lived.) The Waterlanders practiced a milder form of avoidance for many years, but then lost it altogether as they traveled worldward.

By 1557, the Dutch Mennonites' influence for strict shunning had reached Switzerland and southern Germany and caused some commotion among the Swiss Brethren there. The Swiss leaders met in that year and took a position against the Dutch teaching on marital shunning.

From the 1560s through the 1590s, the Dutch Mennonite Church literally flew to pieces over conflicting views of church purity and severity in applying the ban. Around 1566, the mainstream Dutch Mennonite Church divided into three groups: the Frisians, the Flemish, and the High Germans. In 1586, the Flemish split into two groups over this issue, and the Frisians did likewise in 1589. Other groups splintered off in many areas throughout the late 1500s.

From 1590 on, the position on marital shunning was softened. The Concept of Cologne, which brought a number of the divided churches into agreement on various issues, stated that marital shunning was wrong. This was the overwhelming feeling from this time on, with few exceptions. A number of confessions of faith, including the well-known Dordrecht Confession, strongly supported shunning but implied or expressed that marital shunning was not required. From the 1650s on, the Dutch churches apostatized rapidly, and avoidance finally disappeared altogether.

Jacob Ammann took up the struggle in Switzerland in 1693, when he tried to push the Swiss Brethren into a stricter observance of shunning. Chapter 5 gives this story in detail.

Chapter 8

The Hutterites

The Hutterites represented one of the largest groups of faithful Anabaptists. They differed from other Anabaptist groups chiefly in their practice of communal living and their long-lived evangelical vision. While the Swiss Brethren stagnated spiritually and most of the Dutch Mennonites drifted into the world, many of the Hutterites testified faithfully and practiced careful, Biblical discipleship. Eventually, the Hutterites apostatized also, with only a remnant holding to the faith of their fathers.

Moravia—a Land of Religious Toleration

Today, Moravia is a lowland, agricultural and forest region of the Czech Republic, enclosed on three sides by mountains and hills. Moravia lies east of southern Germany and south of Poland. In the 1500s, most of Moravia was divided into manorial estates controlled by lords. In previous centuries, these manors had usually been independent political entities. But as kings gained power and nations formed, the Moravian lords technically became

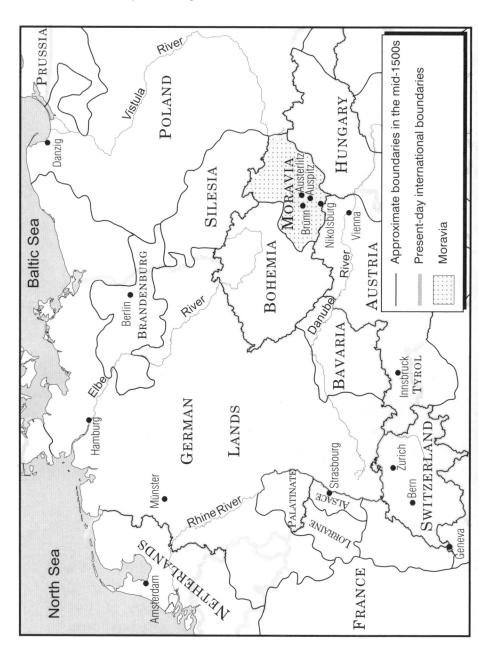

Moravia and Surrounding Lands

subject to the Holy Roman Emperor. However, they did not give up their freedom easily. They continued to control many of their own affairs. They felt little obligation to obey the emperor unless he threatened them with grave consequences.

Some of the Moravian lords prided themselves in their religious toleration. For many years, followers of John Huss,[1] as well as other small religious sects, found a degree of toleration in Moravia unequaled anywhere else in Europe. This toleration extended to the Anabaptists as well.

The lords also tolerated the Anabaptists because they were morally upright people and reliable workers. The native, Catholic Moravians tended to be lazy, dishonest, and immoral. The Anabaptists, on the other hand, were careful, honest workers, who went the second mile, took good care of their land and buildings, and paid their taxes. As a group, they had laborers in almost every type of occupation and provided quality goods for both local and foreign markets. These qualities were an asset to any lord.

Balthasar Hubmaier and the Nikolsburg Scene

Nikolsburg,[2] a city and domain in southern Moravia, became an Anabaptist center in the late 1520s. Until 1566 Nikolsburg belonged to the tolerant Liechtenstein family. Already in 1524 a Lutheran church was established in

---

[1] John Huss (c. 1369–1415) was a reformer among the Bohemian people. From Bohemia, his influence spread into Moravia. By the time the Anabaptist movement came to Moravia, Huss's followers had split into two groups.

John Huss was influenced by the teachings of the reformer John Wycliffe (1320–1384). Wycliffe's followers were called Lollards. They taught against the abuses of the pope and Roman clergy and considered the Bible to be the only standard of truth. Huss taught many truths that later reformers emphasized, such as the belief that Catholic popes were not the head of the church and that one could be a member of an earthly church and yet not be saved.

[2] Nikolsburg is known in modern times as Mikulov.

the area. Several groups of John Huss's followers were there as well.

Balthasar Hubmaier, a former priest, came to Nikolsburg in the spring of 1526, about fifteen months after Swiss Anabaptism began in Zurich. He had been influenced by the Lutheran and Zwinglian reforms, and he had introduced many Biblical teachings in his church at Waldshut, a small city north of Zurich. Hubmaier supported adult baptism and some other Anabaptist beliefs. But, unlike the Anabaptists, he did not reject swearing oaths, physical resistance, and the idea that civil government can be Christian.

Hubmaier had a few contacts with the Swiss Brethren. Conrad Grebel and Wilhelm Reublin had visited him at Waldshut. After Hubmaier left Waldshut, he had been in both Zurich and Schaffhausen for a time before he arrived in Moravia some nineteen months later. It is likely that he had contact with Anabaptists during that time.

Now, in Nikolsburg, Hubmaier became the leader of a large group of Anabaptists, and he labored, with some success, to convert the existing Lutheran congregation to Anabaptism. Around twelve thousand Anabaptists gradually found their way to southern Moravia. The heavy persecution in other areas caused this swell of immigrants. Other leaders also served the Nikolsburg Anabaptists, although Hubmaier seems to have been the main leader.

These Anabaptists held varying beliefs, and soon the people began disputing with each other. Hubmaier and his fellows led a group that accepted the use of the sword and paid military taxes. At least one lord of Nikolsburg was a baptized member of Hubmaier's church.

Jacob Wiedemann and Philip Jager led a party that held to nonresistance and did not pay taxes levied specifically for war. This faction also felt that Hubmaier accepted people into his church without an adequate examination of their faith. They accused Hubmaier's followers of not giving enough material aid to the many poor Anabaptists who were flocking to Nikolsburg. Many of these destitute refugees had left all their possessions and fled for their lives. Wiedemann and his followers soon began meeting separately and broke off fellowship with the larger group.

Early in 1527, Hans Hut entered the troubled waters of Nikolsburg. Hut was a zealous, effective, Anabaptist missionary, who did not agree with the Swiss Brethren on some points.[3] He was a dynamic preacher and soon entered into debate with Hubmaier concerning the Nikolsburg strife. Since Hut strongly believed in nonresistance and in sharing material aid, he sided with the Wiedemann group. The lords of Nikolsburg did not appreciate Hut's aggressiveness. They were trying to keep all the Anabaptists on their estate at peace with each other, and Hut's presence only produced more dissension. They imprisoned him, but he soon escaped and left the territory for good.

---

[3] Hut was somewhat extreme in his views of prophecy. He thought he knew when Christ would return. He made strong comparisons of the events of his day with the Biblical end-time events. He also placed some emphasis on dreams as a method of divine revelation. Hut taught nonresistance, but it seems that it was based as much on his views of prophecy as on Bible teaching. He felt that the Turks (who were at that time a grave threat to Europe) were destined to overcome Europe and its rulers. There was little use in trying to resist them, since they were simply fulfilling God's plan. Hut was also strong on sharing material aid with others. This was good, but it was based on the assumption that since the Turks would devastate Europe, there was little use in keeping many material possessions.

Was Hut an Anabaptist? His message had many elements of Anabaptism, such as a Biblical view of Communion and baptism. Although he does not fit with the more Biblical Anabaptists, such as the early Swiss Brethren and Dutch Mennonites, it seems fair to place Hut within Anabaptism as a whole. He attended the Martyrs' Synod (a 1527 meeting of Anabaptist leaders, some of whom were martyred soon after the gathering). At this meeting, Hut agreed to modify the prophecy in his preaching.

In central and south Germany, the main territory of Hut's labors, the Anabaptist churches deviated on some points from the Swiss Brethren. They were not as stable, and were soon exterminated by persecution and emigration.

Late in 1527, the lords finally told Wiedemann and his group that they could not remain in the area unless they joined the larger church.[4] The authorities did not strongly object to their views, but they could not tolerate the division. Wiedemann's group wanted to move anyway because the lords were protecting the Anabaptists on their estate by force and the group felt that such resistance against the emperor's authority was wrong.

In the spring of 1528, Wiedemann and his followers sold some of their goods and left some behind. About two hundred adults and their children left and camped in a deserted village near Nikolsburg. Here they made the decision to stay together, pool their goods, and live from a common purse. The dire poverty of some of the group forced them to either pool their resources or break up and leave the poor to their fate. In Christian love, they decided to care for each one. At this point, they did not envision the highly organized, essential-for-salvation, communal life that developed among them later.

One of the lords traveled with them for a time, providing them with drink and freeing them from tolls. They soon found a place to live near the town of Austerlitz. The lords here agreed to allow them to live in peace, and were eager for them to settle on their estate. The lords gave the group wood for building and freed them from compulsory labor, rent, and taxes for six years.

The Communal Group Grows and Struggles

By the winter of 1530, less than two years after the Austerlitz group began, there were about six hundred members in the church. Many Anabaptists from Austria, suffering intense persecution, fled to Moravia and joined

---

[4] The Austrian authorities captured Hubmaier soon after Hans Hut left Moravia. He was martyred in Vienna on March 10, 1528. His church at Nikolsburg fragmented in the years following his death.

the Austerlitz group. Jacob Hutter, a leader from Tyrol,[5] had visited Austerlitz in 1529 and appreciated what he found. He returned to Tyrol and organized small bands of refugees for flight to Moravia.

Since so many refugees were coming to Austerlitz, it became almost impossible to properly care for them all. Wiedemann was the main leader, but Jacob Hutter decided that Georg Zaunring, a minister who had immigrated from Tyrol, should be in charge of the large group of Tyrolean immigrants. Wilhelm Reublin, a Swiss Brethren leader who had associated with Grebel, Mantz, and Blaurock in the early days of the Anabaptist movement, also came to Moravia early in 1530 and wanted to assume a leadership role. But Wiedemann did not grant his desire.

Factions develop in the Austerlitz group. In the winter, it became too cold to meet for worship outside, as the group had been doing. There was no building large enough to house them all, so they divided the people into three groups and assigned a minister to each group. These groups soon became factions because the teachings of their ministers differed. In addition, many of the people were dissatisfied with Wiedemann's administration. Reublin, seemingly upset about his rejection as a leader, became the unofficial spokesman for those dissatisfied with Wiedemann. Georg Zaunring sided with Reublin.

When Wiedemann was temporarily absent, Reublin and Zaunring presented their charges against him to the congregation. They blamed Wiedemann for unequal distribution of material goods. Over twenty babies had died that winter for lack of milk, and certain people in the

---

[5] Tyrol was a territory southwest of Moravia and due east of Switzerland.

group had more food and clothes than others. Wiedemann and his fellow leaders also demanded that girls marry the young men the ministers selected for them. When some women resisted this, Wiedemann had threatened to secure heathen wives for the young men. According to Reublin, Wiedemann also believed that water baptism was absolutely necessary for salvation and that children who died unbaptized did not go to heaven.[6] Zaunring and his Tyrolean brethren felt that the church did not receive enough spiritual food. They complained that the preaching was not as comforting and instructive as what they had heard at home in Tyrol. Some people felt that church discipline was weak and that the children were not receiving an adequate education.

Wiedemann, warned of the conditions at home, soon returned from his trip. He made a long speech to the church, defending his administration and opposing Reublin. He refused to allow Reublin to defend himself before the church. Rather, he told his people to have nothing to do with the dissenters. But this refusal to allow Reublin to present his case caused most of the people to go over to Reublin's side. Nevertheless, Wiedemann and his followers excommunicated Reublin and Zaunring.

Sick at heart, the two banned leaders gathered their three hundred fifty followers. Two hundred fifty stayed with Wiedemann. In the middle of winter, amid much hardship, the dissenters relocated to Auspitz and began a commune *(Bruderhof)* there. This group became the one from which the Hutterites sprang.

The division did not please either faction. Both appealed to Jacob Hutter and Simon Schützinger in Tyrol to look into the matter and to discipline those who were

---

[6] Wiedemann may have taught this, but it was probably the fruit of Reublin's questionable attitude toward the leader. Many historians feel that it was not an accurate accusation.

guilty. These leaders sided with the Auspitz group and strongly admonished the Austerlitz brethren, but Wiedemann refused to submit to their judgment.

Administrative difficulties in the Auspitz group. The Auspitz group faced trial after trial. Besides their lack of material goods and their suffering from robbers, spiritual problems continued to plague the church. Soon after the division, a minister from a small group of believers in Swabia came to inquire about the faith and practice of the Bruderhof at Auspitz. When Reublin explained to him the position of the church on certain issues, the minister left in disappointment, but not before sharing the matter with several other Auspitz brethren. The brethren found that Reublin did not truthfully tell the minister what their position was. Besides this, Reublin soon became extremely ill. It then became known that he had been hiding a fair amount of his personal money, even though the church was in tremendous need. Jacob Hutter and Simon Schützinger, who were in the area to look into the division, excommunicated Reublin.[7] They entrusted the Auspitz group entirely to Georg Zaunring and returned to Tyrol.

In the summer of 1531, the church found that Georg Zaunring's wife had committed adultery with a brother in the church. Georg and another leader had secretly excommunicated them and then brought them back into the church, and they considered the matter closed. When the secretive affair came to light, it shocked the whole church. They excommunicated Zaunring, but he repented and the church accepted him again, but not as a leader.

---

[7] Reublin left the communal group after this. For a time, he associated with Anabaptists in other areas, but he finally turned his back on Anabaptism altogether.

Now the church was without a minister, so they once again called Jacob Hutter and Simon Schützinger from Tyrol. These brethren looked into Zaunring's failure and approved of the church action. Simon Schützinger was appointed to lead the church. At this time, the Auspitz brethren united their church with two other Anabaptist groups that were nearby: Philip Plener and his followers at Auspitz (the Philippites) and Gabriel Ascherham and his followers at Rossitz (the Gabrielites). Hutter arranged that the three groups would remain separate communities but that their leaders would counsel together. Gabriel Ascherham became the highest authority in the affiliation.

Problems continued, especially in Simon Schützinger's group. Difficulties with selfishness, jealousy, and family ties abounded. Communal living faced severe testing.

Jacob Hutter takes up residence at Auspitz. The persecution in Tyrol finally became so harsh that it was almost impossible for Anabaptists to remain there, so Jacob Hutter moved to Auspitz in August 1533. The church welcomed him with great joy and immediately asked him to help solve the many internal problems. Some of the dissatisfied members at Auspitz thought that Hutter would begin a new church with them, but he assured the group that he had no such intentions.

Right away, Hutter addressed the many needs. He felt God was calling him to discipline the erring members and put the church in order. But soon Schützinger began to resist him and declared that Hutter had no business trying to administrate the group. Hutter was ready to move on if the church did not want him. He felt he could not remain there, however, and be silent about the church conditions, or he would not be able to answer to God with good conscience.

The leaders of the three groups met and argued bitterly over the matter. A few of them wanted Schützinger and Hutter to serve together, but many of them felt that Hutter should move on to another area. Schützinger seemed to feel threatened because Hutter was a more able leader and speaker than he. He blamed Hutter for pushing to be the shepherd over the church when God had called Schützinger to that position. Hutter, however, realized that there were elements in the church that supported him, so he refused to leave without allowing the church to make the decision.

After much wrangling, the church agreed that Hutter could stay there, but that he should give precedence to Schützinger in church administration. Hutter claimed that this decision was wrong, and maintained that God had sent him to Auspitz. However, for the sake of peace, he finally agreed to abide by their decision. Clearly, obstinate feelings were on both sides.

Within a few weeks, Schützinger became quite ill, so Hutter preached the sermons and admonished the people. For some reason, he suspected that Schützinger's wife was harboring some goods she had not given to the Bruderhof. He asked permission of the other leaders to search Schützinger's apartment. They agreed to it if Hutter would also let his living quarters be searched. Hutter agreed, and the leaders found that Schützinger and his wife had hidden a small fortune in money, as well as extra clothing and bed linen. The church was appalled. Hutter excommunicated Schützinger and his wife immediately.

The *Hutterian Chronicle* describes the situation like this:

> The whole brotherhood had previously chosen Schützinger as elder in preference to Jakob. Now that Schützinger was found to be a deceiver, Jakob exhorted all the brothers and sisters to consider how they had

talked and acted and what sort of decision they had made. Also it had been said that he, Jakob, did not have the gifts to be a shepherd to such a people; instead they had chosen Schützinger as shepherd, a man whose wickedness was now revealed. And so, he said, they were once more completely without a shepherd, for as they had had so little respect for the Lord's Word, he was no longer certain about serving them. He challenged them, however, to pray earnestly, calling on God to raise up a faithful shepherd and servant for them.

For eight days and nights they prayed earnestly to God. They sent two brothers to Gabriel [Ascherham] at Rossitz to tell him of their need and to ask his advice about what they should do. He, too, suggested Jakob Hutter.[8]

In spite of this questionable attitude on Hutter's part, the group appointed him to be the main leader at Auspitz.

The church affiliation with the Philippites and Gabrielites dissolves. The excommunication of Schützinger let loose a torrent of bitterness from Philip Plener, Gabriel Ascherham, and their followers. They blamed Hutter and the church at Auspitz for faulty administration in church discipline. They felt that the church should not have treated Schützinger so harshly. Surely, they said, the church could have punished Schützinger without exposing him to such humiliation. They believed that some of Hutter's members who had been reaccepted after repentance should still be outside the church, and that some excommunicated people had never really done anything that warranted their discipline.

Hutter's church basically stood together in the matter. They made a number of efforts to try to come to peace

---

[8] *The Chronicle of the Hutterian Brethren,* 1:104, 105.

with the others, but when everything failed, they cut off fellowship with both groups. The other groups took in those who left Hutter—excommunicated brethren and all. They put out many slanderous reports about Hutter's group.

Hutter strengthens the communal brotherhood. Despite his rocky beginning with the Auspitz church, the group began to appreciate Hutter, and he contributed to the strength of the church. He established more consistent discipline, and the church experienced spiritual peace and growth. With his fellow leaders, he reorganized the Bruderhof, making it completely communal in both production and consumption.

Hutter had a sound vision of the church as a suffering, despised remnant in the world. His earnest preaching had been born in the midst of terrible persecution in the Tyrol. The Bible does not support his belief that the only valid expression of Christian love is giving up all earthly possessions and joining the Bruderhof. Yet we cannot mock his belief, due to the physical needs present among the Anabaptists of the time. Hutter and his brethren had deep, spiritual concerns at heart when they laid the foundation for a durable community. They had a zealous interest in the salvation of lost souls and did all in their power to keep the church pure as well as to invite sincere seekers into their midst. Although their organization was not the only one that contained true Christians, it was one of the most successful and one of the largest groups of faithful Anabaptists for many years. Many Anabaptist converts from persecution areas continued to flood into Moravia, and the churches built many Bruderhofs. Because of Hutter's contribution to the group, they soon became known as Hutterites.

The history of other Anabaptist groups in Moravia. The Philippites moved to Germany and Austria. Some of them assimilated into the Swiss Brethren, joined other small Anabaptist groups, or recanted. A number of them also joined Hutter's group. There is no record of them surviving beyond the 1540s.[9]

Most of the Gabrielites joined Hutter's group after their leader, Gabriel Ascherham, died. Some of them completely left the Anabaptist movement. Their history as a group was over by 1565.

There were other Anabaptists in Moravia who did not practice community of goods. They were generally called Swiss Brethren, even though they did not necessarily come from Switzerland. A small group of Pilgram Marpeck's followers (Pilgramites) was also present. But all these groups finally died out or moved away.

Persecution Comes to the Hutterites

For nine years, from 1526 to 1535, the Anabaptists in Moravia lived in relative peace. Imprisonment was rare. There was little persecution in Moravia compared with other areas where Anabaptists faced severe trials. Emperor Ferdinand, theoretically the highest authority of Moravia, had demanded as early as 1528 that the Moravian nobles must not tolerate Anabaptists. The nobles refused to comply with his demand, and Ferdinand did not immediately enforce his desire.

Ferdinand increases his efforts to exterminate the Anabaptists. The Münster rebellion in 1534 and 1535 convinced Ferdinand that Anabaptism was a grave political threat to his empire. Fully aroused, he attended the

---

[9] A group of Philippites was imprisoned at Passau from 1535–1540. While there, they wrote fifty-two hymns, which became the first part of the present *Ausbund*.

Moravian Diet[10] of 1535 and threatened the nobles with force unless they immediately expelled the Anabaptists from their estates. The nobles and Anabaptists pleaded for tolerance, but to no avail.

Soldiers drove the Hutterites from their villages in the spring of 1535. The fields and forests became their inhospitable home, and the open sky their roof. Many children, sick people, old folk, and widows suffered severely during this time. Besides being forced to live in the open, the sufferers were harassed by robber gangs and government agents, who captured any Anabaptist they could find. The government paid them for every Anabaptist they turned in.

Hutter wrote a letter concerning their pathetic condition to the rulers, but it fell on deaf ears. The letter put Hutter in great danger of being captured by the persecutors. Since the government was seeking Hutter as an Anabaptist ringleader, some of the brethren felt that it might take some pressure off the group, besides providing more safety for Hutter, if he would return to Tyrol. The church agreed on this move. Hutter chose Hans Amon to lead the group, and returned to his former scene of labors. In November, he was betrayed and captured. After much suffering, he was burned at the stake in February 1536.[11]

For nearly a year, the Hutterites wandered about in small groups, seeking work and food wherever they could find it. Gradually the persecution lessened, and small groups of workers found fairly permanent jobs on the estates of lesser nobles who dared to evade the law. The proceeds from this labor helped to support the whole group.

[10] *Diet* in this sense refers to a legislative assembly of rulers in certain countries.

[11] To relate Hutterite history to Dutch Anabaptism, Jacob Hutter was martyred about the same time that Menno Simons left the Roman church.

A few Hutterites returned to their former homes in Tyrol, but most of them stayed in Moravia. Hans Amon and other leaders traveled about from group to group, encouraging them and trying to help meet their needs. Within a few years, most of the Hutterites regrouped, and the nobles again took them in. They even prospered and enjoyed relative peace in the early 1540s. They also established Bruderhofs in Hungary.

Evangelists in Chains

The storybook *Evangelists in Chains* recounts a persecution experience some of the Hutterites faced.[12] Because of the persecution in Moravia, some brethren had moved to a benevolent lord's domain in northern Austria, not far south of Nikolsburg. For several years, they lived here in peace, but their presence did not go unnoticed by the Austrian authorities. In December 1538, these brethren held a meeting with some Philippite brethren and possibly some other Anabaptist branches to discuss uniting their churches. As the brethren met, imperial soldiers from Vienna, the Austrian capital, surprised and arrested them. The authorities tortured and interrogated some of them and gave them offers of freedom, but they refused to compromise their faith and accept release.

Finally the government sentenced ninety brethren to galley slavery on warships. The soldiers chained them in pairs and fastened them together in a long line. Accompanied by soldiers, the brethren marched approximately four hundred miles in the winter of 1539 to Trieste, a port on the Adriatic Sea. At the port, the soldiers imprisoned them, but God miraculously delivered the Anabaptists from their impending doom.

Using the chains that had bound them, the brethren scaled the prison wall and escaped in the night. They broke into small groups for their homeward journey. Authorities captured twelve of them on their way home, and their fate remains unknown. The rest of them arrived safely in Moravia, praising God for His deliverance.

---

[12] Elizabeth Wagler, *Evangelists in Chains* (Crockett, Ky.: Rod and Staff Publishers, Inc., 1983).

Hans Amon, Peter Riedemann, and Leonard Seiler lead the Hutterites. Hans Amon was a strong, inspiring leader from 1536 to 1542. The Hutterites successfully pulled through the persecution and maintained a strong spiritual vision and dedication. During Amon's time of leadership, the Hutterite churches sent missionaries to take the Gospel to all the German people of Europe. These missionary journeys resulted in many converts who moved to Moravia and joined the communal brotherhoods.

The missionaries' willingness to go forth, even though 80 percent of them never returned, is a monument to the spiritual vitality of the early Hutterite church. The early Swiss and Dutch Anabaptists were also evangelistic but did not organize such a comprehensive program.[13]

After Hans Amon passed away in 1542, Peter Riedemann and Leonard Seiler jointly led the Hutterites. This leadership team worked well. Riedemann was a zealous, kind, spiritual leader, and Seiler efficiently oversaw the practical aspects of the Bruderhofs.

Riedemann made an outstanding contribution to the church by his writings. His chief works are two large doctrinal volumes. He wrote the first one, *An Account of Our Faith,* before he joined the Hutterite brotherhood. Riedemann wrote the second book, *An Account of Our Religion, Doctrine, and Faith,* around 1541, while he traveled as a Hutterite missionary. He wrote these books, as well as many letters, as he lay in various prisons. The Hutterites treasure both of his books, especially the second one, as important, doctrinal expositions of their faith.

---

[13] One reason the Hutterites could organize such an extensive mission program was that the sending churches experienced relative peace at this time. The Swiss and Dutch Anabaptists also zealously evangelized in their early years. However, since their churches were small, often lacked adequate leadership, and often were decimated by persecution and emigration, they were unable to organize a program that made history like the Hutterites' work.

The persecution of 1547–1552. The few peaceful years were soon past. Ferdinand again visited the Moravian nobles in 1546 and demanded that the "heretics" be expelled. At the time, the Hutterites had twenty-six Bruderhofs in Moravia and twelve in Hungary. All of them were financial assets to the local nobles, but all pleas to the emperor fell on deaf ears. The authorities were willing to allow the Anabaptists to dwell on the nobles' estates if they would separate into groups of five or seven persons. But the brethren knew that this meant giving up their faith, so they refused. Once again, the government drove the Hutterites from their homes and robbed them.

For a short time, the Bruderhofs in Hungary escaped the persecution, and the Moravian Hutterites fled there for protection. But by 1548, political pressure was placed on the Hungarian nobles too, and the brethren had nowhere to go. The Hungarian nobles escorted them back to Moravia, where they wandered in a forest for over a month. But soon the Moravian nobles drove them back to Hungary again. They seesawed back and forth in severe suffering.

Robber bands roamed the forests and sometimes even stole the clothes from the Anabaptists' backs. Members who were not willing to endure the suffering finally left the group. But many new members also joined the Hutterites through this time. The *Chronicle* adequately describes the sufferings the church faced.

> Peter Bakisch[14] in particular wreaked his fury on them; he spared no one, neither the old nor the sick nor little children.[15] They were threatened and given short notice: in three days everyone had to be gone.

---

[14] Peter Bakisch was a Hungarian lord.

[15] Not all the Hungarian rulers employed such harsh measures as are here described.

Anyone still found there would see what would happen to him. Guards were posted to stop the believers from taking too much with them. They were ungodly folk, who day and night did everything they could to steal food from the faithful and anything else that took their fancy. . . .

Peter Bakisch sent peasants to cut wood, bring it in front of the brothers' houses, and build gallows right outside their doors as if about to hang them, especially those who did not move away fast enough. The brothers suffered much abuse of this sort.

. . . The believers were forced into the forest, even in the cold of wintertime, to live like wild animals. If only they had been allowed to do this unmolested, they would have been happy. But there was no sparing of anyone, no mercy for the old and gray, for expectant or nursing mothers and their babies. . . .

The treatment was so cruel that it would have been too rough for cattle. . . .

. . . Day and night, for five weeks, they lived in the woods with their wives and children, widows and orphans, the sick, the young and the old, like the animals that live in the wild. During this time they met with much violence and injury. Robbers stripped many of them naked, and one brother was even murdered in the woods.

The brotherhood sent many brothers abroad to see if they could find a home, but word came back saying they had found nothing. Yet they could not remain in the woods; the bitter cold forced them to look for shelter.

The elders spoke comfortingly to the people and exhorted them to hold fast to God and his truth until death, as the saints had done from the beginning through all persecutions and hardships, for the world had treated them in the same way. . . .

When they could no longer maintain themselves in the woods, the elders divided the people into little groups of ten or twelve, as many as could find shelter in one house. Each group was entrusted to one brother, who was to go with them and look for work, and they had to find food where they could. . . . The tears ran down their cheeks as they shook hands, blessed one another over and over again, put themselves in God's hands, and set out, each group in a different direction. Misery was their lot.

They returned to Moravia, from where they had been expelled. They were in grave danger and suffered severely, fleeing as they were driven from place to place. . . .

At Poppitz, where believers were living in holes underground, some godless men built a fire at the entrance and tried to suffocate them or smoke them out, but they were stopped and driven away. . . . Around the Mayberg many lived with their children in holes among the bushes for a time. They also lived in rocky crevasses and caves in the Mayberg cliffs and in other similar places in Moravia, wherever they could. . . .

The faithful were driven out of Moravia into Hungary, out of Hungary back into Moravia, out of Moravia into Austria, out of Austria back into Moravia. . . .

During these times of great tribulation, God added many to the church. People came from many places and believed, changed their lives, and took up the cross. More joined then than later in good times. . . .

After five years of great distress we gathered once more, determined to keep community as wholeheartedly as ever. We had every reason to give our heartfelt praise, honor, and glory to God in heaven, who sends times of tribulation and also frees us from them. . .[16]

Riedemann and his fellow leaders led the Hutterian brotherhood through these difficult times. Gradually the persecution subsided, and they once more gathered in Moravia, where they lived in peace for approximately forty years.

---

[16] *The Chronicle of the Hutterian Brethren,* Vol. I, 299–314.

The Peaceful Period

The peaceful period of Hutterite history, also known as their Golden Age, lasted from about 1554 to 1595. Especially during the reign of Emperor Maximilian II (1564–1576), life was tranquil for the Hutterites. Maximilian sympathized strongly with the Protestants. However, he agreed to support the Catholic religion so that he could rise in political power. But whenever he could, he protected Protestants and other minority religious sects, since he also wanted to win the support of Protestant nobles. Under his reign, independent nobles once again were able to disregard Catholic religious authorities, resulting in religious tolerance in Moravia and Hungary.

Throughout this period, the Hutterites freely met for worship. They could also market their goods and services freely, and they realized their community and church ideals to a greater degree than ever before.

Church vision and growth. There were probably around one hundred Hutterite farm colonies, representing between fifteen and thirty thousand souls.[17] Since persecution was still harsh in all Anabaptist areas except the Netherlands, many believers, especially from Switzerland and south Germany, fled to Moravia and joined the brotherhood. The Hutterites corresponded frequently with persecuted Anabaptists in other areas, which helped to draw believers to their communities.

Another factor in Hutterite growth was their extensive evangelizing. Their zealous concern for lost and seeking

---

[17] Historical sources vary on the number of Hutterites during this period. Estimates range from as low as twelve thousand to as high as seventy thousand. See *The Mennonite Encyclopedia,* Vol. II, 855, and Cornelius J. Dyck, *An Introduction to Mennonite History,* 76.

souls was especially evident early in the peaceful period. They determined to go wherever there was an open door. Any land where they knew the language and where souls were seeking truth became a Hutterite missionary field. Applicants for church membership needed to be willing to engage in this work. As in the early years of their church, many evangelists never returned. And hostile authorities apprehended many seekers on their way to Moravia and executed them.

The high spiritual character of the Hutterites became well known to the world around them. Even though the Catholics spread many malicious tales about them, their true character shone through. They held a high standard of discipline in their large group. They produced many writings, both historical and doctrinal, throughout the peaceful period. They carefully obeyed civil authorities when such obedience was in accord with Christ's commands. They avoided foolishness, swearing, vain dressing, immoderate drinking and feasting, and immorality. They prayed much, sang deeply spiritual songs, and gathered often for worship.

The Catholics complained that even when they were able to convert a Hutterite back into the Roman church, they could never count on his sincerity. Almost never did an apostate Hutterite stay faithful to the Catholic Church. Most of them repented and reverted to the Anabaptists.

Material prosperity. The Hutterites' careful diligence, frugality, and well-organized labors brought them a fairly comfortable life. Appointed men supervised each duty and occupation in the colonies. During the peaceful period, leaders wrote detailed guidelines for performing the various occupations. These guidelines established processes for manufacturing and helped to ensure quality products. Even important government leaders sought

Hutterite products for their quality and fair price.

The *Chronicle* gives a detailed account of Hutterite organization and occupations during this period.

> Some men were carefully chosen to take charge of the management of temporal affairs. They made and received payments, provided for food and supplies, and did the buying and selling.
>
> Others were in charge of organizing the work and sending each one to the job he knew and could do well, in the fields or wherever necessary. These were the work distributors. . . .
>
> There was no usury, no buying and selling for gain. There was only honest labor to earn a living through the daily toil of those who worked as vinedressers and farmers in the vineyards, fields, and gardens. Carpenters and builders went out within Moravia and as far as Austria, Hungary, and Bohemia to build many large mills, breweries, and other buildings at fair wages for the lords, nobles, and other citizens. A brother was especially assigned for this purpose, an experienced builder who organized the carpenters, accepted work, bargained, and made agreements on behalf of the brotherhood.
>
> Many of the brothers were millers, and there were many mills in that area whose owners asked the brothers to take them over and look after the grinding for a third or a fourth share, which was a fair deal according to current practice. So the brotherhood appointed a brother to oversee the mills. With the advice of the elders, he made all the agreements, assigned the millers, and saw to it that the mills were staffed and functioning well.
>
> For a long time the lords and noblemen (especially those on whose land we lived) employed our people to run their farms and other work departments, some for a third share, some for wages, or whatever was acceptable to both parties. A brother was responsible for taking on such farms as the community could manage,

often after repeated requests by the landlords. He made the arrangements and saw to it that enough people were available to staff them.

In short, no one was idle; each did what was required and what he was able to do, whatever he had been before—rich or poor, aristocrat or commoner. Even the priests who joined the community learned to work.

All sorts of honest, useful trades were represented: those of mason, scythesmith, blacksmith, coppersmith, locksmith, clockmaker, cutler, plumber, tanner, furrier, cobbler, saddler, harness maker, bag maker, wagon maker, cooper, joiner, turner, hatter, cloth maker, tailor, blanket maker, weaver, rope maker, sieve maker, glazier, potter, beer brewer, barber-surgeon, and physician. In each work department one brother was in charge of the shop, accepted orders and planned the work, then sold the products at their fair value and handed the proceeds over to the church.[18]

Children's education. The Hutterites were far ahead of their day in sound elementary education. The Catholic Church felt no need of general education. For them, ignorance was an excellent tool in keeping the population subject to the church. But the Hutterites believed that a faithful church depended on brethren and sisters who could read and study the Word of God and the religious writings of their brethren.

Throughout their history, the Hutterite approach to the family unit has varied considerably, depending on their approach to schooling. At the times of highest organization, some communities had little family structure. At the tender age of two, children went to live at the nursery school. Sisters assigned to the task trained them and

---

[18] *The Chronicle of the Hutterian Brethren,* Vol. I, 405, 406.

took care of them until they were five or six. They then moved on to the elementary school, which provided a similar arrangement. Parents could visit their children under these circumstances, but they actually saw little of them until the children were older. The school was the children's home until about age fourteen.[19]

In some Hutterite colonies, however, families lived together. Children left the parents only for the school day. This freed the mothers to perform the community duties assigned to them, such as washing, cleaning, and food preparation. The families gathered again each evening and spent the night together.

Peter Riedemann described the Biblical emphasis of Hutterite elementary education as follows:

> As soon as the mother hath weaned the child she giveth it to the school. Here there are sisters, appointed by the Church . . . ; and, as soon as they can speak, they lay the word of God's testimony in their mouths and . . . tell them of prayer and such things as children can understand. With them children remain until their fifth or sixth year, that is, until they are able to learn to read and write. . . .
>
> When they are thus far they are entrusted to the schoolmaster, who teacheth them the same and thereby instructeth them more and more in the knowledge of God, that they learn to know God and his will and strive to keep the same. He observeth the following order with them: when they all come together in the morning to school he teacheth them to thank the Lord together, and to pray to him. Then he preacheth to them as children for the space of half an hour, telling them how they ought to obey . . . their parents. . . .
>
> From such obedience to parents he teacheth them

---

[19] Such an approach to family life does not seem consistent with passages such as Ephesians 6:1–4, Colossians 3:20, and Deuteronomy 6:7. God instituted marriage and the family to meet the emotional, social, and psychological needs of mankind, not simply to produce offspring.

> obedience to God and the keeping of his will . . . and
> [to] serve and cleave to him alone, as him from whom
> they have all that is good. Thus we teach our children
> from babyhood to seek not what is temporal but what
> is eternal.[20]

Penmanship, reading, and memory were the basic subjects these schools taught. The teachers also instructed the children in sanitation and proper manners. Through all the teaching was woven a strong emphasis on community, sharing, and the necessity of giving up personal ideas and blending with the accepted norms of the Hutterite colony.

Talented Hutterite doctors. The Hutterites carefully maintained good sanitation and medical practices in their colonies. Their doctors likely acquired their medical knowledge before they joined the community or by studying as apprentices under established Hutterite doctors. As far as we know, the Hutterites did not generally send their doctors to study under worldly doctors.[21] With time, experience, and pooled knowledge, Hutterite physicians became masters of their trade.

As was the custom in Europe at that time, doctors were both barbers and physicians. These doctors were knowledgeable in using medicinal herbs and other types of medicine, as well as mineral baths. The doctors obtained some medicinal plants in their local communities, but for some medicines they relied on traveling peddlers from far-off lands.

---

[20] Peter Riedemann, *An Account of Our Religion, Doctrine, and Faith.* Cited in William R. Estep, *The Anabaptist Story,* 143.

[21] One exception should be noted. When the Hutterites were in Russia, the physician practice was dying out among them. The Bruderhof allowed a young married man, father of three children, to leave the community and study as an apprentice under a worldly doctor. The brother fell away from the faith and never returned to his family or the community.

Some of the Hutterite doctors became so skillful that they were known internationally. Many Catholics patronized Hutterite mineral baths and sought medical advice from Hutterite physicians. George Zobel, probably the most famous Hutterite physician, doctored Emperor Rudolph II for six months at the imperial headquarters in Prague. Other Hutterite physicians also became personal doctors to high-ranking religious and civil leaders. Sometimes city authorities asked them to come to cities to help fight plagues.

Renewed Persecution and Suffering

Devastating wars brought an end to the Hutterite peaceful period. From 1593 on, their communities were in a steady decline that did not substantially reverse until they emigrated to America in the 1870s. The *Hutterian Chronicle* records almost unbelievable suffering and abuse that both Catholics and Turks heaped on the Anabaptists.

The Catholic Counter Reformation also inflicted great pressures on the Hutterites. The Counter Reformation was a strong Catholic effort to regain control of lands and people that had followed Protestantism.

War between Turkey and Austria. In 1593, war broke out between Turkey and Austria. Moravia was part of the empire that included Austria, so it also came under the pressures of war. Many soldiers quartered themselves in the colonies and consumed the Hutterites' stores of food and drink. Worse than that, Turkish and Hungarian soldiers occasionally swept through Moravia, killing, looting, and taking men and women captive to Turkey. One Hutterite brother wandered for nearly three years in Turkey, trying without success to locate his captive wife and daughter. He did find and rescue a few other Hutterites.

The monetary cost of the war was high, and the emperor soon began pressuring the Moravian nobles for more money. They in turn levied war taxes on the population, but the Hutterites would not pay taxes used specifically for war.[22] In retaliation, some nobles withheld the wages of Hutterites working for them, raided their colonies of valuable goods such as cattle and hogs, and even drove off some Hutterites and confiscated all their goods. Some of the brethren found refuge in underground passages and rooms.

At the same time, Catholic enemies of the brethren wrote many hateful things against the Anabaptists, stirring up the people against them.

The Thirty Years' War. In 1618, the Bohemians rebelled against their Catholic ruler, Emperor Ferdinand II. Most of the Bohemians were Protestant, and they wanted to shake off Catholic rule. This uprising began a vicious struggle between Protestant and Catholic forces, which soon enveloped many countries and caused terrible devastation in Europe. Moravia joined the struggle on the Protestant side.

For a short time, Moravia managed to drive out the Catholic supporters; but in 1619, a Catholic army entered the country, completely destroyed twelve Hutterite communities, and looted seventeen others. The Catholic soldiers behaved terribly. They killed and raped women wantonly and subjected numerous brethren to horrible tortures. Again the soldiers carried many Hutterites into slavery.

Rumors of the supposed wealth of the Hutterite colonies persisted, and soldiers looted every colony they could. But

---

[22] The Hutterites refused to pay war taxes because they did not want to pay someone to protect them with physical force.

they found little, and the soldiers tortured many brethren to find out where the wealth was hidden. Besides these sufferings, with the soldiers came deadly plagues that killed one-third of the Hutterites in the early 1620s.

When the Catholics gained the victory in Moravia, they soon expelled the remaining brethren from the land. Only those who promised to become Catholic could stay in their homes. A few did so, but most of them chose to leave. They fled to Hungary, where a few lords were still able to protect them from the emperor. A few Hutterites tried to establish themselves in Moravia again, but these efforts were not successful. Hutterite history in Moravia basically came to a close in 1622, almost one hundred years after the movement had started in Nikolsburg.

A small group also fled to Transylvania,[23] east of Hungary, about four hundred miles from Moravia. We will look at this group after discussing the Hungarian colonies.

The Hungarian Colonies

Suffering continues in Hungary.[24] Several thousand Moravian Hutterites moved to the few Hungarian colonies. There was hardly enough food and clothing to go around, and the situation did not improve. In 1626, over fifty thousand soldiers moved into Hungary. Even when they were not fighting, they devastated the land by looting. Famine conditions prevailed various times. Because of these hardships, Hutterite numbers continued to decline. The Hutterites numbered less than one thousand members by 1631.

In 1648, the Thirty Years' War ended, but the conditions did not improve for the colonies. The local people and nobles continued to steal food and supplies from the

---

[23] This area is now in Romania.

[24] The part of Hungary to which the Hutterites moved is now part of Slovakia.

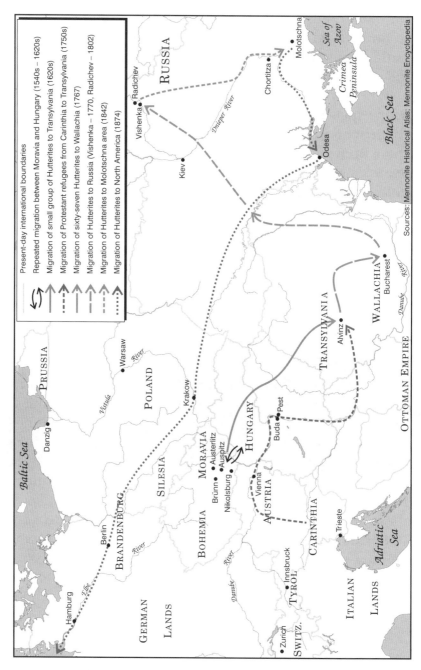

Hutterite Locations and Migrations

nonresistant brethren. The Hutterites in Transylvania and the Dutch Mennonites sent financial aid to the Hungarian colonies, but the help did not substantially change the worsening conditions.

Apostasy and the Jesuits. The pressure and suffering finally took its toll on Hungarian Hutterite spiritual life. In the late 1600s, missionary activity ceased and the church largely lost its spiritual vitality. Many abuses crept into the communal system, and many members were there only for the loaves and fishes. Members kept the proceeds from their labors for themselves, and many worked no more than they had to. The Catholics decreed infant baptism for all babies, and finally the Hutterites gave in to that demand.

In 1685, they decided to dissolve their community of goods and become individual householders. Robbers had sacked their communal storehouses too easily. But they continued to worship together and maintain many Hutterite practices.

Persecution from the Catholic rulers of Hungary increased in the late 1600s. The Jesuits (Catholic missionaries) had full authority to use whatever means necessary to root "heresy" out of the land. They seized many Hutterite books and took some of the children from their parents. They conducted Catholic worship services among the Hutterites and demanded that everyone attend. The government beat, imprisoned, and drove away those who refused to submit. The last of the Hutterites here yielded to a profession of Catholicism in the 1760s. However, the authorities allowed them to continue various aspects of their society. These people became known as Habaners, and a few vestiges of their earlier practices survived into the 1900s.

The Transylvanian Hutterites

In Transylvania, the Hutterites established a single colony in the early 1620s. Here the brethren received kind treatment, and they prospered for about thirty-seven years. From 1658 to 1661, a war ravaged the area and the brethren had to flee to hilly places about five miles from their colony. Here they built shelters of rocks and earth. After a few years, they returned to their ruined colony, but they never recovered from the damage. The group grew smaller and weaker, and finally abandoned communal living in 1690.

Revival through Carinthian refugees. In Carinthia, a strong Catholic region in southern Austria, a small group of Protestants had existed since the 1500s. Finally, the Catholic rulers would no longer tolerate their presence. In the 1750s, the rulers relocated the Carinthian Protestants in Transylvania. They settled close to the Hutterites in Transylvania.

While looking for work, the Protestants met the Hutterites. Some of the Protestants immediately became interested in Hutterite beliefs. Some of them soon became Hutterites and began to live in full community of goods, even though the Hutterites had lost that practice. A remnant of the Hutterites joined the new community. This small group then became the only surviving faithful element of the original Hutterite church.

The Jesuits persecute the new group. It was not long before the Hutterite growth again attracted the attention of the Catholics. The Jesuits wanted to rid Transylvania of these heretics, and they carried out their work as they had done in other Hutterite colonies. They tried to separate the children from their parents, and they forcefully taught Catholic doctrine in the colony. Two men who refused to listen to the priests were driven from the country. The Jesuits scattered the remaining Hutterites throughout the villages, hoping to break down their resolve. Most of the old Hutterites who were no longer practicing communal living gave in under these pressures. But the new group determined to be faithful.

Flight to southern Romania. The two exiled brethren found a fertile farming area in Wallachia (southern Romania). Here the government tolerated various religions. In 1767, they came back to the faithful Hutterites in Transylvania and led them through the mountains to the new area. Sixty-seven people made the excruciating, seven-day journey. They had to leave their wagons behind and cross the high mountains on foot with their baggage and children.

They soon found a piece of land where they could live. But the area had a poor climate, and once again they found themselves in an area where Russian and Turkish armies ravaged the land. Distressed with their new situation, the Hutterites spoke to the Russian army captain about their plight. The captain was sympathetic toward the brethren and advised them to migrate to Russia, since the war had no end in sight. The group decided to take his advice.

The Hutterites in Russia

The captain gave the Hutterites a letter of protection for a safe journey to Russia and told them of an army marshal who would help them there. They set out with their children, wagons, and cattle in the spring of 1770. They were robbed of a few things; and throughout the journey, they were occasionally caught between warring bands of troops. Food was hard to obtain. By the time they reached Russia, they were quite weary of the journey.

The army marshal was kind to them and provided soldiers and food to help them on to their final destination. They received permission to settle at Vishenka, about one hundred twenty miles northeast of Kiev, a large city in western Russia.

The colonies at Vishenka and Radichev. In 1771, the Hutterites built their first buildings at the new location. Here they prospered; and by 1779, they had a well-functioning colony organized. They had freedom to develop and practice trades, exemption from military duty and swearing oaths, and permission to live according to their conscience.

From the beginning in Russia, the brethren were concerned for their apostate relatives, as well as imprisoned, faithful Hutterites, who were still in Transylvania, Hungary, and Moravia. Here in Russia, they were free to serve God. Surely, they thought, some apostate Hutterites would want to return to the church if they knew of this freedom. For twenty-four years, they made contacts with relatives and friends in the old countries. They rescued some faithful, imprisoned Hutterites, but most of their apostate friends had become indifferent to truth and no longer desired the Anabaptist life.

In 1787, the benevolent owner of the estate where the Hutterites lived passed away. His sons tried to take away some of the freedoms their father had granted to the brethren. The brethren appealed to the Russian emperor. The emperor gave them permission to live on his lands and keep all their original freedoms and privileges. A government representative visited the colony and advised them to take the new offer and move to the emperor's lands at Radichev, eight miles northeast of Vishenka. The group had lived at Vishenka thirty-two years, but they decided to move.

In 1802, they built a Bruderhof at Radichev. This colony prospered materially. A visitor to the Radichev colony described it as follows:

> To the right of the entry into the village square, at the foot of a gently rising hillside covered with the most beautiful orchards, stands a not unattractive stone house with a thatched roof; it contains a spacious dining room adequate for the commune which now also serves as a chapel, and also a kitchen which is served by a regular cook assisted by two sisters who are changed daily. Beside the kitchen are various pantries and below them are arched cellars.
>
> Besides this building we found a blacksmith shop with coal sheds, further a tannery with a supply of leather, a cobbler's shop, a distillery with three boilers and the laundry beside a well six *Faden* (36 feet) deep; then the general bakery, where only one kind of bread is baked for all the inhabitants by a sister and her daily changing assistant; a temporary weaving-mill besides other temporary buildings; and finally the head teacher's house which consisted of a spacious room. On the left side of the square are two rooms which are now occupied by eighteen mothers, each with an infant. They remain in this room for the first year-and-a-half; their food is brought to them from the common kitchen. Finally there are two schoolhouses for larger and smaller children where the children of both sexes are taught together, but separated on the two sides, under the very careful supervision of the head teacher and his wife and several unmarried brethren and sisters; they are taught reading, writing, Christianity, and all of them are taught to knit, spin and sew until they are grown or receive baptismal instruction.
>
> Of the unpleasantness one fears in such arrangements there was no evidence. Still it is noticeable that these children, generally quiet rather than wild or

noisy, although free, have an unbroken, stiff streak—one would like to call it an unchristened streak.

Besides these schools are a shop for cabinet-making and several business buildings. A sisters' house is being built where all the sisters, single, married or widowed, will work when they are not otherwise occupied. That this is possible, indeed even suitable, results from their arrangement by which no woman conducts her own household, but man and wife and children are provided with all necessities; in return, each contributes what she is able to the community. In the same way all the men after learning their trade, work in shops, and have their sleeping quarters there. The unmarried boys, however, sleep in the room for brothers. The workshops of the potters, hatters, and dyers along one street form the fourth side of the quadrangle. Besides all these buildings, stables for the assigned cattle and several granaries are to be built.

The men wear the beards unshorn, a round hat, a jacket similar to the Russian except that it has fewer pleats, does not overlap in front, is generally blue in color and instead of buttons has only hooks and eyes. Men and women have neither buckles or ribbons or buttons, or anything that is unnecessary, but confine themselves to what is absolutely necessary. Therefore, also no sugar, coffee, tea, tobacco, etc., are used. The women wear a black woolen cap [*Mütze*] with a simple linen band and in cold weather a coarse white head shawl, a cloth jacket and a skirt of homemade material with an apron of plain linen.[25]

As time went on, the colony at Radichev faced problems. Many of their members became spiritually weak and were not fully committed to communal life. Members began withholding profits from the communal treasury. There was plenty of opportunity for small trade with

---

[25] Zieglschmid, *Das Klein-Geschichtsbuch.* Cited in John A. Hostetler, *Hutterite Society,* 101, 102.

Russian natives, which could escape the Bruderhof's supervision. The managers of the shops and those who did buying and selling with outsiders began to live more sumptuously than their brethren. Many of the brethren became disheartened and shirked their work. The absence of outside pressure and persecution seemed to result in inner laxity and turmoil.

The two ministers, Jakob Walther and Johannes Waldner, disagreed on the solution to the problems. Jakob wanted to dissolve the community, and Johannes wanted to return to a careful adherence to the communal principle. A split followed the disputing, and Jakob moved with his followers (thirty families) to the Mennonite settlement at Chortitza, about 300 miles to the south. The remaining twenty families stayed with Johannes at Radichev.

Soon the Radichev colony suffered more financial reverses. A fire broke out and destroyed many of the buildings. The discouraged members then gave up their communal efforts and divided the community assets among themselves. Hearing this, Jakob and his thirty families returned from Chortitza and settled at Radichev again. But there was not enough available land at Radichev to give the Hutterites a decent living, and their spiritual life continued to stagnate. Even their children's education no longer held importance. By 1842, their young people were illiterate.

The Hutterites settle at Molotschna. Because of the need for more farmland, the group asked the government to provide a new area for them. They received permission to settle near the Mennonite colony at Molotschna, about 400 miles south of Chortitza. The Hutterites moved in 1842.

At Molotschna, they prospered financially and numerically. They maintained their Hutterite worship services and did not assimilate into the Mennonite communities. However, they still had spiritual problems, and there was some friction between the Hutterites and the Mennonites. Not all the Hutterites were satisfied with the private approach to economy. Several men attempted to reintroduce communal living, but they met with failure. Finally, in the late 1850s and early 1860s, the leaders agreed that the old Bruderhof approach was right, and they made a united effort to return to it. Many Hutterites joined with the effort, but some continued practicing a private economy.

Emigration to America

In 1871, the Russian government made military service mandatory. The Hutterites and Mennonites sought exemption from this law, but the government was firm. However, the Russians soon saw they would lose thousands of their best farmers to America if they did not make an exemption for military service. So they proposed that the nonresistant[26] people could do some alternate, nonmilitary service. Their plan worked. Only 18,000 of the 45,000 Mennonites and Hutterites emigrated.

Almost all the Hutterites were included in that 18,000.

---

[26] The Mennonites and Hutterites were basically nonresistant at this time, but there were some outstanding inconsistencies in their practice of the doctrine, especially among the Mennonites. The Mennonite colonies were self-governing. Since many of them, at this point, were only cultural Mennonites and not born-again Christians, lawbreaking occurred among them. The Mennonite "police" then physically punished or jailed the offenders.

Such circumstances show us the great gulf between early Anabaptist thinking and the lives of their Mennonite descendants in later years. The Anabaptists had taken seriously the Bible command for the church to stay out of civil affairs. But the Russian Mennonites' organization, especially in their later Mexican settlements, came very close to a church-state arrangement. This, of course, was because many of them were not Christians. If they had been, they could have lived in such colonies with little civil government necessary. In a truly spiritual setting, practical or economic issues could have been resolved by the brethren and deacons with love and submission.

There were around 1,200 Hutterites at the time. By 1879, almost all of this number, both those living communally and those on private farms, had emigrated to America. Most of them settled on South Dakota's rich agricultural prairies. According to some sources, only two Hutterite families chose to stay in Russia.

The South Dakota Hutterite settlements grew and spread. Today, Hutterite colonies are established in a number of western prairie states and Canadian provinces. Most of the Russian Hutterites who did not join the communal group in the United States lost their Hutterite identity and joined the Mennonite Church.

Conclusion

The Hutterites who organized into communes have retained their identity to the present day. They continue to have a problem with spiritual carelessness. It seems that many of them are not truly born-again. The criteria for being a Hutterite seems to be accepting the culture and way of thinking, instead of being committed to the Lord Jesus Christ. Evangelism also has been neglected since the late 1600s.

One Hutterite preacher around 1970 said, "If I tried to bring in converts, I'd be excommunicated from the church. My job is to keep watch over my own flock—not to gather stray sheep. Converts to our way are very rare. You are *born* a Hutterite."[27] It is evident that a Biblical revival is needed among them.

However, this need is not unique to the Hutterites. Large segments of the three groups of Anabaptist descendants—Mennonites, Amish, and Hutterites—are spiritually lukewarm or dead. There is little of the early

---

[27] William Albert Allard, "The Hutterites, Plain People of the West," *National Geographic,* July 1970, 117.

Anabaptist vision in the mainstream of these groups.

How did communal living affect the Hutterites' spiritual life? In the early days of love and joyful service to each other, the brethren and sisters probably reached a better understanding of self-denial than many of us have today. The Hutterites also maintained a pure, evangelistic faith long after the Dutch Mennonite and Swiss Brethren spiritual life had cooled. Their systematic organization tended to provide for adequate leadership, missionary personnel, and written materials—areas often lacking in other Anabaptist circles.

Communal living did not adversely affect the Hutterites' ability to keep the faith. In fact, it may have strengthened it by providing a close-knit setting that tended to unify the group more than what was experienced in other Anabaptist circles. But it is also true that the organization eventually became such a part of Hutterite life that they believed that the communal life was the only Christian approach.[28] The heavy organization tended to squelch revival when it was most needed. It also gave a false spiritual security to some Hutterites who were not truly saved.

As with other Anabaptist groups, when the Hutterites truly committed themselves to Christ, they prospered. But when they no longer appreciated cross bearing and lost a personal relationship with Christ, the movement decayed rapidly.

---

[28] According to the *Hutterian Chronicle,* the Swiss Brethren asked the Hutterites in 1567 for an explanation of some of their beliefs, including why they practiced community of goods and why they shunned the Swiss Brethren. In their reply, the Hutterites pointed out "errors" in the Swiss Brethren's teaching. The Chronicle reports that the Swiss Brethren paid little attention to their reply and that this would be a judgment against the Swiss on the last day. See *The Chronicle of the Hutterian Brethren,* Vol. I, 394.

Part Two

Anabaptist Beliefs

Introduction

Two Types of Anabaptists

In Chapters 9–12, we will mention *faithful Anabaptists* and *fringe Anabaptists*. Faithful Anabaptists included most of the Swiss Brethren, Dutch Mennonites, and Hutterites. These Anabaptists esteemed the Scriptures properly, understood the difference between the Testaments, submitted to a Scriptural brotherhood, and practiced holy living.

Fringe Anabaptists varied, but they generally believed in visions and dreams, emphasized millennial prophecy, and did not subject themselves to a brotherhood. Fringe Anabaptists often rejected or wavered on Biblical nonresistance, and they varied much in their concept of discipleship.

The division between faithful and fringe Anabaptists is not a division between perfect and imperfect people. Rather, it is a division between those Anabaptists who struggled to do right and fulfill the Biblical ideal of the church and those who allowed their individualism to separate themselves from God's people and His Word. The faithful Anabaptists failed at times, just as Christians today do. Sometimes their faults may seem rather glaring to us, but our imperfections will be just as obvious to future generations. The intense pressure of persecution, the difficulty of communicating between Anabaptist churches, and their inexperience in Biblical church life created a situation in which some problems and misunderstandings were bound to appear. In light of this, we should be willing to view the fringe Anabaptists with some toleration too, even though we cannot agree with the road they took.

Various Views of Anabaptism

Many Protestant and Catholic historians, up to the mid-1900s, viewed Anabaptists as fanatical revolutionaries intent on destroying medieval society. They interpreted instances such as the Münsterite rebellion as the logical outcome of Anabaptism. In spite of the holy testimony of the majority of Anabaptists, these historians charged them all with heinous crimes and sinister motives.

Most of these historians were simply repeating the same old story that anti-Anabaptist writers handed down from medieval times. Few people bothered to check if the information was actually correct. Many historical sources "substantiated" this wrong view, so even an honest historian could have picked it up without knowing it was false.

During the twentieth century, Mennonite historians and a few others worked hard at trying to find the truth about Anabaptism.[1] They found that many older ideas were based primarily on false accusations. They found solid evidence that the faithful Anabaptists were holy, Christian people, not fanatics who conspired to overthrow civil order.

---

[1] Mennonites always knew that their ancestors were not the criminals some histories made them out to be. The *Martyrs Mirror* is an early Mennonite history book that completely disagreed with what other denominations said about the Anabaptists. But later Mennonite historians wanted more evidence than simply Mennonite writings to prove the facts about their history. They searched European libraries and city records and found many documents proving that the Anabaptists were in fact a genuinely Christian people.

Most of this evidence that showed earlier Protestant and Catholic accusations to be false was found in the twentieth century. Also during this time, some previously unknown Anabaptist writings came to light, which ruled in favor of the Anabaptists as well. Even some scholars who disliked Anabaptism admitted that they were wrong in their earlier evaluations.

Since the picture of Anabaptism has been cleared up, it is more honorable now to have Anabaptist roots. Mennonites of all types, Amish, some Baptists, and others became proud of their Anabaptist heritage. This presented another problem. As these people gained a new interest in their heritage, they began to interpret Anabaptism according to their modern lifestyle. They all wanted assurance that they were in line with these dedicated martyrs of the past. As a result, many widely differing people now claim to be following the principles of Anabaptism.

For example, the Anabaptists regulated the conduct and dress of their members. They viewed this as an integral part of holiness, practical discipleship, and Scriptural church administration. Since many present-day Mennonites are far from such a position, they need to reconcile the obvious difference between them and their ancestors. So worldly Mennonite scholars now call the Anabaptist emphasis on holiness and separation "a regulative principle that helped establish theological direction" instead of recognizing it as a part of Scriptural church administration.[2]

However, such scholarly phrases do not erase the facts. The faithful Anabaptists did require strict accountability to their churches; they taught and lived the narrow way. They were very concerned about clear doctrine and Biblical practice, but they never mentioned "regulative principles" and "theological direction." Such terms would have likely confused them, just as they confuse us. This is only one example of how modern historians shift emphases to make room for themselves.

The same problem surfaces occasionally among conservative Mennonites and Amish. Some of these groups, feeling that they are *the* Anabaptists, also want the

---

[2] Cornelius J. Dyck, *An Introduction to Mennonite History,* 136.

assurance that they are right in line with the medieval Anabaptists. And so they are tempted to stretch history—just like the modern, worldly Mennonites—to make a version of Anabaptism that fits their mold.

A Biblical church is concerned about lining up its practice with the Bible. That is the only position from which we can safely evaluate our predecessors. Only when we are solidly based on Bible truth can we claim to be spiritual descendants of the faithful Anabaptists.

Principles for Profitable History Study

Some of the following principles were covered in the introduction to this book. Here is a summary to guide you as you study the remaining chapters.

Regardless of what any church in the past has believed or practiced, the final authority in our doctrine and life must be the Word of God. The Bible, not history, is the foundation for Christian doctrine and practice. History helps us understand what positions and practices have stood the test of time and have been a blessing to the church, but the foundation for right practice is Bible truth applied by every generation under Holy Spirit guidance.

All people and movements of the past, including the Anabaptists, were human. We should not idolize historical movements and men. We need to pour all historical teachings, even the history of faithful churches, through a Biblical screen. On the other hand, we do not write off any historical movements as unworthy of our attention. Either approach will keep us from learning the lessons God has for us in history.

All written history except the Bible is fallible. History can be easily twisted, and probably no historian can completely free himself from this. Because of our background and personal beliefs, our minds color the information we receive. However, if we are as honest as possible with history and do not base our faith in it, we will not be swept away with false interpretations of the past.

History should not be used as a tool to support preconceived conclusions. In an effort to promote certain beliefs or practices, some people try to manufacture "Anabaptist" support for some "un-Anabaptist" ideas. They pick out isolated incidents in history that seem to prove their point. If our beliefs are Biblically correct, they will stand without our misusing history.

Historical conclusions should not be based on sensational incidents. Focusing on dramatic stories and sensational moments in history usually produces ill-founded conclusions.

A similar trap we should avoid is indiscriminately accepting the basic theory of every history book we read. Today, apostate Mennonite historians are questioning older conclusions that were based on the idea that Anabaptists were a people of committed discipleship and practical holiness. The questions arise because modern, mainstream Mennonites, who have drifted far from committed discipleship and practical holiness, want to redefine Anabaptism to fit themselves more comfortably. Generally, it is unfair to history to give precedence to a new, untried theory over established conclusions that many historians over a period of time have agreed upon.

We can seldom understand a historical situation completely. For some historical situations, we have enough information available to gain a fairly accurate picture. But often we know too little about many circumstances to nail down technical and final conclusions. Historical settings and the backgrounds of people several hundred years ago were so different from our own that it is often impossible for us to understand the picture completely. Because of this, we should not be too adamant in our opinions about history.

How can you make your history study worthwhile? Pray that God would teach you through your studies. Look for historical errors that you might be repeating in your own life to your spiritual detriment. Look for spiritual triumphs, and by God's grace determine to make a contribution to the triumphing church today.

Chapter 9

"The Word Is Plain"

The Anabaptist View
of the Scriptures

When writing to people who questioned the Anabaptists' ability to understand the Bible, Menno Simons said, "You say, we are inexpert, unlearned, and know not the Scriptures. I reply: The Word is plain and needs no interpretation."[1] Menno went on to point out clear Bible passages that condemned the supposed wisdom of the "Christians" of his day. The established authorities saw danger in the common man interpreting the Scriptures—not because he might interpret it wrongly, but because he might discover its correct meaning.

The Catholics looked to the pope and their councils to interpret the Bible. The Lutherans, Zwinglians, and

---

[1] *The Complete Writings of Menno Simons,* 214.

Calvinists looked to early theologians such as Augustine and Origen for most of their beliefs. Many fringe Anabaptists looked to personal dreams and visions for direction. The faithful Anabaptists, however, sorted through the religious confusion on a group level and adhered to the Word of God.[2]

The Authority of the Scriptures

The classical cry of the Protestant Reformation was "Scripture alone, faith alone, grace alone."[3] The Anabaptists agreed with the first part of the Protestant emphasis: "Scripture alone." In a letter to an Anabaptist church, leader Leonhard Schiemer wrote, "One finds everything in the New Testament."[4] In Menno Simons's book *The Foundation of Christian Doctrine* (1539), he said:

> We certainly hope no one of a rational mind will be so foolish a man as to deny that the whole Scriptures, both the Old and New Testament, were written for our instruction, admonition, and correction, and that they are the true scepter and rule by which the Lord's kingdom, house, church, and congregation must be ruled and governed. Everything contrary to Scripture, therefore, whether it be in doctrines, beliefs, sacraments, worship, or life, should be measured by this infallible rule and demolished by this just and divine scepter, and destroyed without any respect of persons.

The Protestant and the Anabaptist emphases on the

---

[2] Note that they did this almost invariably as a group, rather than on an individual basis, especially after the church became more established and mature in the faith. The Dutch Anabaptists tended to place more emphasis on the bishop's role, while the Swiss emphasized the role of the congregation, but both expected major Biblical interpretation to be done on a group level, not by the individual. Only the fringe Anabaptists, like Hut, emphasized an individualistic interpretation of the Scriptures.

[3] The difference between this trifold Lutheran emphasis and the Anabaptists' central theme will be discussed more at length in Chapter 11.

[4] Walter Klaassen, ed., *Anabaptism in Outline,* 148–151.

Scriptures appear similar at first glance, yet the two were far apart in their concepts and church life. There are five basic reasons for this.

1. *The Anabaptists did not believe in "faith alone, grace alone" as the Protestants taught it.* For the Protestants, in practice at least, salvation by "faith alone" meant that salvation had little or no effect on actual life. Their emphasis on "grace alone" basically meant depending on the supposed, loving *graciousness* of God to *overlook sin.* The Anabaptists, on the other hand, depended on the enabling *grace* of God to *live in victory.* If we follow this thought to its logical conclusion, we can see that this unscriptural emphasis on "faith alone, grace alone" of the Protestants invalidated their claim to believe in "Scripture alone." For the Protestants, "Scripture alone" did not necessarily mean a return to Scriptural life and church patterns. It simply meant that they would not submit to the Catholic interpretation of the Scriptures. Instead, the Protestants erected their own system—a mixture of Bible teaching and postapostolic theology.

The Anabaptists believed that true faith and a true experience of God's grace always result in a righteous life. They rejected Protestant doctrine because it did not produce Scriptural people or Biblical churches. If the world persecuted the Christian because he followed Christ, so be it. The Anabaptists confidently believed that God would give them grace to live righteously and suffer patiently, because the Bible said He would. This contrasts sharply with the Protestant attitude that by grace, through faith, people could avoid the narrow way and still be Christians.

2. *The Protestants allowed postapostolic theology to govern their interpretation of the Scriptures, but the*

Anabaptists rejected this. The Anabaptists believed that Christ and the apostles were pure examples of Bible truth. They saw that later theologians, such as Augustine, had wrested the Gospel message through human reasoning. But the Protestants and Catholics believed that the apostolic church was doctrinally undeveloped and intellectually simple. They called it the primitive church.

To the Anabaptists, it was obvious, as many Protestants now also admit, that postapostolic theologians did not hold completely to Bible truth. For example, Augustine taught that the church can physically force people to be church members, that the Bible commands infant baptism, and that God predestines some people to eternal punishment and other people to eternal bliss. Although many Protestants still hold to the last two points, they have discarded the first.

The early Protestant leaders held to postapostolic theology because it was an easier road than the Bible way. It allowed for state-controlled churches, political popularity, and a church accepted by the world. In contrast, faithful Anabaptists followed the New Testament regardless of the self-denial and physical suffering this commitment brought.

3. *The Anabaptists refused to accept the Protestant "love and tolerance" gospel.* When some of Zwingli's followers challenged him and said he was erring in his church reforms, Zwingli countered that the church needed to tolerate those who were weak and could not stand to change the old Catholic practices yet. At one point, he said, "Even if the Anabaptists had the Scripture to support their views, these things should be decided by love."[5] When Michael Sattler proved the Scriptural validity of believer's

---

[5] John Horsch, *Mennonites in Europe*, 353.

baptism to the leading reformers in Strasbourg, they told him that he had to give up such strict, Biblical positions. If he did not, they said, he was not acting according to Biblical love and charity. Numerous times when the Protestant reformers had to admit that the Anabaptists were right, their last-ditch stand was that tolerance and charity must finally govern how to apply the Scriptures. If people were not ready to accept Bible truth about church life, the mainline Reformers would compromise rather than stand with truth and lose their followers.

The Reformers' charity and tolerance, however, was often political. The Anabaptists did not agree with them, yet the Reformers did not quietly tolerate them. The Reformers knew that the Anabaptists would not become their followers through kindness and toleration. They knew that Anabaptism would continue to thin Protestant ranks. So they persecuted the Anabaptists to death, making it clear that they were willing to do anything to preserve their Protestant following. Tolerance meant nothing to them unless it gained them a political advantage.

Actually, the faithful Anabaptists were the most loving and tolerant people in Reformation times. Who else risked their lives and gave up all earthly security to help others into the kingdom? They did not tolerate sin in their own ranks, but they did peacefully tolerate terrible persecution. If someone rejected Anabaptism, the Anabaptists still loved that person as a neighbor. They never forced people to agree with them. Instead, they acted according to 2 Corinthians 5:20: "Now then we are ambassadors for Christ, as though God did beseech you by us: we pray you in Christ's stead, be ye reconciled to God." They held strongly to the principles of freedom of conscience and voluntary church membership, while the Protestants denied both.

227

4. *The Anabaptists applied the authority of the Scriptures to their church life, which the Protestants generally refused to do.* Luther recognized the high demands of the Scriptures and made a few futile attempts to bring his churches in line with that, but he soon decided that true Christianity could only be maintained in a small group of dedicated Christians who would represent a higher level of spirituality than the "average" Christian. He often talked about establishing such a church, but he was unwilling to pay the price such an action would exact.[6]

The early Anabaptists accepted no substitutes for truth. Certainly, they recognized that no one was perfect. They believed in growing in the grace of God. But they consistently demanded practical evidence that a person was walking in the Spirit before he became part of the believers' fellowship. Further, they required continuing proof of holiness for a person to remain in the church. They dealt with sin as fatal poison, believing that a little leaven infects the whole lump (Galatians 5:9).

Martin Luther believed that sound preaching would convert the masses to true Christianity, but it did not, as he himself lamented. He actually referred to his own followers as well-nigh heathen under a Christian name. Luther's emphasis on teaching, at the expense of Biblical church discipline, could have added "preaching alone" to the Protestant "alone" list.

Luther's policy made it impossible for him to establish a Biblical church; he was simply the leader of people who interpreted Christianity to suit their whims. In contrast, the Anabaptists believed in faithful preaching as well as Biblical church action with erring members. They believed that sound church life consisted of Biblical preaching

---

[6] Ibid., 26–29.

and godly "fruit inspection."[7] While contending against abrupt, harsh excommunication, Pilgram Marpeck said:

> The natural body cannot lose a member without pain. Nor does it immediately cut it off, even if it is failing and weak; rather it uses all kinds of medicines. As long as it is not dead and is only painful, the body bears it with patience and long-suffering, and delays the penalty to allow for improvement. If, however, it allows the body no rest, nor does it improve by means of any medicine from the Lord Jesus Christ, through suffering and pain, it must be cut off in order that the other members of the body of Christ remain healthy in the fear and love of God.[8]

The Protestants' retention of the state church system and its sacramental "salvation" kept them from applying the Bible to their church life. Organizations bound by nationality, community, or ceremony, as the Protestant churches were, cannot consistently apply Biblical church principles. God designed those principles for a redemption-bound body, and that is the only place they fit.

5. *The Anabaptists divided correctly between the Old and New Testaments.* Even though the Anabaptists believed that all of the Scriptures were authoritative and inspired, they understood that the New Testament fulfilled the Old.

Both the Catholics and the Protestants erred on this point, since they held to the errors of Augustine and other ancient theologians. As the early church drifted away from Bible truth, theologians reached into the Old Testament to find support for their wrong beliefs. War, infant baptism, persecution of "heretics," sacramental "salvation,"

---

[7] See Matthew 7:16–21; John 15:1–6; Galatians 5:22, 23; 1 Corinthians 11:28; and 2 Corinthians 13:5.

[8] *The Writings of Pilgram Marpeck,* 356, 357.

and a host of other evils became part of "Christianity" through this mishandling of the Testaments. Of course, the mainstream churches thought the Old Testament was partially fulfilled. But they could not put the whole Old Testament in that category (as the New Testament expressly does[9]), or many of their favorite doctrines would have been without Bible basis.

Fringe Anabaptists held varying views on the place of the two Testaments. Usually they, like the mainstream churches, used the Old Testament to support pet theories. The Münsterites were the most outstanding example of this when they used the Old Testament to support war and polygamy.

The faithful Anabaptist belief that the Old Testament was fulfilled and that the New is final came up often in court trials, tracts, and letters to churches. Over and over, as both Protestant and Catholic prosecutors defended their conduct by using the Old Testament, the Anabaptists patiently explained their beliefs on the issue.[10]

> The New Testament is more complete than the Old. The Old has been fulfilled and explained by Christ. What Christ has explained and helped us to understand, I will adhere to. . . . I accept the Old Testament wherever it points to Christ. However, Christ came with a more exalted and perfect teaching. He showed his people a new covenant which they would need if their righteousness were to exceed that of the scribes and hypocrites. *—Hans Pfistermeyer, Swiss Anabaptist preacher, 1531*

> Firstly, we acknowledge the law insofar as it agrees with the New Testament and is an announcement, witness, type or sign of Christ, and that it is useful for

---

[9] See Romans 10:4 and Hebrews 10:9.

[10] Walter Klaassen, ed., *Anabaptism in Outline*, 149–157.

the faithful in strengthening their faith. To that extent we grant it validity, for Moses himself witnessed to the prophet whom God would raise up and whom we should hear. It is valid insofar as it illuminates and reveals Christ. We are also satisfied with the way it deals with judicial matters and the punishment of evil and have nothing to criticize. But we do not find that Christ established and commanded the punishment of the body even to death. Instead he instituted the Christian ban.

–Swiss Brethren at a disputation, 1538

Wherefore is the law our schoolmaster until we are in Christ, through whom the promise of the Father is poured out on all who believe in his name, which promise is the Spirit of grace through whom, if we suffer him to rule and lead us, we are set free from the law, as Paul says. . . .

. . . Not that God's covenant is finished and done with, but the imperfect revelation and darkness of the same is ended and ceases that the covenant itself might be revealed in its strength and clarity and brought to light, as has been done in Christ.

–Peter Riedemann, Hutterite bishop, 1542

Interpreting the Scriptures

Menno Simons said, "The Word is plain and needs no interpretation." This simple, firm belief helped to lead the Anabaptists away from the mainstream, medieval view of the Scriptures and into the light of truth.

When Menno made that remark, it seems that he was referring to wrong interpretation born of human philosophies and carnal desires. All the faithful Anabaptists interpreted the Scriptures, but they tried to do it according to Scriptural principles rather than according to human philosophy. The Anabaptists rightly believed that understanding various Bible verses within their context and the tenor of Scripture erases seeming contradictions.

They also believed that if an interpretation of a Scripture passage does not lead the Christian to holiness and practical discipleship, then that interpretation is not reliable.

In relation to Bible interpretation, several significant thoughts constantly come through in Anabaptist literature.

The clarity of the Scriptures. The Anabaptists believed that God's Word as a whole was complete and self-explanatory. No popes, priests, councils, or other "enlightening" agencies were necessary. The common man, if given an opportunity, could read the Bible and know God's will for his life.

This Biblical belief aroused much opposition from the Catholics. For hundreds of years, the Catholic church had kept its power by teaching that only a few high church leaders could understand the Bible. Even priests believed that the Bible was a dangerous book. And it did represent a real danger to the Catholic system because the exposure of Bible truth spelled doom to the Catholic monopoly of power.

The place of faith in understanding God's Word. The Bible says that without faith hearing God's Word will not profit man. "For unto us was the gospel preached, as well as unto them: but the word preached did not profit them, not being mixed with faith in them that heard it" (Hebrews 4:2).

Here lies one of the reasons that the Lutheran reform efforts did not produce disciplined soldiers of the cross. Luther believed that if preachers proclaimed the Word of God, the masses of medieval humanity would believe in God and experience salvation. However, to whatever degree this happened, it did not result in sanctified living. The

Anabaptists saw this, and some of them felt that Luther did not recognize that a work of the Spirit needs to happen in man's heart so that he will respond to the preached Word. A degree of faith and spiritual desire is necessary before the Word can have a positive effect.

Some Anabaptists, in an effort to give the Spirit of God His proper place, called the Bible the *outer Word* and the work of the Spirit the *inner Word*.[11] Both were necessary for salvation, said Anabaptists such as Hans Denck and Hans Hut, who were on the fringes of South German and Swiss Anabaptism. A Hutterite leader, Ulrich Stadler, also freely used these terms.

The Swiss Brethren shied away from using such terms, probably because the words could mean that individual visions and dreams were authoritative sources of revelation. Some people supported fanaticism by the idea that "the Spirit" could give a person license to do things the Bible did not allow. But most of the Anabaptists that used these terms seemed to be combating "cheap grace" rather than teaching that the written Word of God was not authoritative. While Luther was saying, "Just believe the Word of God and you will be saved," these men were saying, "It takes more than an outward assent to some words on paper. You must have faith and an inner communion with the Spirit of God that results in a changed life."

Ulrich Stadler explained his convictions about the matter in clear terms:

> It does not suffice to confess: I believe the written Word and consider it God's Word. Such faith does not save and is not followed by improvement of conduct. Biblical faith is a work of grace of the Holy Spirit who brings to life the read or heard Word, so that it becomes a power in man to live righteously and suffer patiently.

---

[11] The Anabaptists did not invent these terms. They had been used throughout medieval times.

> Indeed, suffering becomes for those who believe from
> the heart a means of strengthening faith.[12]

The Anabaptists demanded that professed faith be proved by Biblical conduct. They believed that unless the truth of a Bible verse or passage penetrated a person's heart and was proved by his life, that person could not interpret the Scriptures properly.

The dangers of theology and scholars. Protestant and Catholic theologians hated the Anabaptists bitterly. With spiteful booklets and sermons, they stirred up government leaders and communities against the peaceful brethren. This was one reason why the Anabaptists rejected professional, religious scholarship.

Both Luther and Zwingli began by teaching that the Scriptures could be correctly interpreted by all true believers. But when their own followers did just that and came up with conclusions that challenged them, both Luther and Zwingli reverted to another principle of authority.

> At the Bern Disputation the Anabaptists were told
> that they, as laymen, were not capable of dealing with
> theological matters. The sheep should not presume to
> teach the shepherd; they ought rather to go and look
> after their families and their trades, and leave the inter-
> pretation of the Scriptures to the educated.[13]

The theologians constantly disputed and twisted the plain words of the Scriptures. They often reasoned, when confronted with their wrong views, that the Bible does not actually mean what a normal person would understand from it. Because scholarly learning was usually used to evade the clear meaning of the Scriptures, the

---

[12] Cited in Wilhelm Wiswedel, "The Inner and the Outer Word," *The Mennonite Quarterly Review,* July 1952, 189.

[13] Walter Klaassen, "Word, Spirit, and Scripture," *Mennonite Life,* XV (1960), 184.

Anabaptists rejected theologians and the tools of education as unworthy interpreters of the Scriptures.[14]

For example, in 1524, Zwingli discussed infant baptism as follows:

> If one baptizes infants they [the Anabaptists] cry out that there is no greater abomination, atrocity, or sin in Christendom than baptizing infants. And they daily bring forth more silly arguments than Africa produces strange beasts. . . .
>
> . . . when speaking of the baptism of infants, those who refuse to baptize them have no clear prohibition against baptizing infants. On the other hand, those who baptize them have no clear word commanding that they be baptized. . . . Now we do not find in the New Testament that infant baptism is either commanded or forbidden. For by raising the objection that the apostles did not baptize infants, and therefore they should not be baptized, they prove nothing; else I could also argue: the apostles baptized no one in Calcutta, hence nobody in Calcutta should be baptized. We must therefore see whether there is anything in the Old Testament about it. We find nothing on baptism, but we do on the practice followed in the place of baptism, namely, circumcision. . . . Paul also touches on the same point in Colossians 2: "In whom (Christ) you are circumcised with the circumcision made without hands in that you have put off the body of sin by the circumcision of Christ, that you are buried with him in baptism, etc."[15] I know, of course, what Paul is speaking of. I quote this passage simply to show that we know a verse that shows baptism as taking the place

---

[14] The Anabaptists' opinion about theology coincided with a statement from Ambrose, bishop of Milan (c. 340–397). Ambrose said that pagans and heretics "dyed their impieties in the vats of philosophy." It is doubtful whether Ambrose was entirely free from the vats of philosophy himself, but his statement does bring out an important truth. (*Encyclopedia Britannica,* 1993, article "Ambrose.")

[15] It did not escape Zwingli's notice that Colossians 2:11, 12 is speaking of a spiritual circumcision, one "made without hands." It follows then that the burying with

of circumcision. . . . Besides, it is better to assume that the apostles baptized the infants of believers than not, as Paul says in 1 Corinthians 1: "I also baptized the household of Stephanas." And in Acts 16: "When Lydia was baptized with her household, etc." And soon after this: "He was baptized that very hour, he and all his household." It is more likely than not that in such households there were children.[16]

The basis of Anabaptism was practical obedience to the Bible, not speculation and philosophy. Since the united testimony of the Scriptures was that teaching and repentance needed to precede water baptism, and since infants could not meet these requirements, they changed their former practice to match Bible teaching. It was that simple. They did not spend days coming up with philosophical arguments about why a clear Scripture passage was not clear; they spent their time telling others about the truth.

They believed that Christianity was a life, not a set of mental propositions. They believed that speculation and philosophy of theology destroyed simple, obedient devotion to God.

Theology as practiced by nearly all theologians obscures the Word of God. As theologians study, they apply the tools of literary analysis to the text of the Bible.

Christ in baptism and the rising with Him through faith are also spiritual operations. These references do not refer to literal water baptism, or we would have to literally be buried and rise with Christ, which is a physical impossibility. Zwingli rationalized, " What cause would there be for making a comparison analogically between baptism and circumcision, when without that [Paul] could have spoken of the spirit being renewed, unless he wished in the same way to make equal the internals as well as the externals? . . . It must be therefore that Paul entertained this opinion, that our circumcision is baptism. This he would never have held unless he had seen at that time the children of Christians baptized as he had formerly seen them circumcised." (Ulrich Zwingli, *Refutation of the Tricks of the Anabaptists* [1527]. Cited in Leland Harder, ed., *The Sources of Swiss Anabaptism*, 505.)

[16] Ulrich Zwingli, *Treatise on Rebels and Rebellion* (1524). Cited in Leland Harder, ed., *The Sources of Swiss Anabaptism*, 316–320.

By taking the background of the Bible "authors" into consideration, searching out the ancient context and languages in which the Bible text was written, and bringing scientific and archaeological data to bear on the message of the Scriptures, most theologians have obscured simple, direct Bible truth. Zwingli, Luther, and Calvin were no exceptions to this rule.[17]

Again we can use Zwingli's rationalizations for an example of this. Notice how he uses human conjecture and background to establish his version of "truth" instead of accepting the clear Scriptures.

> Circumcision was abrogated by decree of the church gathered in the Spirit. Infants were with their parents within the church. If, then, according to the Anabaptists' opinion, those infants or little children were not baptized, yet were circumcised, it follows that by a decree of the church children of Christians were cast out of the church and were sent back to the circumcision. For who is circumcised becomes a debtor to do the whole law. And there is no reason why we should plead here that account must be taken of the time. For the strife about circumcision believers arose at Antioch, not at Jerusalem, where either circumcision or baptism was bound to have flourished.
>
> . . . we should consider the race from which the first believers came. They were of a race that so clung to externals that the apostles believed even after the

---

[17] It is not wrong to benefit from archaeology, language, and other resources. But to use such things to disprove the Bible or to twist it to make room for carnality is wrong. Such resources may have a valuable place in Bible study, but we must use them with caution. We should saturate our minds with God's Word and use other resources carefully.

Not all theologians have deliberately tried to obscure God's Word. But many of them have twisted the Scriptures to suit their whims. We should not write off all theologians as deliberate deceivers, but we need to guard against incorporating their methods in our Bible study.

We should remember that sound exegesis requires going from the Scriptures to an application. Most theologians begin with a preferred idea or application and try to find Biblical support for it.

resurrection that Christ would rule corporeally. It is not therefore likely that they left their children unbaptized. I leave the rest to you, reader, for much can be educed from these bases.

The fourth I have touched on in the foregoing, i.e., that Paul in 1 Corinthians 10 makes us and the Hebrews equal. "All," he said, "were baptized, all ate the same spiritual bread." And since all their children were baptized in the sea and in the cloud, they would not be equal if our children were not baptized, as has been said. . . .

[The Anabaptists]: If they ate the same spiritual bread, therefore our children will also celebrate the Eucharist.

[Reply]: . . . But since we have a precept for the celebration of the Eucharist—"Let each man prove himself"—children are not competent for this, while they are for baptism and circumcision.[18] It is clear that with Paul infant baptism was in use, but not infant Eucharist. . . .[19]

Instead of depending on theologians and scholars to interpret the Scriptures, the Anabaptists depended on the local group of "unlearned" believers. Instead of a "professional" analysis of a given text, they depended on a congregational analysis. They believed that a group of sincere, born-again believers, gathered in worship and readiness to hear God speak to their current needs, would be able to understand the Scriptures. That was exactly what Anabaptism was—a group of united, Spirit-filled common people responding to the obvious meaning of the Bible and learning what God was saying for their day. First Corinthians 14 and other Scripture passages provided the basis for this conviction.

---

[18] Since Zwingli could see the preconditions for Communion, it seems strange that he did not also see the preconditions for baptism.

[19] Ulrich Zwingli, *Refutation of the Tricks of the Anabaptists* (1527). Cited in Leland Harder, ed., *The Sources of Swiss Anabaptism,* 504, 505.

"Let the prophets speak two or three, and let the other judge. If any thing be revealed to another that sitteth by, let the first hold his peace. For ye may all prophesy one by one, that all may learn, and all may be comforted. And the spirits of the prophets are subject to the prophets. For God is not the author of confusion, but of peace, as in all churches of the saints" (1 Corinthians 14:29–33).

Anabaptist literature bears abundant testimony that this was exactly the pattern of their worship services.

> The brothers and sisters should meet at least three or four times a week, to exercise themselves in the teaching of Christ and His apostles and heartily to exhort one another to remain faithful to the Lord as they have pledged.
>
> When the brothers and sisters are together, they shall take up something to read together. The one to whom God has given the best understanding shall explain it, the others should be still and listen, so that there are not two or three carrying on a private conversation, bothering the others.
>
> *–Agreement of some Swiss Brethren, 1527*[20]

> They have no special gathering places. When there is peace and unity and when none of those who have been baptized are scattered they come together wherever the people are. They send messages to each other by a boy or girl. When they have come together they teach one another the divine Word and one asks the other: how do you understand this saying? Thus there is among them a diligent living according to the divine Word.
>
> *—Court record of an Anabaptist trial, 1527*[21]

Along with their emphasis on entire church involvement in the decision-making process, the Anabaptists

---

[20] John H. Yoder, ed., *The Legacy of Michael Sattler,* 44.

[21] Excerpt from the interrogation of Ambrosius Spitelmaier. Cited in Walter Klaassen, ed., *Anabaptism in Outline,* 124.

believed in church order and the ministers' responsibility to guide the church.

> Through our faith we have received grace and the apostolic office from God. However, we do not believe that all who believe and receive the faith in Christ should therefore be preachers. For there are different offices which are distinguished from each other but all belong to the one body. . . .
>
> We also confess that not everyone who is called to the godly life should teach. We believe that there is a variety of gifts and offices. A person may not appoint himself; he must be chosen by the church. I too, for my own part, did not preach until the faithful, who are called to a Christian life through the teaching of Christ, and gathered through a penitent life, called me to do so.
>
> *–Hans Hotz, Swiss Anabaptist preacher, 1538*[22]

No traditions, man-made creeds, or government arms may disrupt this process. When Luther and Zwingli accepted some unscriptural, postapostolic traditions, the Anabaptists ceased to support the mainline church reform efforts. They did not deny the possibility of right traditions; they simply held that any tradition is right only when the New Testament confirms it. They did not believe that the New Testament church was primitive and simple; rather, they understood it to be a well-developed, pure Christian church.

The faithful Anabaptists taught that every true believer could know and do God's will. This attitude was also evident in Luther and Zwingli in the beginning of their reform efforts. The differences between the Reformers and the Anabaptists stemmed from their actions at the crucial point when the government put the brakes on religious reform. At that point, the Reformers abandoned their

---

[22] Ibid., 125, 126.

vision of a pure, committed church in order to include everyone in given localities. Because their churches were impure, they depended on technically "qualified" theologians and scholars to "make" the Bible say what they wanted to hear. The Anabaptists, however, remained committed to the Bible ideal—an honest, obedient membership discerning God's will together.

Lessons for Today

In today's world, theology has become the application of human reasoning to the Bible. The further a church drifts from Scriptural obedience, the more theology it generates to support the direction it is taking. For the remainder of this chapter, we will discuss some areas in which the "theological tendency"—appreciating human philosophies instead of obeying God's clear Word—may affect us today.

When a church drifts away from God, intellectual, theological skills become more impressive than simple, sound doctrine preached by God-fearing shepherds. When preaching becomes more historical than practical, more philosophical than Biblical, more mind-stretching than heart-strengthening, or more eloquent than God-fearing, that flock will starve.[23] Typology, prophecy, and similar studies have a proper role. But "Jesus Christ, and him crucified" always permeates the entire message of faithful churches. The apostle Paul set the matter clearly before his Corinthian brethren:

> "And I, brethren, when I came to you, came not with excellency of speech or of wisdom, declaring unto you the testimony of God. For I determined not to know

---

[23] Genuine spiritual food sometimes involves history and things that stretch our minds. And if God gives a man eloquence, he should use it to glorify his Maker. But beware of messages that do not challenge the disciple in practical doctrine and discipleship. That is a mark of waning devotion to God.

any thing among you, save Jesus Christ, and him crucified. And I was with you in weakness, and in fear,
and in much trembling. And my speech and my
preaching was not with enticing words of man's wisdom, but in demonstration of the Spirit and of power:
that your faith should not stand in the wisdom of men,
but in the power of God" (1 Corinthians 2:1–5).

*On the heels of a theological approach to God's Word
comes the tendency to solve problems by a logical analysis instead of by following the Bible.*

If the church firmly deals with sin, it will be purified.
But applying human logic to sin only leads to more problems. If the church excuses sin because the person had
a poor background, because other people in the church
have problems too, or because they want to deal "redemp-
tively" and not drive people away by doing what the Bible
says, the church is excusing sin.

In Mennonite church history, two errors have often
cropped up in troubled situations. Sometimes leaders
tried to give equal weight to all the voices in the church
and to chart a middle course. In other situations, the
leaders forced their own way instead of taking the counsel of the faithful brethren in the church. These errors
may seem logical, depending on the situation, but they
are not Biblical. Both have contributed to the mainstream
Mennonite apostasy.

The true church is a theocracy, not a democracy or a
dictatorship. It respects the gifts and offices as God has
given them in the church, without abusing them. It
applies truth to every situation. We never need to violate
the principles of love, purity, humility, brotherhood counsel, and leadership in order to be faithful.

To a large extent, we can judge the spiritual quality
of our brotherhoods by how we make decisions and on
what basis we are united. A church that is moved by

logic, personality, and polish is apostatizing. But a church that is moved by prayer and simple Bible truth will go on conquering till the end of time.

The theological tendency can also become evident in how the church indoctrinates new members. We appreciate our instruction booklets as a valuable aid for new Christians. But understanding a denominational catechism should not be the primary basis for church membership. When a Scriptural church welcomes new members, the primary requirement is that the new members be conformed to the Scriptures. Appreciating and having strong conviction for Bible doctrines and discipleship must have first place. A Scriptural church is maintained only by an influx of Scriptural members, who are generated by God's work and Word.

The church of Jesus Christ grows and thrives because it works on the spiritual level to meet spiritual needs. It allows Christ to build His church.

Whether we are laymen or leaders, we can be faithful in the church only by being faithful to God and His Word. We need to approach the Bible with absolute trust that it is God's rule for our lives. And we must commit ourselves to follow that rule, whatever it may involve. That was the Anabaptist emphasis.

> "These were more noble than those in Thessalonica, in that they received the word with all readiness of mind, and searched the scriptures daily, whether those things were so" (Acts 17:11).
>
> "All scripture is given by inspiration of God, and is profitable for doctrine, for reproof, for correction, for instruction in righteousness: that the man of God may be perfect, throughly furnished unto all good works" (2 Timothy 3:16, 17).
>
> "As I besought thee to abide still at Ephesus, when I went into Macedonia, that thou mightest charge some

that they teach no other doctrine, neither give heed to fables and endless genealogies, which minister questions, rather than godly edifying which is in faith: so do. Now the end of the commandment is charity out of a pure heart, and of a good conscience, and of faith unfeigned: from which some having swerved have turned aside unto vain jangling; desiring to be teachers of the law; understanding neither what they say, nor whereof they affirm" (1 Timothy 1:3–7).

Chapter 10

"An Assembly of the Children of God"

The Anabaptist View of the Church

The Hutterite leader Peter Riedemann, in his *Account of Our Religion, Doctrine, and Faith,* described the Anabaptist church as "an assembly of the children of God."[1] The Anabaptists based their view of the church on Scripture passages such as 2 Corinthians 6:17, 18: "Wherefore come out from among them, and be ye separate, saith the Lord, and touch not the unclean thing; and I will receive you, and will be a Father unto you, and ye shall be my sons and daughters, saith the Lord Almighty." A

---

[1] Peter Riedemann, *An Account of Our Religion, Doctrine, and Faith,* 1542. Cited in Walter Klaassen, ed., *Anabaptism in Outline,* 111.

Biblical church is a pure and committed assembly of God's children.

Restoration or Reformation?

Reformers and restorers have different goals in mind. A *restorer* takes an old item, such as a piece of furniture, and tries to return it to its original condition in every detail. A *reformer,* on the other hand, is more like the person who wants to make an old item functional again, but is not particularly concerned about returning it to its original state. A restorer will painstakingly strip a piece of furniture to bare wood and refinish it, while the reformer will be satisfied with giving it a coat of paint.

The Anabaptists wanted to restore the fellowship of believers to apostolic standards, while their Lutheran and Zwinglian contemporaries were satisfied to reform the existing church. The Anabaptists had no agenda of their own. Rather, they believed and obeyed the original blueprint, the Bible. The reformers, however, wanted to retain the structure of the fallen church but replace some practices and beliefs with new ones from the Bible. They worked to make the fallen church functional again, but failed to deal with its fallen nature.

Since Zwingli's and Luther's reform blueprints were taken from postapostolic theologians, they could not regain the apostolic character of the church, *nor did they want to.* Zwingli and Luther knew that when they retained certain fallen elements of the church, they were not attaining to the purity of the church as the New Testament explained it. But this did not greatly trouble them, for they believed the Catholic teaching that the apostolic church was doctrinally undeveloped and intellectually primitive. They believed that God had sanctioned some alterations in the simple New Testament plan so that the apostolic church could survive in the "real" world.

Many evils have come from this belief because it releases Christianity from its founding principles and examples. Actually, it releases Christianity from accountability to God! If man can alter the New Testament at his will, what meaning does God's Word have for the church? It is accepted almost universally in "Christianity" that the simple relationships and teachings of apostolic Christians are not a standard for believers today.

This issue is the main dividing line between the true church and the false church. The true church believes that the New Testament message is to be practiced and believed. Much of nominal Christianity thinks that the New Testament church evolved from a primitive beginning to spiritual maturity as it adjusted to its environment. The true church calls this evolution apostasy; the false church terms it a "blossoming into its real element."[2]

The faithful Anabaptists simply accepted the New Testament as their standard. They literally believed what Jesus said in John 12:48: "He that rejecteth me, and receiveth not my words, hath one that judgeth him: the word that I have spoken, the same shall judge him in the last day."

The following sections discuss some basic Biblical church concepts and how the Anabaptists fulfilled or obeyed them.

The True Church Is Voluntary and Personal

Most members of the medieval state churches supported their church because it was all they ever knew. From birth, they had existed within that church. Those who thought for themselves and came to conclusions that

---

[2] See Appendix I, footnote 10.

were different from the state church faced persecution.

The Anabaptists realized that a church could fulfill its evangelistic duty and keep itself in Biblical order only with the voluntary commitment of each member. They saw that New Testament church leaders did not force people to be church members or physically discipline erring members. The Anabaptists considered Luther and Zwingli to be part of the fallen church just like the Catholics, since they enforced their religious ideas with civil power. Pilgram Marpeck said:

> Such children of God in the kingdom of Christ have authority, so that whatever they loose on earth is loosed and free in heaven, and what they have bound on earth is bound in heaven. This ban is externally administered by the Holy Spirit in the manner of God's love. . . .
>
> Whoever is not ruled by love, and acts contrary to it, belongs outside. . . .
>
> Here there is no coercion, but rather a voluntary spirit in Christ Jesus our Lord. Whoever does not desire [this spirit] let him remain outside; whoever desires it let him come and drink freely, without price.[3]

In Lutheran and Zwinglian churches, a person could be a member even if he had no spiritual interest. He did not need to agree with the Bible or even with the church. He simply needed to partake of the sacraments, to say the right things, and to perform the correct motions. So Luther and Zwingli were essentially no different from the Catholics, for they did not require holy living.[4] The basic differences between the Reformers and the Catholics were and are theological, not practical.

---

[3] *The Writings of Pilgram Marpeck,* 112, 113.

[4] Certainly, Luther and Zwingli wanted to promote and maintain godliness among their membership, but they never required it and always assumed that it was not altogether possible. This is still the case today in most Protestant churches.

Anabaptism was not primarily a new doctrine. Doctrinally and practically, they simply accepted Bible truths the Catholics and Reformers had abused and glossed over. *Anabaptism was a commitment to put New Testament doctrine to actual practice and to gather into small, voluntary, responsible fellowships all those who were willing to do this.* In these voluntary fellowships, each member was responsible for his own spiritual life and was expected to spiritually interact with his fellow believers. Hypocrites were few because the intense sharing and learning experience made transparent, spiritual interaction a dominant factor in church life.[5] Michael Sattler placed great confidence in the local brotherhood to discover hypocritical hearts. Shortly before his death, he wrote:

> Forget not the assembly, but apply yourselves to coming together constantly and that you may be united in prayer for all men and the breaking of bread, and this all the more fervently, as the day of the Lord draws nearer. In such meeting together you will make manifest the heart of the false brothers, and will be freed of them more rapidly.[6]

In a sense, the Anabaptists did not *go* to a church, for they *were* the church. Infant baptism became a live issue in the Reformation because it was an expression of *in*voluntary, *im*personal church life. The Anabaptists insisted on adult baptism because the New Testament teaching on conscious repentance and commitment to Christ could not possibly be an infant experience.

The True Church Is Visible

Faithful Anabaptists faced the temptation to hold their faith in secret. How much easier their lives could have

---

[5] Persecution also weeded out hypocrites.

[6] Michael Sattler, *Letter to the Church at Horb.* Cited in *The Legacy of Michael Sattler,* 62.

been if they had simply lived for God in their hearts and given up a few of their radical, social differences. The temptation was strong, but the faithful Anabaptists did not give in to it. Why?

The Anabaptists believed that the New Testament could only be fulfilled in a *gathered* church—a visible church that met together, practiced the ordinances, and interacted as members of a unit. When questioned by the Reformers about church history, some Bernese Anabaptists replied, "We do not insist that there was no one that pleased God even in the blindness and darkness [of pre-Reformation times]. We commit that to God; He will have known them. . . . For it cannot be that there was a church of which no one knew and that was not recognized."[7]

Peter Riedemann wrote:

> We confess also that God has, through Christ, chosen, accepted, and sought a people for himself. . . . Therefore is such a people, community, assembly or church gathered and led together by the Holy Spirit, which from henceforth rules, controls and orders everything in her. . . .
>
> . . . Thus, it is evident that the church is gathered together by the Holy Spirit: also that she has being and is kept in being by him, and that there is no other church apart from that which the Holy Spirit builds and gathers.[8]

Echoing the same beliefs, Dirk Philips wrote:

> The church of the Lord, although existing in spirit and in truth, is nevertheless also visible. . . . The name church or congregation indicates that it is not only invisible, but also visible, for the term used is "ecclesia," that is, a gathering or meeting or congregating

---

[7] Martin Haas, *Quellen zur Geschichte der Täufer in der Schweiz:* IV, 1538. Cited in Walter Klaassen, ed., *Anabaptism in Outline,* 110.

[8] Peter Riedemann, *An Account of Our Religion, Doctrine, and Faith,* 1542. Cited in Walter Klaassen, ed., *Anabaptism in Outline,* 111, 112.

together. . . . The apostles, according to the command of the Lord . . . gathered a church out of all nations (Matt. 28:19, 20; Mark 16:15, 16). This was not an invisible body, for they did not write nor send their epistles in a general or indiscriminate way to all people, but specifically denominating the believers and God-fearing people, and designating many places and calling many persons by name. How is it possible for all this to be invisible?[9]

As time went on, persecution wore down this firm resolve to have a visible church. Many Anabaptists fell to Pietism. Pietists were content to worship God and hold some right beliefs in their hearts, without openly defying the state church system. Since they were not as visible as the original Anabaptists, they did not face stiff persecution.

There was also another pietistic concept that worked against Biblical, visible church life. Pietists taught that Christians are responsible only to God. However, as Riedemann and Philips indicated, the visible church calls for commitment and a practical working together. Christians have a responsibility to God, but that includes a definite, visible responsibility to and for their brethren. Without personal commitment to a visible group of Christians, this brotherly relationship cannot exist. The Anabaptists believed that part of Biblical, spiritual unity was practical unity and brotherly admonition in a responsible church setting. They willingly died for the visible-church concept, knowing that they could have saved their lives by going quietly underground.

The True Church Is Pure

Both the Anabaptists and the state churches dealt with members who did not meet the conditions their

---

[9] Dietrich Philip, *Enchiridion or Hand Book,* 483, 484.

respective groups required for church membership. But because the state churches did not have a Biblical view of the church, they could not use Biblical church discipline.[10] To medieval state church authorities, imprisonment, torture, and execution were all legitimate means of church discipline. The state churches regarded Anabaptists as heretical members; therefore, they felt responsible to punish them. In medieval society, everyone was considered to be Christian, so there was no "world" into which a heretical member could be excommunicated. Killing the stubborn heretic was the only way to remove him from the church.

The Anabaptists believed that society was divided into a church and a world. An excommunicated church member, therefore, did not have to be killed to be sent out of the church. The true church could be Scripturally nonresistant *and* exercise Scriptural excommunication.

Anabaptist church discipline did not settle into a stable pattern immediately. The Swiss, Dutch, and South German Anabaptists all had their unique ideas about excommunication. It seems that the Dutch Anabaptists sometimes neglected private, charitable admonition, became too hasty in excommunication, and shunned the excommunicated person to the extent that they were not fulfilling the Great Commission.

Pilgram Marpeck blamed the Swiss Brethren for a harsh and legalistic application of discipline. Whether his accusation was just is unknown, but the Swiss

---

[10] The absence of this kind of punishment today in Catholic and Lutheran churches is due, not to the will of the founders, but to the changing political circumstances, in which these churches found it unwise and impossible to act on their original foundations. Some members of these religions, especially in North America, are now rather embarrassed about their church's part in Anabaptist persecution. However, they should note that essentially, especially in the Catholic Church, the doctrinal framework that originally caused the persecution remains intact and could serve as an agent of persecution in the future, should the political climate change.

Brethren were not nearly as extreme as the Dutch Anabaptists. Jacob Ammann left the Swiss Brethren because he wanted to institute some of the hard-line Dutch practices.

The first concise statement of the Swiss Anabaptist position was in the Schleitheim Confession.

> We have been united as follows concerning the ban. The ban shall be employed with all those who have given over to the Lord, to walk after [Him] in his commandments; those who have been baptized into the one body of Christ, and let themselves be called brothers or sisters, and still somehow slip and fall into error and sin, being inadvertently overtaken. The same [shall] be warned twice privately and the third time be publicly admonished before the entire congregation according to the command of Christ (Mt. 18). But this shall be done according to the ordering of the Spirit of God before the breaking of bread, so that we may all in one spirit and in one love break and eat from one bread and drink from one cup.[11]

Several important principles are woven into this statement. Exclusion from the church is on the basis of error and sin, not on the basis of disagreements over nonessential matters. Timely admonition needs to be given to the erring individual. The whole church should be aware of what is happening before an excommunication takes place. The church needs to be pure so that its testimony of spiritual unity, Communion, is not soiled.

In 1532, some Swiss Brethren told some Reformed leaders:

> If your brother sins against you, go and chastise him in private. . . . But that among you this does not function, we will show. When people, papists and

---

[11] *The Schleitheim Confession.* (See Appendix II.)

Lutherans assemble in the drinking-houses, where is the chastisement? If someone blasphemes the name of the Lord no one admonishes him. Nor, if he does not improve his ways after admonition with two witnesses, does anyone take the matter to the congregation and thence to a servant of the Word! . . . If someone has gambled, spoken profanity, etc.; if he has been admonished, and there is no fruit, we exclude him. We no longer consider him a brother until he improves, abandons his evil and receives God's grace.[12]

In a letter to the Swiss Brethren in 1531, Pilgram Marpeck especially emphasized the patient admonition that should precede church discipline.

This is a copy of an epistle written to those called the Swiss Brethren, and it concerns hasty judgments and decisions in which some may not concur. . . .

My dear ones, constrained by the love in Jesus Christ, I write this letter because of the schism which, until now, has existed between us, because we have never recognized in our hearts and consciences the acknowledgment and understanding of Christ Jesus in each other, nor have we ever been able to meet. . . .

. . . The natural body cannot lose a member without pain. Nor does it immediately cut it off, even if it is failing and weak; rather it uses all kinds of medicines. As long as it is not dead and is only painful, the body bears it with patience and long-suffering, and delays the penalty to allow for improvement. If, however, it allows the body no rest, nor does it improve by means of any medicine from the Lord Jesus Christ, through suffering and pain, it must be cut off in order that the other members of the body of Christ remain healthy in the fear and love of God. . . .

Oh, my dear brothers, if our hearts and consciences

---

[12] Martin Haas, *Quellen zur Geschichte der Täufer in der Schweiz:* IV, "Zofingen Colloquy of 1532." Cited in Walter Klaassen, ed., *Anabaptism in Outline,* 217.

could only meet on the above-mentioned matter! This is my concern about you. I would hope that, through the grace of God, we would soon be united on the other matters.[13]

All the material we have from both the Swiss Brethren and Marpeck about church discipline seems Biblical. Evidently, they disagreed in the actual working out of those beliefs. The Swiss Brethren thought that Marpeck was too careless in what he allowed in the church, and Marpeck thought that the Swiss Brethren were too careless in what they put out of the church.

A valuable, concise treatment of church discipline has come down to us from Peter Riedemann. This selection details what we today call *probation*. Evidently, the Hutterites did not excommunicate for every failure regardless of the attitude of the erring one.

> But where one will not accept the rebuke, but disregards it, the matter is brought before the church, and if he hear not the church, then he is excluded and put out.
>
> If, however, one be discovered in the gross and deadly sins of which Paul says, "If any man that is called a brother be a fornicator, or covetous, or an idolater, or a railer, or a drunkard, or a thief or a robber, with such an one ye must not even eat." Such an one is put out and excluded or separated from the church without admonition, since the judgment of Paul is already spoken.
>
> And if one is so excluded, we have nothing to do with him: have no company with him, that he may be ashamed. Yet is he called to repentance, that perchance he may be moved thereby and return the more quickly to God; and where not, that the church may remain pure and innocent of his sin, and bear not guilt and rebuke from God on his behalf.

---

[13] *The Writings of Pilgram Marpeck,* 311, 312, 356, 357.

In all such cases, however, a distinction is made, that he who sins willfully be punished according to the weight of his sin; and the more willful the sin, the sharper the punishment. If, however, he sin in the haste of the flesh and not willfully or recklessly, but through the weakness of the flesh, he is punished, but not completely separated from the church or excluded from all fellowship; but he is not permitted to use the Lord's greeting, to give or accept "Peace," that he may humble himself before God for his sin, and thereafter watch all the more carefully against it.

Concerning Readmission

Now when one is excluded we have no fellowship with him until he has truly repented: though he may run with entreaty and desire, he is not accepted until he has received from the church the good report of a truly repentant life; yea, he is not accepted until one senses that the Lord has again drawn nigh to him, been gracious to and accepted him. . . . When this has taken place he is accepted again in full love; all suspicion, complaint and disinclination are swept away and cut off—lest Satan should get the advantage of us—and one has a right and completely trusting heart toward him as toward all the other members of the church.[14]

In the third paragraph of this excerpt, Riedemann is clear that the brotherhood has an evangelical obligation to the excommunicated individual. He indicates that a church which does not verbally call an excommunicated member to repentance, even after the punitive action, might be guilty before God.

The True Church Is Evangelistic

To be an Anabaptist meant that you were an active

---

[14] Peter Riedemann, *An Account of Our Religion, Doctrine, and Faith,* 1542. Cited in Walter Klaasen, ed., *Anabaptism in Outline,* Walter Klaassen 220, 221.

evangelist of the Gospel.[15] It meant that you were part of a group whose business was spreading the truth as rapidly and effectively as possible.[16] Most modern Mennonites think of themselves as evangelistic churches because they have foreign missions and local outreach committees. While all that can be a part of evangelism, it is only a fraction of being an evangelist. The true Christian looks

---

[15] This does not mean that every Anabaptist was ordained or led in worship services. Evangelists are not necessarily ordained. All Christians are called to evangelism upon their conversion. Some evangelists are subsequently ordained to fill various offices in the church in addition to their personal evangelistic responsibilities. The equation of ordination and evangelism is devastating to the Biblical concept of Christian mission. It was an equation the mainstream Reformers loved to hurl at the Anabaptist missionaries, accusing them of not being authorized to explain the Gospel to the common man.

The Anabaptists ordained church leaders according to the Biblical pattern. Generally, Anabaptists did not preach unless the church specifically called them to do so. However, they did not limit evangelism to preaching.

[16] Some Anabaptist-related churches use Dirk Philips's teaching to avoid the Biblical call to evangelism. On pages 211 and 212 of Dirk's *Hand Book of the Christian Doctrine and Religion,* Dirk indicates that the commands in Matthew 28 and Mark 16 do not apply to Christians today. See also this section of his writings as translated by Isaac Horst in *Close Ups of the Great Awakening,* pages 123–125.

A cursory examination of Dirk's writings contradicts the theory that he was not evangelistic. First, Dirk was replying to accusers who blamed him for not preaching openly. He was defending the Mennonites for witnessing only in their homeland, saying that at the time, in light of persecution and resistance against the truth, it was impossible for Christians to fulfill the Great Commission. In defending his view, he contradicted himself, much as he did when discussing the incarnation of Christ. (This conclusion is based on Isaac Horst's translation.) It is hardly fair to use writings out of context as the only basis for deciding that Dirk did not believe in evangelism. Second, of Dirk's fifteen extant writings (as divided in the *Hand Book*), five seem to be directly written to nominal Christians of the Netherlands, urging them to consider their ways and join the true Christian church. This falls directly into the category of evangelism. Third, in Dirk's treatise on the church, he said that the apostles and all pious witnesses of truth reprove the world of unbelief (John 16:8) by God's Word and power. This teaching leaves no room for the silence of many Anabaptist descendants. Fourth, the most effective evangelist in all of Anabaptist history (in terms of adding members to the church) was Menno's and Dirk's co-worker, Leenaert Bouwens. He baptized over ten thousand persons during his ministry. Some of these were probably converted children of Mennonite parents; many others were the first members of new fellowships sprinkled all over Holland. The way Dirk, Menno, and Leenaert held to their positions and excommunicated those who did not agree with them, would have made it impossible for Leenaert and Dirk to co-exist peacefully, unless Dirk supported Leenaert's work. (See Cornelius Krahn, *Dutch Anabaptism,* 208, 229, 230.)

for opportunities in daily life to speak a word for Christ. He scrutinizes his life to ensure that it is consistently speaking for Christ. He subjects his business interests and family interests to the cause of truth.

Some Anabaptists carried this too far. Some newly converted men left their families without proper care and wandered around the countryside, teaching the Gospel. The Protestant preachers who accused these men of not providing for their families had some basis for their accusation. As time went on, however, Anabaptist evangelism became more orderly. The Martyrs' Synod in 1527 and the later Hutterite mission program are examples of this. These planned missionary activities divided up the land and sent evangelists forth by twos and threes to each area. Local churches, though under persecution, supported the evangelists' families. When threatened by the authorities, evangelist Hanss Schmidt told them that he had suffered all his life as a pilgrim loose from the world, and his brethren would take care of his wife and children.[17]

To the Anabaptists, the church existed for the purpose of spreading the Gospel and maintaining sound, local fellowships of evangelists. In Anabaptist court testimonies and confessions of faith, Matthew 28:18–20 and Mark 16:15, 16 are the most prominent Scripture passages.[18] Menno Simons set forth his view plainly:

> But after it had all been accomplished according to the Scriptures, and had been made new in Christ, He did not then send out the scribes and Pharisees with Moses' law, but His disciples with His own doctrine, saying: Go ye into all the world and preach the gospel to every creature, teaching them to observe all things whatsoever I have commanded you.[19]

---

[17] Franklin H. Littell, *The Anabaptist View of the Church,* 132.

[18] Ibid., 109.

[19] *The Complete Writings of Menno Simons,* 178

In another writing, Menno said of Christ:

> His command is eternal life. He sent out His mes-
> sengers preaching this peace, His apostles who spread
> this grace abroad through the whole world, who shone
> as bright, burning torches before all men, so that they
> might lead me and all erring sinners into the right way.
> O Lord, not unto me, but unto Thee be praise and
> honor. Their words I love, their practices I follow.[20]

The evangelistic character of the Anabaptists did not
develop over a period of time; it was present immediately
at their beginning, in 1525. The clear Bible command
sent them out immediately to the surrounding villages
and countryside. To Zwingli, the Anabaptists' wrong view
of evangelism was second only to their wrong view of baptism. In May 1525, several months after Anabaptism
began, he wrote a treatise against their view of baptism,
and in June he published a tract against their "unauthorized" evangelism. His writing verifies the intense evangelistic campaign the Swiss Anabaptists had under way.

> Therefore those who pretend to be apostles or
> prophets do not, in expositing the Scripture, act
> according to the practice of the apostles. They do not
> stay in their own churches but run to other churches
> and speak there without the prophets. And whereas
> they use this passage by Paul to prove that they may
> also interrupt by speaking from Scripture, they refuse
> to be interrupted themselves. . . .
>
> . . . At Jerusalem there were thousands of believ-
> ers, but there were no more than twelve apostles.
> Here all of them are apostles. I believe there are more
> apostles than believers! If one has attended a Ger-
> man school and has learned to spell, he appears in
> public and spells it out to the congregation.[21]

---

[20] Ibid., 71.

[21] Ulrich Zwingli, *Concerning the Office of Preaching,* June 3, 1525. Cited in Leland
Harder, ed., *The Sources of Swiss Anabaptism,* 393, 403.

Throughout Catholic history, a few groups of people, mostly monks and nuns, had tried in their own way to fulfill the Great Commission. However, the Anabaptists did not merely join cells of piety[22] existing within a great, corrupt church. Neither were they a protest group who withdrew from the mainstream church until it would mend itself. They separated themselves entirely from the old church and made every member of their group an evangelist. They controlled no territory politically, they fought no wars, and they observed no political borders as they went about establishing Christian churches. They constantly challenged the Reformers with the Great Commission.

The Reformers held that the Commission had expired. Only the apostles, they said, were sent into all the world. They believed that one had to be ordained by the church in order to teach the Gospel. The idea that every member had an evangelistic responsibility was heresy to them. Further, they still believed the Catholic teaching that faith was limited and defined by political territories. They expected everyone in their territory to be a Protestant, and they did not generally send missionaries to Catholic areas to establish Protestant churches. Their idea of spreading their religion was to acquire political control of an area by force and then to force their religion on their new subjects.

Due to the disparity between the mainstream church and the Anabaptists' beliefs, Anabaptist evangelism was carried out in a bloodbath. Far from smothering the fervent Anabaptist evangelism, the persecution fanned the flames of witness. Many of them seemed to expect to die for their activities, but they nevertheless went forth undaunted to preach Christ. Records tell us the testimony

---

[22] Some of the monasteries and convents were as corrupt as the church they were a part of. Others were concerned about purity and tried in their own way to achieve peace with God. In this sense, we can call some of them "cells of piety."

of Matthias Binder, who was on a missionary journey, sent by the Hutterian Brethren. "The question if he would leave the principality he answered with a clear 'No', for the earth was the Lord's. He didn't know yet where the Lord was leading him, or in what land his death was fixed."[23]

Death was expected; suffering was inevitable. If the Anabaptists had considered evangelism as a side focus or only supplementary to the concept of the true church, they would have faded into the countryside and probably been largely unmolested. But they saw evangelism as an undeniable part of discipleship. Further testimonies bear this out.

> Firstly, Christ said, go forth into the whole world, preach the Gospel to every creature. Secondly, he said, whoever believes, thirdly—and is baptized, the same shall be saved. This order must be maintained if a true Christianity is to be prepared and though the whole world rage against it.[24]

> Therefore we seek, to the extent of our opportunity, to make known and proclaim to all mankind the grace of God which has appeared. . . . To this end we preach as much as opportunity and possibility affords, both in day time and by night, in houses and in fields, in forests and wildernesses, in this land and abroad, in prison and bonds, in the water, the fire and on the scaffold, on the gallows and upon the wheel, before lords and princes, orally and by writing, at the risk of possessions and life, as we have done these many years without ceasing.[25] (Menno Simons)

Lessons for Today

Are we willing to commit ourselves to the kind of voluntary and personal church life that the early Anabaptists

---

[23] Franklin H. Littell, *The Anabaptist View of the Church,* 120.

[24] Ibid., 111.

[25] John Horsch, *Mennonites in Europe,* 316.

maintained? Here are a few principles that will help us to maintain long-range faithfulness to the Word of God in our church life.

Churches need to be small enough that the members personally know each other well. The ministry needs to be sufficiently staffed and to take the initiative in fulfilling Acts 20:28: "Take heed therefore unto yourselves, and to all the flock, over the which the Holy Ghost hath made you overseers, to feed the church of God, which he hath purchased with his own blood." It is difficult for the leaders or the members to fulfill their Biblical obligation when a congregation is so large that they are no longer personally acquainted with every member. In any congregation, both members and leaders need to take personal responsibility to make sure that such a relationship remains in place.

We need to appreciate the kind of help and admonition we personally receive in a close-knit church. Many Anabaptist descendants do not want close-knit churches. They do not want their hypocrisy to show up or their wrong thinking to be exposed. They simply want to be left alone and to remain as church members, because being a church member gives them some assurance of being a Christian. If our churches shelter hypocrisy simply because the communication gap is too wide, we are in the tradition of the Protestant and Catholic churches, not of the believers' church.

We need to understand that the ministry and the unordained members are one, yet give the leaders their proper authority. Every church needs leadership, and we need to respect our godly leaders. However, the leaders of a congregation are on the same level as the rest of the group. They have an important function to fill, but that does not make them more important to the congregation than the least esteemed member in the pew. Jesus set the pattern for the New Testament brotherhood: "But be not ye called Rabbi: for one is your Master, even Christ; and all ye are brethren. And call no man your father upon the earth: for one is your Father, which is in heaven. Neither be ye called masters: for one is your Master, even Christ. But he that is greatest among you shall be your servant" (Matthew 23:8–11).

We need to be evangelistic. The dreadful persecution in the 1500s finally succeeded in quieting the Anabaptist missionaries. By 1650, the Swiss and German Anabaptists had become the "quiet in the land," content simply to have their own children follow them in their faith.

Anabaptist emigrants to America carried this concept with them. Even in the New World, the Anabaptist descendants did not recover the Biblical character that they had lost under persecution.

The New Testament requirements, however, are clear. In addition to the Great Commission, the Scriptures are full of evangelistic commands. Acts 1 and 2 show that there were a number of people *besides the apostles* present when Christ sent the Holy Spirit and charged the church to "be witnesses unto me both in Jerusalem, and in all Judaea, and in Samaria, and unto the uttermost part of the earth" (Acts 1:8). After distinctly describing both heathen and nominal believers in Romans 10, the apostle Paul pointed out the necessity of the Christian church to take the Gospel to all men. In 2 Corinthians 5, Paul described the new Christian and immediately said that unto Christians was committed the ministry of reconciliation. While this does have an application within the church, it goes much further than that. Verse 19 expressly indicates that this responsibility is *to the world.* Verse 20 shows that we are ambassadors—laborers in a foreign nation—who are calling non-Christians to God.

All these commands are positive. They picture the church on a mission, not a passive church reclining in the background and saying, "Here we are. If you want truth, come and get it." The church does not keep an office and wait for men to come for business. She preaches and publishes the Gospel, because that is how God uses the church to reveal Himself to the world. She is sent and active. Christians do not feel like fish out of water when they are evangelizing; they understand this to be one of their primary duties.

> "I pray not that thou shouldest take them out of the world, but that thou shouldest keep them from the evil. They are not of the world, even as I am not of the world. Sanctify them through thy truth: thy word is truth. As thou hast sent me into the world, even so have I also sent them into the world" (John 17:15–18).

> "Therefore said he unto them, The harvest truly is great, but the labourers are few: pray ye therefore the Lord of the harvest, that he would send forth labourers into his harvest. . . . He that heareth you heareth me; and he that despiseth you despiseth me; and he that despiseth me despiseth him that sent me" (Luke 10:2, 16).

Chapter 11

"The Pressing Cross of Christ"

The Anabaptist View of Discipleship

When we consider, worthy brethren, our very weak and sinful nature, how that we are prone to evil from our youth, how that in our flesh no good thing dwelleth, . . . and when we consider how that we have a tendency at all times (although we do seek and fear God) to mind earthly and perishable things, then we see that the gracious God and Father, who through His eternal love always cares for His children, has left behind in His house an excellent remedy against all this, namely, the pressing cross of Christ.[1]

---

[1] *The Complete Writings of Menno Simons,* 614.

The faithful Anabaptists did not mope and pine at heavy persecution. They believed that God allowed it for their good and for the separation of hypocrites from true believers. Many times they compared it to Christ's suffering and quoted John 15:20: "The servant is not greater than his lord. If they have persecuted me, they will also persecute you."

The Two Kingdoms

Anabaptists did not try to reconcile the Bible message with the condition of the world, as did the mainline Reformers and the Catholics. Rather, they saw the world as a kingdom of darkness, evil, and falsehood. They saw the true church as a regenerated band of believers who existed in the world *but were not of the world.* The Catholics and the Reformers also divided the world into two categories—heathen, or those who lived in nations that did not serve God; and "Christian," or those who lived in nations that claimed to serve God. Because "Christian" nations had largely subdued Europe, the entire continent was therefore considered to be Christian.

The Catholics believed that being Christian meant to partake of the sacraments and church-prescribed ceremonies. The Reformers differed little from this, except to add that being Christian meant to be taught correct doctrine. In essence, both Catholics and Reformers believed that the Christian church did not depend on the discipleship of her members; it only depended on the correctness of her liturgy and ceremony. Performing these rites required no change of heart.

The Halfway Anabaptists (discussed in Chapter 4) endeavored to find a middle ground. They assented to Anabaptist teachings in their hearts, and some

Anabaptists called them the "truehearted" and "good-hearted."[2] But they would not fully commit themselves and thus rejected the cross of Christ. Fear kept them from doing what they knew was right, so they were not true Anabaptists. When someone became an Anabaptist, he did not just think like an Anabaptist; he lived like an Anabaptist.

The unlearned Anabaptists understood the relation of the church to the world much better than the theology-minded Reformers and Catholics. They correctly saw that within one physical universe there existed two spiritual kingdoms. For them, following Christ included a Biblical change of heart and a commitment to discipleship. This is how the Christian church could prosper and maintain Biblical preaching and ordinances. They did not include everyone within the church and then try to change them. Rather, they considered everyone outside the church until they committed their lives to Christ and proved their discipleship in daily living. Two years after Anabaptism began, the Swiss Brethren, assembled at Schleitheim, said it this way:

> All those who have fellowship with the dead works of darkness have no part in the light. Thus all who follow the devil and the world have no part with those who have been called out of the world unto God. All those who lie in evil have no part in the good. . . .
>
> . . . Now there is nothing else in the world and all creation than good or evil, believing or unbelieving, darkness and light, the world and those who are [come] out of the world, God's temple and idols, Christ and Belial, and none will have part with the other.
>
> To us, then, the commandment of the Lord is also

---

[2] Some Anabaptists felt quite adamant about the spiritual condition of the truehearted. Hans Reist and his brethren refused to label the truehearted as sinners, but Jacob Ammann and his followers insisted that they were. This issue contributed to the Amish and Mennonite division of 1693.

obvious, whereby He orders us to be and become separate from the evil one, and thus He will be our God and we shall be His sons and daughters.[3]

Among the Hutterite writings, we find this description of the two kingdoms, probably written by bishop Peter Walpot around 1577:

> Between the Christian and the world there exists a vast difference like that between heaven and earth. The world is the world, always remains the world, behaves like the world and all the world is nothing but world. The Christian, on the other hand, has been called away from the world. He has been called never to conform to the world, never to be a consort, never to run along with the crowd of the world and never to pull its yoke.[4]

The spiritual difference between these kingdoms made the children of the world hate the children of light. In Reformation times, that hatred resulted in bloodshed. This gave rise to the Anabaptist concept of martyrdom, discussed later in this chapter.

Worship and Obedience

The Reformers and Catholics depended on the right ceremonies for justification. Their worship consisted of the performance of these ceremonies. The Anabaptists, however, considered a life of discipleship, with a correct relationship to the Christian church, to be worship.

Many Anabaptist protests against the state churches were against their formal, dead motions of "worship," which anyone could perform regardless of his spiritual condition. Chanting, ceremonies, and liturgical prayers went on whether or not there were any true believers in

---

[3] *The Schleitheim Confession of Faith,* Articles 3 and 4, 1527. (See Appendix II.)

[4] Robert Friedmann and Lydia Muller, *Glaubenszeugnisse oberdeutscher Taufgesinnter,* II, 1967. Cited in Robert Friedmann, *The Theology of Anabaptism,* 39.

the church. Images and paintings decorated the walls and ceilings, but they changed nothing in the worshipers' hearts. To the Anabaptists, these things were signs of apostasy. Such things had little to do with true Christianity, as they understood it, which was to *obey Christ* in daily life. Worship was not chanting to Christ, or keeping many ceremonies, or fingering a rosary while glorifying His mother, but believing and doing what Christ said His disciples must believe and do. Menno Simons hammered this point throughout his writings. To quote but one example:

> My beloved children in Christ Jesus, you are aware that all the world by its blind and foolish unbelief has hitherto followed adulterously after outward works and ceremonies. Yet you should not do likewise. You should know that the righteousness which avails before God consists not in any ceremony and outward work, but exclusively in a true, pious, and fruitful faith. . . . it leads into all manner of righteousness, causes men willingly to submit in all obedience, and it gives willingness cheerfully to comply not only with baptism, but with all the words and ceremonies which God, the gracious Father, through His blessed Son, has so clearly taught and commanded in His holy Gospel.[5]

Pilgram Marpeck, in his writings, condemned the apostates and blessed God's true followers.

> Whoever retains, practices, or accepts baptism, the Lord's Supper, or anything else, even Scriptures, word or deed, according to the command, attitude, form, essence, or example of the Antichrist is a child, member, and brother of the Antichrist, worships the image of his being, and with him will inherit destruction.
>
> But whoever retains, practices, and accepts such ceremonies according to the command, attitude, form, essence, and example of Christ and the apostles,

---

[5] *The Complete Writings of Menno Simons*, 267.

indeed according to the instruction and urging of the free Spirit, participates without blemish, misunderstanding, or abomination in the truly reenacted, spiritual apostolic order.

Whoever practices or receives such ceremonies and matters without true faith, because of an external urge or other reasons, errs even though there is, externally, correctness of words and procedures.[6]

These writings show that the Anabaptists did believe in the correct observance of the ordinances. However, they saw all Biblical ceremonies as part of active discipleship instead of channels whereby passive men received God's approval.

Because of this emphasis, the Anabaptists often faced the accusation that they believed in justification by works. It is no wonder that the Catholics and Reformers made this charge. When comparing the Anabaptists' active discipleship with the Reformers' passive reception of God's grace or with the Catholics' passive reception of sacraments, it could appear that the Anabaptists were works oriented.

In July 1527, when Zwingli wrote his last tract against the Anabaptists, he accused them:

It is time to prove your spirit. You openly teach that blessedness can come to none but by works of righteousness. So Christ, whom the Father sent into the world to become a sacrifice for the despairing, is made void.[7]

Johann Kessler, a Swiss chronicler and contemporary of Zwingli, wrote:

They insisted more powerfully on justification by works than the papists [Catholics]. Thereby those

---

[6] *The Writings of Pilgram Marpeck,* 64.

[7] Ulrich Zwingli, *Refutation of the Tricks of the Anabaptists,* July 31, 1527. Cited in Leland Harder, ed., *The Sources of Swiss Anabaptism,* 486.

newly born through the gospel became quite confused in their conscience and were made depressed, for they had just recently learned that it is the grace of Jesus Christ, received by faith, that saves.[8]

The idea that the Anabaptists did not believe that justification came by faith persists even today among those who are unwilling to submit to the demands of Biblical discipleship. A Protestant high school history textbook says it this way:

> Unfortunately, many of the early Anabaptists also questioned the doctrine of justification by faith alone. They feared that this teaching might encourage men to think that justification apart from good works allowed them to sin as much as they wanted and still have forgiveness from God. These Anabaptists did not understand, as most of the other reformers did, that the Bible teaches that justification—although by faith without works (Gal. 3:11; Eph. 2:8-9)—always *results* in good works in the life of the justified believer (Eph. 2:10).[9]

Yes, the Anabaptists did question justification by faith alone. They saw that, to the average Reformed member, justification by faith alone meant that people could sin as much as they wanted and still be saved. In the Reformation, *only the Anabaptists put to practice the belief that justification produces righteous living,* contrary to the assumption quoted above.[10] Part of the problem between the two lines of thought springs from the fact that Luther

---

[8] Johann Kessler, *Sabbata.* Cited in Leland Harder, ed., *The Sources of Swiss Anabaptism,* 382.

[9] David A. Fisher, *World History for Christian Schools,* 2nd ed. (Greenville, S.C.: Bob Jones University Press, 1994), 293.

[10] John Calvin tried harder than the other Reformers to enforce righteousness, only to fail because righteousness cannot be enforced. He used the police to try to enforce Biblical morality among his people. The Anabaptists did not need to enforce righteous living, because their people were committed to it before they entered the church. Calvin, like the Catholics and the other Reformers, included all men in the church and then tried to change them.

saw justification as something done *to* man, while the Anabaptists saw it as something done *in* man. The first kind required nothing on the part of the receiver; the second kind required a conscious choice and a change by God's power in the nature of the receiver. A quote from Luther's advice to a friend underscores his error: "Sin boldly . . . but believe and rejoice in Christ more boldly still."[11]

As the Anabaptists and Reformers debated doctrine in state churches and civil halls, the Anabaptists did strongly emphasize the importance of righteous works as a fruit of salvation. They may have made some emphatic statements that could have been taken out of context to support works-religion. However, no one can argue with the Biblical quality of their extant writings. Listen to the Anabaptists as they answer these challenges in their own words.

> It is a great work of God to create man out of nothing, but it is an equally great work to justify a sinful man. But that can in no way happen outside of the conception, birth, death, and resurrection in us of Christ who is our righteousness. Whoever will be my disciple, says Christ, must follow me. Again he says that without me you can do nothing. *(From a 1527 letter to an Anabaptist church, by Leonhard Schiemer, a South German Anabaptist)*[12]

> Again when one speaks of works, one must preach not, after the manner of the work-righteous, the works of law but the works of faith; that is a turning away from works, creatures, and your own self, through faith in Christ the crucified one, not as what man can do from himself, but what he really can do in the power of faith; which thereby are not man's works but God's. . . .

---

[11] Martin Luther, *Briefwechsel.* Cited in Robert Friedmann, *The Theology of Anabaptism,* 88.

[12] Cited in Walter Klaassen, ed., *Anabaptism in Outline,* 54.

Verily, blessed be he who remains on the middle path, who turns aside neither to the work-righteous. . . . Nor to the side of the scribes,[13] who although they have forsaken works, then turn aside to the right, and teach in the name of "gospel" a faith without works. . . .

. . . They say much about faith and yet know neither what Christ nor faith is. They reject works without faith in order to raise up faith without works. They would like to obey God with the soul and not also with the body, so that they might be without persecution. They believe that faith is a lazy and empty fiction, whereby they are also able to say that infants have faith, even though no works of faith can be discerned in them, even when they grow up. *(Swiss Anabaptist Michael Sattler, from a tract entitled* On the Satisfaction of Christ*)*[14]

Thus the godless [Catholics and Reformers] say to the godly [Anabaptists]: O yes, you boast about your good works, act like the hypocrite in the temple, and think that therefore you are without sin. To this we reply that we can take no credit for good as natural men, but we give all glory and praise to God to whom it rightfully belongs. For it is obvious that man in himself cannot think anything good, let alone do it, as Paul says. For because of the grace of God we know that the works which we do and carry out as men count for nothing before God on that day. Inasmuch, however, as God does them in us through his grace and his spirit by whom all the believers are governed, they are good, just, pleasing and acceptable to God. *(Hutterite leader Jacob Hutter, in a writing entitled* Plots and Excuses*, ca. 1535)*[15]

You see, kind reader, we do not seek our salvation in works, words, or sacraments as do the learned ones,

---

[13] It appears that Sattler was referring to the mainline Reformation leaders as scribes.

[14] Cited in John H. Yoder, ed., *The Legacy of Michael Sattler,* 115–117.

[15] Cited in Walter Klaassen, ed., *Anabaptism in Outline,* 60.

although they accuse us of that very thing, but we seek them only in Christ Jesus and in no other means in heaven or on earth. We rejoice exclusively in this only means. We trust by the grace of God to continue thus unto death.

But that we abhor carnal works and desire to conform ourselves to His Word and commandment, according to our weakness, we do because He so taught and commanded us. For whosoever does not walk according to His doctrine, proves in fact that he does not believe on Him or know Him and that he is not in the communion of the saints. *(Dutch Anabaptist leader Menno Simons, in a writing entitled* Confession of the Distressed Christians, *1552)*[16]

These quotations, taken from all four major sectors of Biblical Anabaptism, are only a fraction of the available writings on this subject. The Anabaptists spent considerable effort trying to clear up the Reformed assumption that because they taught discipleship, they were not sound on grace and justification.

Why did the Reformers assume that discipleship and works-religion were the same thing? Because they believed Augustine's idea that man could not choose to do right. If man could not choose to do anything right, nothing he did could have an effect on his relationship with God. In light of that theory, the Reformers occupied themselves with how a man with no ability to commit himself or choose could be justified in spite of himself. The Anabaptists, on the other hand, believed in man's free will—that is, man's God-given ability to choose which spiritual master he will serve. So the Anabaptists were not preoccupied with justification; they knew that it was a work God performed when man, by God's grace, turned to his Creator in repentance. Rather, they occupied

---

[16] *The Complete Writings of Menno Simons,* 504, 505.

themselves with discipleship—that is, what did God want man to do and be after He justified them?

God wants His children to be righteous here and now. The Catholics did not expect their average member to be holy. Rather, they regarded sacraments and ceremonies as covering present sin, and saw future suffering in purgatory as a major step God used to make His followers fit for heaven. Neither did the mainline Reformers realize that God wanted to give the Christian victory over sin in his earthly life.

The difference between the mainline Reformers and the Anabaptists can be stated in several other ways. The Reformers emphasized the forgiven *status* that God confers upon a justified individual, while the Anabaptists emphasized the radical *change* that follows justification. The Anabaptists believed that salvation was not primarily a *status* but rather a *transformation.* The Reformers saw repentance as an admission of guilt, while the Anabaptists saw repentance as admitting guilt and turning away from the old life. The Reformers saw faith primarily as passive acceptance of God's offer of salvation, while the Anabaptists understood faith as the positive response of an open heart and life that invited the transforming work of God. In this response is commitment to discipleship. The Anabaptists "walked in the resurrection,"[17] while the Reformers rested in "grace."[18]

A Theology of Martyrdom

We know that being a true Christian will bring some scoffing, but we do not expect to die for our faith. In fact, we expect the civil government to respect Christian

---

[17] *The Schleitheim Confession of Faith,* Article 1. (See Appendix II.)

[18] In his tract on *The True Christian Faith,* 1541, Menno Simons gave a valuable description of what type of faith the Catholics and Lutherans had, and why it was wrong. See *The Complete Writings of Menno Simons,* 332–334.

honesty and godly living. It is hardly possible for us to imagine a time when commitment to Christ meant commitment to martyrdom. Because the Anabaptists faced martyrdom so often, they developed some doctrinal ideas about it that strengthened them for faithfulness to the end.

To the Anabaptists, martyrdom was a normal result of the universal struggle between God and Satan. The Anabaptists were not surprised at all to find themselves the object of the state church's wrath. Before Anabaptism began,[19] Conrad Grebel must have had a premonition of things to come as he wrote:

> Moreover, the gospel and its adherents are not to be protected by the sword, nor should they protect themselves. . . . True believing Christians are sheep among wolves, sheep for the slaughter. They must be baptized in anguish and tribulation, persecution, suffering, and death, tried in fire, and must reach the fatherland of eternal rest not by slaying the physical but the spiritual.[20]

In one of Menno Simons's writings, he listed a number of martyrs from the Old and New Testaments and the period between the Testaments. His evaluation:

> It seems to me, dear brethren, that this is a good example and a fair indication as to the way the righteous have always been offscourings and a prey to the unrighteous, and how they will continue to be that, even as the Scriptures testify sufficiently and as daily experience plainly teaches.[21]

---

[19] Catholic authorities had executed a few Protestants for their faith at this point, but there had been as yet no Anabaptist martyrs. Grebel probably knew about the Protestant martyrs.

[20] From Grebel's letter to Thomas Müntzer, September 5, 1524. Cited in Leland Harder, ed., *The Sources of Swiss Anabaptism,* 290.

[21] *The Complete Writings of Menno Simons,* 588.

Conrad, Menno, and their brethren had a different frame of reference about the true church and the world than we do. We too know that the world persecutes the true church, but the pressure we face is mostly mental and social. We can look back at a time of unparalleled peace and physical freedom for part of the true church, but the Anabaptists enjoyed no such perspective. They believed that since New Testament times, almost every generation had shed the blood of God's children.[22] They believed that physical persecution would always be the lot of God's people.[23] Jacob Hutter wrote:

> [Suffering] is a beautiful honour in the sight of God and all the saints; a deserved glory and wreath of joy from them. For this was the way of the holy prophets and patriarchs and of Christ the holy Lord and all his disciples, in fact of all the elect from the beginning of time.[24]

Why would persecution always continue? Because it is an expression of the age-old conflict between heaven and hell, truth and falsehood. Wherever Christ builds His church, there Satan will concentrate his greatest powers. Wherever the light of truth shines, the darkness of falsehood will struggle fiercely. "The whole volume of holy Scriptures," said the *Martyrs Mirror* writer, "seems to be nothing else than a book of martyrs."[25] These truths gave the Anabaptists great courage. They realized that they were in a battle that went far beyond

---

[22] They also pointed out Old Testament characters whom they considered martyrs, such as Abel and some of the faithful Israelite prophets.

[23] Persecution is the lot of the true church, even today. Physical freedom in the Americas can give us a warped view of reality. Throughout the world, Christians still suffer for their faith. In the future, American Christians could easily face the same pressures.

[24] From Jacob Hutter's *Letter to the Prisoners at the Hohenwart,* 1535. Cited in Walter Klaassen, ed., *Anabaptism in Outline,* 92.

[25] Thieleman J. van Braght, *Martyrs Mirror,* 12.

their own martyrdom. They did not see the persecution as merely a tussle between magistrates and disobedient citizens, but as the hatred between Darkness and Light.

Martyrdom was not just a personal matter; it had great implications for the cause of Christ. It was the greatest damage that Darkness was able to inflict on Light. But for all its bitterness, it held promise of great things to come. Though saints were killed, truth would triumph at last. This is why the martyrs could go to the stake joyfully, testifying that by their death they would give witness to the truth that they had preached. They knew that, far from being destroyed, the truth was actually spreading by the persecution. This growth was the very thing that the persecutors were trying to stamp out! Killing the Christians, which the persecutors thought was an ultimate expression of their power, was only an expression of their weakness. Taking physical life was *all they could do*. Realizing this, a political leader in the Palatinate exclaimed, "What shall I do? The more I kill, the greater becomes their number."[26]

For the Christian, death was only a doorway to a greater life. The cause of truth would grow regardless of evil men. In this spirit, Menno encouraged his suffering brethren.

> Nevertheless, my brethren, do not fear, for all your persecutors and enemies will become old like a garment no matter how mighty, how glorious and great, they may be esteemed. All flesh is as grass and all the goodliness thereof is as the flower of the field. But ye shall flourish and increase in God, and your fruit shall never wilt, for the kingdom of Jerusalem is given to you and the glorious Lord will be honored in you and He will give you, no matter how Saul may rage,[27] the

---

[26] John Horsch, *Mennonites in Europe,* 301.

[27] Menno here is comparing the suffering Christians to David under the oppressive King Saul.

eternal habitation which He has prepared and set apart from all eternity for you and for all the elect.[28]

To the Anabaptists, martyrdom was a continuation of the sufferings of Christ, the Head, in His body, the church. To be a part of Christ's body meant experiencing the suffering that the Head had faced. The world had persecuted and killed the Head; why would they do less to the body? South German Anabaptist Leonhard Schiemer put it this way:

> As soon as a man wants to begin to live as a Christian he will experience exactly those things that Christ experienced. . . . That is the lot of all Christians for the disciple is no greater than the master. For it is grace if someone for the sake of conscience suffers godly sorrow. . . . For to this you were called, since Christ also suffered for us and left us an example that you should follow in his footsteps. . . . Christ suffered in the flesh. Arm yourselves with the thought that whoever suffers in the flesh ceases from sin. . . . It is given to you that you not only believe in Christ but also suffer for him and fight the same battle.[29]

The Anabaptists saw the Lord Jesus Christ as the captain of the hosts of martyrs. The new age that Christ ushered in intensified the struggle between sin and righteousness. The enemy who thought to slay the Lord of glory now directs all his fury upon the Lord's followers. Stephen's death as a martyr, which brought this fury into full play for the first time after the Lord's crucifixion, is an example of how the Christian follows the Lord in accepting this lot and expressing love and concern for his persecutors. "[Those] who rebuke the world's shame

---

[28] *The Complete Writings of Menno Simons,* 590.

[29] From Leonhard Schiemer's *Letter to the Church at Rattenberg,* 1527. Cited in Walter Klaassen, ed., *Anabaptism in Outline,* 90.

and sin," said Menno, ". . . must with Stephen be cast out of the city and get a taste of flying stones."[30]

The Anabaptist concept of baptism and martyrdom. "True believing Christians," said Conrad Grebel, "must be baptized in anguish and tribulation, persecution, suffering, and death." The Anabaptists revived the Biblical doctrine of baptism and especially the truth that water baptism signified death to the old life, a truth not recognized by infant baptism. They realized the deep meaning behind Jesus' words in Luke 12:50: "But I have a baptism to be baptized with; and how am I straitened till it be accomplished!"[31] The Anabaptists realized, of course, that Christ's cup of suffering was far more significant than theirs. Christ was not a Christian who suffered for conscience' sake; He was God incarnate. Yet they could not help comparing their baptism of blood with His crucifixion, drawing strength from His faithful example of suffering victoriously.

"There are three that bear witness in earth," said the apostle John, "the Spirit, and the water, and the blood: and these three agree in one."[32] To the Anabaptists, this meant that the Spirit, water, and blood are the three Christian baptisms. The baptism of the Spirit comes at conversion, the Christian later publicly seals his commitment with water baptism, and later yet he gives his physical life for Christ, a baptism in blood.[33]

---

[30] *The Complete Writings of Menno Simons*, 594.

[31] Similar expressions are in Matthew 20:22 and Mark 10:38.

[32] First John 5:8.

[33] Although we understand why the Anabaptists came to this conclusion about 1 John 5:8, its meaning is not limited to their explanation. I appreciate the view that the Spirit is the Holy Spirit's work in men, the water is the written Word of God, and the blood represents Christ's sacrificial work on Calvary.

Lessons for Today

As long as the spirit of early Anabaptism remained strong, the Anabaptists held fast to the idea of the two kingdoms and preached it to those around them. That witness brought on them the full wrath of the kingdom of darkness. When they began to be silent to avoid that wrath, the dual-kingdom concept began to fade.[34]

Even after ceasing their verbal testimony, the Swiss Anabaptists preserved many of their traditional forms, which gave them the illusion of being faithful Anabaptists. But in reality, they had lost that dual-kingdom tension and Christian witness, which was the essence of faithful Anabaptism. Many Anabaptist descendants have inherited that laxity.

The true disciple of Christ will always suffer for his commitment. Scoffing, social rejection, or physical abuse are normal in the Christian life.[35] The world is uncomfortable with the church when she is truly the church. The spirit of slumber is at right angles to the spirit of holiness. The world will accept the religion of spectators, or the piety of traditional people who cause few ripples of consternation in the swamp of sin around them, but the world does not love true cross bearers.[36]

What can we learn from the Anabaptists' attitude toward martyrdom? The Anabaptists lived in fear, while

---

[34] As an example, by the end of the 1600s, some Swiss Anabaptists did not feel it was wrong to attend the state churches regularly, in order to pacify the civil authorities.

[35] Any Christian will face one or more of these trials. Although physical abuse has not been a common experience for New World Christians, it has always been the common experience in the world as a whole.

[36] Today in some areas of North America, the world respects some Christian principles. We appreciate that. We should not feel that we are not genuine Christians if our neighbors do not hate us. We do what the Bible teaches, and whether our neighbors hate us or like us is not really important. We know that they do not love the principles of true Christianity, or they would become believers too.

we live in relative security. The Anabaptists were often quite poor, while we have more than we need. The Anabaptists crouched in the cold shadows under ancient firs and sang martyr hymns, while we relax comfortably in ample, heated meetinghouses and sing about "an honored life, a peaceful end, and heaven to crown it all."[37]

It is impossible and unhealthy to try to recreate an "Anabaptist situation" for ourselves, but we should take the challenge to maintain the kind of commitment they had. The pressing cross is just as real today as it was in Anabaptist times. However, for us, those struggles usually do not have a physical element—or if they do, it is minor compared to what the Anabaptists endured. This can dim the vision of the true kingdom in our minds.

We need to hone our spiritual senses to a greater precision. Satan tried to exterminate the church by persecution, but that failed. Today he is trying to lure us away from the Remnant by religious confusion. He is trying to blur the differences between right and wrong. But God certainly knows right from wrong, and we must follow Him with the same earnest devotion that the Anabaptists expressed. Our experiences may be different, our situations may vary, but our destination can be the same.

Let us not trap ourselves by thinking that peace will always be our lot. We do not know. The true church has usually faced persecution almost everywhere. North America, where Christians have usually been free except for some wartime persecution, is an exception to the rule. We are thankful for the blessings of freedom, but it tests us at least as much as persecution would. Whether we will be faithful depends on whether we will be Christ's disciples regardless of the circumstances.

---

[37] Henry F. Lyte, "Beneath His Wings," *Church Hymnal* (Scottdale, Pa.: Mennonite Publishing House, 1927), #484.

True Christians bear the disciplines of discipleship in any age, in any surroundings.

"The disciple is not above his master, nor the servant above his lord. It is enough for the disciple that he be as his master, and the servant as his lord. If they have called the master of the house Beelzebub, how much more shall they call them of his household? Fear them not therefore: for there is nothing covered, that shall not be revealed; and hid, that shall not be known. What I tell you in darkness, that speak ye in light: and what ye hear in the ear, that preach ye upon the housetops. And fear not them which kill the body, but are not able to kill the soul: but rather fear him which is able to destroy both soul and body in hell" (Matthew 10:24–28).

"Whosoever therefore shall confess me before men, him will I confess also before my Father which is in heaven. But whosoever shall deny me before men, him will I also deny before my Father which is in heaven. Think not that I am come to send peace on earth: I came not to send peace, but a sword. For I am come to set a man at variance against his father, and the daughter against her mother, and the daughter in law against her mother in law. And a man's foes shall be they of his own household. He that loveth father or mother more than me is not worthy of me: and he that loveth son or daughter more than me is not worthy of me. And he that taketh not his cross, and followeth after me is not worthy of me. He that findeth his life shall lose it: and he that loseth his life for my sake shall find it" (Matthew 10:32–39).

"If any man come to me, and hate not his father, and mother, and wife, and children, and brethren, and sisters, yea, and his own life also, he cannot be my disciple. And whosoever doth not bear his cross, and come after me, cannot be my disciple" (Luke 14:26, 27).

Chapter 12

"Give Me Freedom for My Faith"

The Anabaptist View of the State

In 1529, the Zurich civil authorities arrested Anabaptist Hans Müller for his faith. While lying in a filthy prison, he wrote, in a letter to the city council:

> Honoured, dear sirs, I beg you in all friendliness that you would have fatherly compassion on me as a father has compassion on his children. Please do not burden my conscience since faith is a free gift of God. . . .
>
> So I beg you, you servants of God, that you will give me freedom for my faith. . . . Have compassion on my four little children and let me go home for a

little while. As you wish that men should do to you do also to them.[1]

Many an Anabaptist echoed Hans Müller's cry. The faithful Anabaptists did not wish to establish an "Anabaptist state," as was done at Münster, nor did they want to live as renegades and criminals. They simply wanted to honor their civil leaders in every matter that did not go against their faith, and be free to raise their families and spread the Gospel. In the following sections, we will explore some basic factors in the faithful Anabaptist's relationship to civil powers.

Defenseless Christians

Civil states need defense. Loyal citizens are one of their greatest assets because they help protect their country in times of national danger. Defense is not the only asset that citizens give their state; many nations appreciate peacefulness, obedience to laws, and good work ethics. In a crisis, however, the most important thing to a nation is whether its citizens will defend themselves and the nation.

Because the faithful Anabaptists would not use weapons to defend themselves or others, they did not fit into this "model citizen" stereotype. Peter Riedemann wrote in his *Account of Our Religion, Doctrine, and Faith:*

> Now since Christ, the Prince of Peace, has prepared and won for himself a kingdom, that is a church, through his own blood; in this same kingdom all worldly warfare has an end, as was promised aforetime, "Out of Zion shall go forth the law, and the word of the Lord from Jerusalem, and shall judge among the heathen and shall draw many peoples, so that they shall beat their swords into ploughshares and their lances or spears into pruning hooks, sickles and scythes, for

---

[1] *Letter of Hans Müller,* 1530. Cited in Walter Klaassen, ed., *Anabaptism in Outline,* 293.

from henceforth nation shall not lift up sword against
nation, nor shall they learn war any more.[2]

Menno Simons said:

> We teach and acknowledge no other sword, nor
> tumult in the kingdom or church of Christ than the
> sharp sword of the Spirit, God's Word. . . . But the civil
> sword we leave to those to whom it is committed.[3]

Neither Riedemann nor Simons denied that the world
would use a sword. Their point was that since Christians
follow the New Testament, they do not participate in the
world's bloodshed.

When the Anabaptists commented on the sword, they
were thinking of the persecution they experienced. They
did not think in terms of the political wars we know of,
but rather in terms of "holy war" in defense of the "Christian" faith.[4] Because of this, they often commented that
the state and its "church" should use reasoning and not
the sword to convince people of the correctness of its religion. "Only love to God through Christ shall stand and
prevail," said Felix Mantz, "not boasting, denouncing, or
threatening. It is love alone that is pleasing to God: he
that cannot show love shall not stand in the sight of God.
The true love of Christ shall not destroy the enemy; he
that would be an heir with Christ is taught that he must
be merciful, as the Father in heaven is merciful."[5]

To the Anabaptists, nonresistance was more than

---

[2] Cited in Walter Klaassen, ed., *Anabaptism in Outline*, 277.

[3] *The Complete Writings of Menno Simons*, 200.

[4] One exception to this might be found in the accusations against Michael Sattler.
When the court accused him of teaching that Christians should not fight the Turks
(Muslims), should they overrun Europe, Sattler admitted that the charge was true.
Such a war would have been both political and "holy," whereas the fight against
the Anabaptists was only a "holy war," a fight against choice making in religion.
The Reformers and Catholics said that it was a political war; but in their more honest moments, they realized that the faithful Anabaptists posed no political threat.

[5] Thieleman J. van Braght, *Martyrs Mirror*, 415.

refraining from war; it was a Biblical ideal that governed all human relationships. Whether an enemy exerted physical or mental pressure, Christians should respond with patience, meekness, and forgiveness. Jacob Hutter explained this well, as follows:

> We desire to molest no one; not to prejudice our foes, not even King Ferdinand. Our manner of life, our customs and conversation, are known everywhere to all. Rather than wrong any man of a single penny, we would suffer the loss of a hundred gulden; and sooner than strike our enemy with the hand, much less with the spear, or sword, or halbert, as the world does, we would die and surrender life.[6]

Menno Simons said:

> All of you who would fight with the sword of David, and also be the servants of the Lord, consider these words. . . . If he is not to strive, and quarrel, how then can he fight? If he is to be gentle to all men, how can he then hate and harm them? If he is to be ready to learn, how can he lay aside the apostolic weapons? He will need them. If he is to instruct in meekness those that oppose, how can he destroy them?[7]

Do such writings mean that the Anabaptists tried to convince the world that they should use nonviolent means instead of war to achieve their goals? Certainly, the Anabaptists did urge the state church to use nonviolent means of dealing with supposed spiritual transgressors. Such a plea does not seem to contradict the Scriptures. But the Anabaptists did not try to take the sword from the government. They understood Romans 13 to mean that God had ordained the government for civil order and that force was its main tool. All the faithful Anabaptists,

---

[6] Jacob Hutter, *Letter to the Vice-Regent.* Cited in Walter Klaassen, ed., *Anabaptism in Outline,* 275.

[7] *The Complete Writings of Menno Simons,* 46.

except the Hutterites, paid their taxes regardless of the way the government used the proceeds. Several quotes may clearly set forth their position.

In 1531, the Swiss Brethren said:

> According to Romans 13, the sword, the power, and the authority which is to be deployed and used in the world has been established to punish the evil and protect the good. . . . Thus the apostles taught the churches everywhere that they should not resist . . . the law insofar as it agrees with the gospel. . . . We, therefore, confess and accept the government and authority of the world because it is everywhere ordained by God. That is why taxes and duties must be paid.[8]

In 1532, Pilgram Marpeck wrote:

> I admit worldly, carnal, and earthly rulers as servants of God, in earthly matters, but not in the kingdom of Christ; according to the words of Paul, to them rightfully belongs all carnal honor, fear, obedience, tax, toll, and tribute.[9]

A major difference between the faithful Anabaptists and the fringe Anabaptists, such as the Münsterites, was that most fringe Anabaptists thought that nonresistance was commanded only until the last days. At that time, they thought, God would again command His people to destroy the ungodly with a sword, as in the Old Testament. We think of the Münsterites as quite repugnant because of their polygamy and violence, but they based their doctrine on a mixture of the Old and New Covenant principles. It was time, they thought, to take up the sword against the ungodly and return to the militant Old Testament character of God's people.[10]

---

[8] "Zofingen Colloquy," 1531. Cited in Walter Klaassen, ed., *Anabaptism in Outline,* 250, 251.

[9] *The Writings of Pilgram Marpeck,* 150.

[10] Cornelius Krahn, *Dutch Anabaptism,* 138–145.

This covenants confusion was the main reason for the Münster tragedy. The faithful Anabaptists guarded themselves against such error by realizing that the Old Testament was forever finished.[11]

Can a Christian Be a Magistrate?

The faithful Anabaptist could not be a magistrate, because he was nonresistant, but the reasons for his refusal to be a part of government went much deeper than that. In this section, we will explore these reasons.

The faithful Anabaptists rejected government involvement because they understood the Biblical dual-kingdom concept, explained in Chapter 11. The church functions within the kingdom of truth and light, but the world and its authority serves the kingdom of darkness. This does not deny that God ordains earthly government. Rather, it means that earthly government belongs to the world and will pass away with it at the end of time. The government functions within *common grace,* that is, the blessings and provisions that God generally gives to all people, saved and unsaved, to enjoy. But the government does not belong to *redemptive grace,* the privileges and blessings that accompany eternal salvation and the fellowship of saints.

There is no contradiction between the fact that God ordains the government and the fact that it belongs to the world and will pass away. God raised up Pharaoh, but this raising up did not save Pharaoh.[12] God sometimes sets up the basest of men, but setting up base men does not save them or justify them for any evil they might do while in office.[13] Pilgram Marpeck said:

---

[11] See Romans 10:4.

[12] See Romans 9:17.

[13] See Daniel 4:17.

The kingdom of Christ is not of this world. For this reason no true Christian may administer cities and protect countries. . . . that is the function of earthly and temporal rulers but never of true Christians. . . . This is what many false [Christians] have undertaken to do in our time, among them the Papists and the Evangelicals (as they call themselves). . . .

It is difficult for a Christian to be a worldly ruler. . . . And if he did, and if everything concerning the kingdom of this world was done properly according to the true human and divine order and he ruled and ordered everything without fault . . . how long would his conscience allow him to be a magistrate, assuming that he did not want to forsake the Lord Jesus Christ and Christian patience, . . . or at least that he did not want to sustain some injury to his soul or Christianity, since no one can serve two masters, that is the king or emperor in the worldly magistracy, and Christ in the spiritual, heavenly kingdom.[14]

Here Marpeck brought up the interesting question of what would happen to a magistrate who became a Christian. His conscience would soon condemn him, and he would need to leave office or leave Christ. To the Protestant argument that the best government was a Christian one, Marpeck replied:

But Saint Paul distinguishes this wisdom of the worldly magistrates from the wisdom of Christ when he says: It is not the wisdom of the rulers of this world 1 Corinthians 2:6. It is thus clear that worldly rulers have a special wisdom for their service. For Christian wisdom is not suited to their office nor will it serve them since it brings about only grace, mercy, love for the enemy, spiritual supernatural things, cross, tribulation, patience and faith in Christ without coercion . . . only through the Word of God. The wisdom of the office of

---

[14] Pilgram Marpeck, "Defence." Cited in Walter Klaassen, ed., *Anabaptism in Outline,* 263.

the worldly rulers is designed to work through the external sword in vindictiveness, mercilessness . . . and similar things. It is therefore without foundation to say that no one can exercise worldly government better than a Christian. That would imply that he needed the wisdom of Christ for it or that Christ's wisdom is his wisdom of office. Christ's wisdom is merciful and will not serve him in his office because he is not merciful in his office but rather an avenger.[15]

This logic is Scriptural. Since a Christian cannot exercise himself in a Christian way in civil office, the idea that a Christian would make the best civil leader is not valid. Peter Riedemann, a Hutterite leader, agreed.

Thus no Christian is a ruler and no ruler is a Christian, for the child of blessing cannot be the servant of wrath. . . .

. . . the power of the sword has passed to the heathen, that they may therewith punish their evildoers. But that is no concern of ours; as Paul says, "What have I to do to judge them that are without?" Thus no Christian can rule over the world.

To this someone might say, "Then according to this view, the way to life is closed to those in governmental authority!" We say, "No", for Christ says, "Come unto me all ye that are weary and heavy laden. I will refresh you and give rest unto your souls." Therefore is this free to all—to rulers as well as to subjects. . . .

Therefore if rulers divest themselves of their glory as Christ did, and humble themselves with him and allow Christ, only, to use them, then the way to life would be as open to them as to others. But when Christ begins to work in men, he does nothing except what he himself did—and he fled when men sought to make him a king.[16]

---

[15] *The Writings of Pilgram Marpeck,* 558.

[16] Peter Riedemann, *An Account of Our Religion, Doctrine, and Faith.* Cited in Walter Klaassen, ed., *Anabaptism in Outline,* 261, 262.

Riedemann came to the same conclusion as Marpeck. If a ruler began to serve Christ, he would need to flee his civil leadership.

Working for the State

In April 1525, Pilgram Marpeck became a mining magistrate in Austrian territory. A mining magistrate administered mining laws in a region, leased new mines, and settled legal controversies in the mining and smelting business. He also collected royalties for the government and kept records of the mining and financial activity.

It seems that many miners in the area Marpeck administrated became interested in Anabaptism, and through them Marpeck himself was attracted to the movement. Two years after Marpeck began his job, the authorities of his area issued a mandate against Anabaptism. By the end of 1527, the authorities instructed Marpeck to apprehend and report Anabaptists in his area, but he, perhaps already an Anabaptist himself, would not do this. In 1528, the government confiscated his property and he was forced to flee. Later in the year, he found his way to Strasbourg.

In Strasbourg, he went about his Anabaptist activities with more freedom. For his living, he worked for the city as an engineer. His labors here included forestry, mining, and engineering waterways from the nearby mountains to Strasbourg for lumber transportation. In 1532, Strasbourg banished him. Marpeck then went to St. Gall, Switzerland, where he engineered a fulling mill and likely also a water conduit around the mountains to supply the weaving business in the city. In 1544, the city of Augsburg, in Bavaria, hired Marpeck to redesign and repair their water canals. They seemed uneasy about his Anabaptism and repeatedly warned him about his religious activities. But they continued to employ him until his death in 1556.

Marpeck's convictions regarding public service seem to be among the most consistent in the Anabaptist record. His quality workmanship and engineering skills spared him from some persecution. He probably lost his first job because he refused to perform duties inconsistent with his growing convictions. However, he willingly worked for the state in public service jobs that did not violate his principles. We know of no other Swiss or South German Anabaptist who worked for the state. Due to persecution, very few of them would have had opportunities to serve the public in a Scriptural way, such as Marpeck did.

The Hutterites believed similarly, though their political situation was a bit different. They generally lived in the countryside, under benevolent estate lords. They willingly labored for these estate owners and manufactured all sorts of things for themselves as well as others, but they would not fight for the estate lord or manufacture weapons.

The Dutch Anabaptists related to civil service inconsistently in their early days. Some civil leaders became Anabaptists without quitting their offices.[17] However, it seems that conviction against holding civil offices grew. We know of no office holding in the mainstream Mennonite church from the 1550s through the late 1600s. The less traditional Waterlanders, who had divided from the mainstream Mennonite group in 1556, permitted their members to hold some civil offices by 1581.

During the last half of the 1600s and the 1700s, conviction against government offices gradually faded from the Dutch Mennonites. However, only a small number of Mennonites before 1800 actually held office. After that, participation increased.

At first, the Mennonites held only offices such as

---

[17] Franklin Hamlin Littell, *The Anabaptist View of the Church*, 105.
The Mennonite Encyclopedia, article "Anabaptist—Mennonite Attitude Toward State."

inspectors or trustees of a polder. Later they became sheriffs, ministers of finance and reclamation, burgomasters, governors, judges, and even generals of the army.

Did the Anabaptists Invent Freedom of Religion?

The Anabaptists held that civil governments were of the world and would pass away with it. These governments were composed of unbelievers and operated on non-Christian principles, so the Christian could not be a part of them. Therefore, the true church was separate from the state.

Their conviction in this regard did not spring from social considerations or from studying civil government. None of the early Anabaptists had any knowledge of societies that functioned as we have come to expect in the New World. None of them were government leaders and few, if any, were schooled in theories of government function. Their conviction on separating the church from the state sprang purely from the Biblical teaching of the place and function of the church. They commented on church and state separation in the context of pleading that *they* be allowed to have church separately.

Such statements, of course, always indicated that separating these institutions was Biblical. That inevitably meant the Reformers should separate their churches from the state too, since they claimed to be Biblical. Other than that inference, however, the Anabaptists did not champion freedom of religion as a social concept for society, but rather as a Biblical concept for the church. They would have welcomed national freedom of worship, but that was a side issue. As the true church, they practiced church and state separation and voluntary membership, not because it made sense politically, but because that was the pattern of Biblical church life.

The Anabaptists did not invent the separation of church

and state; they derived it from the Bible. In that, they followed the pattern of faithful believers throughout the Middle Ages. The Anabaptists' greatest contribution to the world was their faithful example of Christian discipleship, not freedom of religion and separation of church and state.

Nevertheless, they did make a contribution to this concept. The fact that they refused to go away, that they did not die out, and that they continued to resist the prevailing state church patterns made them an influence that pushed toward greater tolerance in society. Except for their refusal to bow to the state in religious matters, they were usually model citizens. Some governments tolerated them because they benefited the country despite their religious differences. Civil powers slowly discovered that differing religious beliefs did not have to produce social disorder.

Every sect of the Reformers, and the Catholics, would have continued to persecute minorities if the increasingly irreligious civil leaders had not stopped them. The mainline Reformers did not champion religious freedom. True, some of their writings contain pleas for religious freedom, but *the Reformers only pleaded for freedom while they personally faced oppression.* John Robinson, a Puritan minister, described the situation this way:

> Protestants living in the countries of papists commonly plead for toleration of religions: so do papists that live where Protestants bear sway: though few of either, especially of the clergy . . . would have the other tolerated, where the world goes on their side.[18]

When Luther faced excommunication and possible death for his beliefs, he said:

> Princes are not to be obeyed when they command submission to superstitious errors, but their aid is not to be invoked in support of the Word of God. . . .

---

[18] M. Searle Bates, *Religious Liberty: An Inquiry* (New York, N.Y.: International Missionary Council, 1945), 155.

> I say, then, neither pope, nor bishop, nor any man whatever has the right of making one syllable binding on a Christian man, unless it be done with his own consent. Whatever is done otherwise is done in the spirit of tyranny. . . . I cry aloud on behalf of liberty and conscience, and I proclaim with confidence that no kind of law can with any justice be imposed on Christians, except so far as they themselves will; for we are free from all.[19]

This sounds rather lawless, but Luther was speaking of religious laws, not of civil laws designed to keep national order. Later, however, when Luther had gained the protection of some lords and was fairly sure of the success of his program, he stated:

> Heretics are not to be disputed with, but to be condemned unheard, and whilst they perish by fire, the faithful ought to pursue the evil to its source, and bathe their hands in the blood of the Catholic bishops, and of the Pope, who is a devil in disguise.[20]

To the Duke of Saxony, he wrote:

> It will lie heavy on your conscience if you tolerate the Catholic worship; for no secular prince can permit his subjects to be divided by the preaching of opposite doctrines.[21]

John Calvin, in his early years, asserted that the church

> has no power of the sword to punish or to coerce, no authority to compel, no prisons, fines, or other punishments, like those inflicted by the civil magistrate. Besides, the object of this power is, not that he who has transgressed may be punished against his will, but that he may profess his repentance by a voluntary submission to chastisement. The difference therefore is very great; because the Church does not assume to

---

[19] Leo Pfeffer, *Church, State, and Freedom* (Boston: The Beacon Press, 1953), 21.

[20] Ibid., 21.

[21] Ibid., 21.

itself what belongs to the magistrate, nor can the magistrate execute that which is executed by the Church.[22]

However, when Calvin had established his church in Geneva, he made absence from worship services a crime. If someone missed Communion, the city could banish him for one year. Criticizing church leaders was considered blasphemy, and blasphemy was punishable by death. Calvin wrote:

> Whoever shall now contend that it is unjust to put heretics and blasphemers to death, will, knowingly and willingly, incur their very guilt. This is not laid down on human authority; it is God that speaks and prescribes a perpetual rule for His Church.[23]

The Reformation period was an unprecedented[24] outburst of cruelty and intolerance, in which both Catholics and Protestants participated. The Reformation as a whole represented no progress for freedom of religion. It actually arrested any tendencies toward religious freedom. Because of it, fighting over religion became a significant part of European life for the next century and a half. The freedom of religion that finally prevailed in Europe was due, not to the churches, but to the government leaders' increasing feeling that religion was not worth fighting over.[25]

When settlers came to the New World, most colonies and towns adopted the religion of the majority and persecuted those who did not agree with them, in the same pattern as the Old World. Early colonists used

---

[22] Ibid., 22

[23] Ibid., 22.

[24] I say *unprecedented* because a number of sources agree that the persecution against the true church was more fierce during the Reformation than at any other time in history. And not only was there persecution against the true church, but also parties within the nominal church persecuted each other dreadfully.

[25] In a sense, the Reformation did provide a gain for the concept of religious freedom in that the Reformation escalated religious conflict, which eventually served to make political leaders aggravated at religious conflict.

execution,[26] whippings, and other punishments for dissenters. Many people, such as the Puritan settlers who populated parts of New England from 1630 on, came to the New World to find religious freedom *for themselves.* In their settlements, however, many of them actively persecuted any dissenters. This included the Dutch settlements in New York, the Catholic settlements in Maryland,[27] and the Anglican settlements in the South. A number of areas fined any parents who had scruples against infant baptism. However, this persecution changed because of the rising tide of nationalism in the colonies, the growing number of people who cared for no particular religion at all, the increasing distaste for persecution, and the evident success of free colonies such as Pennsylvania[28] and Rhode Island. From 1650 on, persecution was on the decline, but vestiges of it persisted until it was effectively ended by the First Amendment in 1791.[29] A close study of American history shows that separation of church and state came about because religion became too unimportant to fight over. It was not

---

[26] In New England, the Puritans executed four Quakers. In Virginia, the Anglican state church established the death penalty for impious speaking, blasphemy, or Sabbath breaking. The Catholic government of Maryland imposed the death penalty on blasphemy and atheistic speaking. See Leo Pfeffer, *Church, State, and Freedom,* 63–75.

[27] Later, Maryland changed to Protestant hands. The oppression remained for the segment without political power.

[28] William Penn did not begin his colonization until the late 1600s. A few Dutch Mennonites were in New York as early as the 1640s. The first Mennonite settlements of any size, however, did not begin until the late 1600s and early 1700s. These settlements were all in Pennsylvania, where the settlers could practice their religion freely.

[29] This era of persecution is not discussed in many elementary or secondary history textbooks. To help substantiate it, I quote from Leo Pfeffer, *Church, State, and Freedom,* (81, 82), a respected history on religious freedom.

In August 1700 the province of New York enacted a law under which any Jesuit, priest, or other ecclesiastic ordained by the Pope who remained in the province after November 1, 1700, teaching or practicing Catholic doctrines or rites or granting absolutions "shall be deemed and accounted an incendiary and disturber of the public peace and safety and an enemy of the true Christian religion and shall be adjudged to suffer perpetual banishment."

brought about by Americans rallying to the Bible doctrine of separating the true church from the civil government. Historians agree that the percent of Americans belonging to any church was very low at the founding of the nation, likely no more than four percent.

The most plausible link from Anabaptism to American religious freedom is in the Baptist movement. London became an Anabaptist refuge haven in the late 1530s. The Anabaptist church did not continue in England, but the ideas they deposited there may have influenced the rise of John Smyth's separatist congregation, from which the first Baptist churches came. Later, John Smyth and part of his church applied for membership in the Mennonite Church in Amsterdam. The remainder of Smyth's church did not agree with the Mennonite views of war and the oath. They began the General Arminian Baptist Church in London around 1610. The Calvinistic Baptists began independently about thirty years after this.

The Baptist groups in America were the most active of all religious bodies in their struggle for religious freedom. They had a European background of separatism

---

In 1704 Maryland forbade Roman Catholic priests to baptize children, and in 1716 imposed severe penalties on public officials who participated in the mass after taking an oath of office. As late as the eve of the Revolution, the governor of Pennsylvania, the only colony that did not interfere with the public exercise of Catholic rites, expressed the opinion that such practice was illegal even in that colony.

Nor were Catholics the only victims of colonial restrictions on religious liberty. In Virginia up to the time of the Revolution, denial of the Trinity was punishable by imprisonment for three years, and a Unitarian or freethinker could be adjudged an unfit custodian of his own children. Baptists, particularly during the "period of the Great Persecution," 1768 to 1774, were whipped, beaten, arrested, fined, and imprisoned, sometimes on bread and water. In 1774 Madison wrote to a friend: "That diabolical, hell-conceived principle of persecution rages among some. . . . This vexes me the worst of anything whatever. There are at this time in the adjacent county not less than five or six well-meaning men in close jail for publishing their religious sentiments, which in the main are very orthodox."

This Madison was James Madison (1751–1836), also known as "The Father of the Constitution."

and hostility toward church and state unions. Part of this background came from their associations with Anabaptist fugitives in England and the Mennonites in Holland.

Lessons for Today

We live in a different climate than our Anabaptist brethren did. They had no experience in religious freedom or with a government that allows its citizens many personal freedoms. Most Mennonites now believe that it is unnecessary and impossible to view government as the Anabaptists did. We live in such a different situation, they reason, that we have different opportunities and responsibilities. That is partly true. *But it in no way erases the Bible doctrine of the Christian's noninvolvement with the political realm.*

The faithful Anabaptists strongly resisted the Protestant view of government as long as they faced persecution and for some time thereafter. Eventually, however, ideological pressure from Protestantism changed this, first in Europe and later in America. This process outlines the danger we face. If we presently paid for our beliefs with our blood, the pressure to slowly or slightly change our views probably would not be as great. We would either be a Christian or not be a Christian. But since we face tremendous ideological pressure from Christendom to change our views, we are in danger of unconsciously injecting worldly concepts into the Bible principles we hold.[30]

---

[30] Democracy brings many blessings to the Remnant in the New World, but it also poses some dangers. In America, unless there is a very strong reason to oppose the majority opinion, it always prevails. For the Remnant, the dangerous factor in the rule of the majority is not that it might at some point actively persecute minorities, but that in times of freedom it can break the Remnant's inner will to resist spiritual decay. The rule of the majority can condition the church to believe that might is right and that numbers are a solid platform for doctrinal decisions. Every church that has not actively and positively held up the Bible as superior to public opinion has degenerated to the moral level of the masses.

The faithful Anabaptists did not share John Calvin's hope of using the government to eradicate moral evil. They understood government as necessary because evil, selfish men will frequently trample down others in society to gain their own ends. They realized that the magistrate, bearing a sword and executing wrath upon civil lawbreakers, was a servant employed by God in His common-grace plan (Romans 13:4). They also knew that God taught men redemptive truths through the Bible and His people, *not* through the unredeemed civil government. Peter Riedemann said:

> Therefore the government is a picture, sign and reminder of man's departure from God, and ought well to be to all men an urge to retire within themselves and to consider to what they have come and to what they have fallen, that they might with all the more haste turn back to God to receive again the grace they had lost.[31]

We tend to translate the Biblical truth about the government repressing evil to mean that the government should support Christian ideals. We are sometimes too optimistic about the idea of government improving moral conditions in society. Several areas of concern are as follows:

We should not make supportive or nonsupportive statements about candidates for political office. The Bible is clear that elections are in God's hand and that He does as He wills in the kingdoms of men. It is impossible to avoid contemplating who, in our opinion, is most morally fit for an office, but we must leave such choices in God's hands. The Bible and history show that God does not necessarily choose political leaders by their moral qualities. Despite

---

[31] Peter Riedemann, *An Account of Our Religion, Doctrine, and Faith.* Cited in Walter Klaassen, ed., *Anabaptism in Outline,* 259.

the clamor of Christendom, God has never yet asked for their advice about His doings in the worldly kingdoms.

Every statement of true Christians should support God's standard for us, which is

> "Let every soul be subject unto the higher powers. For there is no power but of God: the powers that be are ordained of God. Whosoever therefore resisteth the power, resisteth the ordinance of God: and they that resist shall receive to themselves damnation" (Romans 13:1, 2).

We should call the world to salvation through Jesus Christ, rather than expecting to improve the world through political legislation. Nominal Christianity tries to increase national morality through legislation. However, the New Testament, the example of Christ, and the example of the early church do not support such an approach.[32]

Christians testify of salvation; they do not tell unbelievers how to function better while remaining in their sin. Our message to all non-Christians is "Ye must be born again" (John 3:7). Christians are not primarily social restorers; they are bearers of the Word of Life. When people accept God's Word and will, they become socially restored, but that happens after salvation. Christians are called to be ambassadors for Christ, "as though God did beseech [men] by us: we pray you in Christ's stead, be ye reconciled to God" (2 Corinthians 5:20).

Every attempt at national moral therapy places the Christian in a realm where he has no authority to speak. Every attempt at changing the conduct of people instead of presenting them with the heart-changing Word dilutes the Gospel and defeats the purpose of the true church.

---

[32] God has ordained the government to keep order and subdue evil. It is a benefit to Christianity when the government does this. But to expect to "Christianize" a nation through political means is not a Scriptural approach.

It leads to viewing Christianity as simply practicing good morals. The church will maintain within itself the standard of righteousness it tells the world is acceptable. If we give up on calling people to the full New Testament message because few respond, and switch to promoting such external morals as the Ten Commandments represent, the spiritual condition of our churches will soon reflect that ideology.

We should not put pressure on the government to use New Testament principles in deciding political issues, such as capital punishment. Some Bible principles are useful for civil government, and the Old Testament contained specific advice for Israel's government. The New Testament, however, contains no formulas for successful civil government. It expressly places involvement in government outside the Christian's field. Even Romans 13 contains no direction to civil rulers as to how they should carry out their office. It simply informs the Christian that God has planned that unsaved persons maintain civil order. Whether they use methods such as capital punishment is their business, not ours. Christians do not have Biblical support for instructing the government on such matters.

Civil government methods are only employed by those who have rejected Christ. Such methods are symbols of the fallen nature, not signs of righteousness. The fact that God has ordained (arranged, determined, set up) civil power does not mean that there are righteous ways of handling civil power. God knew that some people would reject salvation, and He knew that such people would be selfish, monopolize others, and naturally become anarchists. So He established a plan to maintain a degree of social justice. In this plan, God uses unsaved people to maintain law and order, thus making a tolerable situation for His creation. God's relationship to civil government is basically impersonal utilization. Impersonal utilization is not eternal salvation.

Christendom tries to control morality through civil means because they have failed to uphold the truth in their own assemblies. They have diluted the Gospel and rendered themselves savorless salt. Now they turn to human government to do what the church should have done through Christian influence.

The Remnant who takes God at His Word will flourish. Wherefore, brethren and sisters, "lift up thy prayer for the remnant that is left" (Isaiah 37:4).

> "Blessed are ye, when men shall revile you, and persecute you, and shall say all manner of evil against you falsely, for my sake. Rejoice, and be exceeding glad: for great is your reward in heaven: for so persecuted they the prophets which were before you.
>
> "Ye are the salt of the earth: but if the salt have lost his savour, wherewith shall it be salted? it is thenceforth good for nothing, but to be cast out, and to be trodden under foot of men. Ye are the light of the world. A city that is set on an hill cannot be hid. Neither do men light a candle, and put it under a bushel, but on a candlestick; and it giveth light unto all that are in the house. Let your light so shine before men, that they may see your good works, and glorify your Father which is in heaven" (Matthew 5:11–16).
>
> "Then he answered and spake unto me, saying, This is the word of the LORD unto Zerubbabel, saying, Not by might, nor by power, but by my spirit, saith the LORD of hosts. Who art thou, O great mountain? before Zerubbabel thou shalt become a plain: and he shall bring forth the headstone thereof with shoutings, crying, Grace, grace unto it. . . . For who hath despised the day of small things?" (Zechariah 4:6, 7, 10).

Part Three
Appendixes

Appendix I

Anabaptist Origins

What hat medieval roots, if any, did Anabaptism have? Can we physically trace the faithful Remnant back to the apostles' time or to Constantine's time, or did Anabaptism begin in 1525?

Since this specialized treatise does not fit into the general run of the main chapters of this book, I have included it as an appendix. For deeper study, you can refer to the books listed in the footnotes.

Of special note is Leonard Verduin's work, The Reformers and Their Stepchildren. *With Mr. Verduin's permission, I have adapted and condensed some of his material for the section entitled "Tracing Medieval Currents of Religious Dissent."*

Two Prominent Views

The view of Zurich origin. Some Mennonite and Protestant historians have taught that Anabaptism originated in 1525 in the Zurich area. This view is characterized by statements such as

> The rise of the Anabaptist group in Zollikon was the birth of a brotherhood of a purely religious character.
>
> The young plant was soon violently suppressed, but that does not decrease its significance. In Zollikon a new type of Church had begun to differentiate itself, the Free Church type. Zollikon is the cradle of this idea, which from here entered upon its triumphal march through four centuries and through the whole world. *(Fritz Blanke)*[1]

When the thoroughgoing Reformation supporters realized that Luther and Zwingli[2] were not fully returning to the New Testament church pattern, they left those men and gathered a pure church, free from civil control. When they did this, they became the originators, according to some historians, of a new movement.

In favor of this theory is the fact that wherever Anabaptism arose, there seemed to be some influence from the Zurich group. The connection may be firsthand or secondhand or even more obscure, but when studying the origins of Anabaptism in particular areas, one generally finds a link back to the Zurich area.[3]

The view of pre-Reformation origin. This view holds that Anabaptism was an outgrowth or resurgence of medieval anti-Catholic movements. The following quotations are examples of this theory.

> In the twelve centuries that went before the Reformation it has never lacked for attempts to get away

---

[1] Franklin Hamlin Littell, *The Anabaptist View of the Church,* 1.

[2] Here Luther and Zwingli are mentioned together. Remember, however, that there were conflicts between these Reformers. They began separate churches in separate countries. They represented different factions of the Protestant Reformation. They argued over doctrinal differences and had a cold relationship.

[3] This is true of the Dutch Anabaptists as well as the Swiss/German groups. See Chapter 6 for more information.

from the State-Church Priests' Church and to rein-
stitute the apostolic congregational structurization.[4]

The Protestant Left[5] was the heir of the medieval
underworld. It had categories of thought and a vocabulary emerging from late medieval heresies . . . , a
vocabulary which pre-existed the Reformation and had
its own power and momentum quite apart from Luther.[6]

Supporters of this view point out that there was resistance to the Catholic Church throughout much of the Middle Ages. They believe that these grassroots convictions
sprang forth in the Reformation and came to be known
as the Anabaptist movement.

Many medieval records of martyrs and their beliefs
seem to support this view. Many of the documented beliefs
sound exactly or nearly like the concepts the Anabaptists taught. Catholic arguments against medieval dissenters are also quite similar to what the Catholics of the
Reformation threw at the Anabaptists.

This view has been supported by many historians and,
to some degree, by Anabaptist traditions.[7] Some recent
students of this theory teach that through these medieval

---

[4] Adolf von Harnack, *Texte und Untersuchungen zur Geschichte der Altchristliche Literatur* (Leipzig, 1886). Cited in Leonard Verduin, *The Reformers and Their Stepchildren,* 35.

[5] The term *Protestant Left* is sometimes used in reference to the Anabaptists. In political terms, the *left* is a faction that wishes to go further and faster than the *center,* and much further and faster than the *right.* Generally, the left is liberal, or radical, in moral and economic policies, when compared with the past. Since the Anabaptists were considered radicals, they are sometimes referred to as the Protestant Left or the left wing of the Reformation. Since the Reformation was swinging away from the Catholic Church, that can be considered the right wing. Protestant historians consider the mainline Reformers "the center." These terms refer to where one stood in the spectrum of religion, but they do not adequately describe the doctrinal positions of the Catholics, Reformers, and Anabaptists.

[6] Gordon Rupp, *Archiv für Reformationsgeschichte,* Vol. IV (1958). Cited in Leonard Verduin, *The Reformers and Their Stepchildren,* 35, 36.

[7] Some Anabaptists did not appreciate that the Reformers and Catholics threw them into a mold with all the "heretics" of generations past. Sometimes they denied that they were connected with the previous "heretics," which was true as

"heretics," the true church can be physically traced back to the apostolic days. Along with this, some teach that the beginning of Anabaptism was back around the time of Constantine rather than in the 1500s.

A careful evaluation of history seems to show that there are some elements of truth in both theories. Now we will look at medieval resistance to the Catholic Church, see how the Reformation contributed to the rise of Anabaptism, and then draw some conclusions about Anabaptist origins.

Tracing Medieval Currents of Religious Dissent

Before the Reformation had progressed very far, the mainline Reformers realized that they faced not only a duel with the Catholics but also a severe struggle with another Reformation faction, Anabaptism. Zwingli testified that his struggle with the Catholics was "but child's play" when compared with his fight with the Anabaptists.

In this three-sided struggle, the Reformers and the Catholics used much the same arsenal against the Anabaptists. Both of them heaped derisive names on the Anabaptists, indicating that they were "heretics."[8] Many of these names or terms were used long before the Anabaptist movement, as we know it, came to the foreground. When we understand what those names meant in medieval times, it will help us to evaluate Anabaptism's spiritual roots. In the following paragraphs, we will look at six of these names.

---

far as a physical link was concerned. They had a more completely Biblical message than some of the previous "heretics," so it is understandable that they did not want to be considered the same as everyone who went before them. But in general, most Anabaptists recognized a kinship between their teachings and those of previous "heretic" movements.

[8] To be a heretic was to disagree with the prevailing religious ideas. It was good that the Anabaptists were that kind of heretics because the Bible did not agree with the prevailing religious ideas either.

Neo-Donatists. Numerous times, the Reformers and Catholics referred to the Anabaptists as Donatists or neo-Donatists (new Donatists). Among other things, the fourth-century Donatists held that the Roman integration of church and state was wrong. They were named for one of their prominent leaders, Donatus (died c. 355).

When Constantine legalized Christianity, he brought it under his civil authority. The mainline church accepted this new "advantage" to its cause and adjusted its doctrine to fit the new order of things. As the "church" and state melded into one, this view no longer fit. So theologians invented the idea that God had ushered in a new era for the church. In this new era, basic New Testament truths, such as voluntary conversion and nonresistance, were no longer necessary.[9] The new, powerful church no longer heeded the truths that had originally guided it.[10]

The idea that a whole society may be made Christian sounds ideal but is impossible due to man's nature. Some men in every society will refuse personal regeneration.

---

[9] This process of apostasy had begun long before the church was liberated from persecution, of course. What we see here is the culmination of that process in an unprecedented slide away from truth.

[10] The theologian Augustine used Jesus' parable of the great supper (Luke 14) to support the new order. In the parable, some of the guests voluntarily refused to accept the supper invitation, so the lord's servant went out and gathered others to fill the house. When that was done, there was still room in the house, so the lord commanded the servant to *compel* more to come. Augustine saw this progression as a foundation for the church to use physical force in enlarging its borders. He said the apostolic time was the first era of the church, in which the church suffered and men joined it voluntarily. But now God's will had changed—the suffering church was blossoming into its real element. It was time for the church to compel people into its fold. Augustine believed that on this basis men could be forced into the church, and the Catholic Church acted on this belief.

However, a cursory examination of this parable and its context will disprove Augustine's interpretation. In the verses following, Jesus plainly taught that there would be some men who would forsake all and become His disciples, and there would be some who would follow their own devices. Jesus did not expect that all men would follow Him. The entire New Testament depicts the church as a voluntary unit. And the New Testament church vision can be fulfilled only in a voluntary unit of regenerated individuals.

Those who do so place themselves outside the true church. So when the church tries to embrace everyone, she loses her New Testament character. She becomes a pseudo church, an impostor, that neither looks nor functions like the original. The people of God always reject such arrangements and regroup in a voluntary, regenerated, and holy body—the true church.

That was what the Donatists did.[11] One of their main emphases was resisting the melding of church and society that took place under Constantine and Theodosius. They refused to believe that a divinely authorized change had taken place in the nature of the church.[12] The Donatists saw the change as nothing more than a new tactic of the devil. Previously he had inspired the state to persecute the church; now he had gained strong allies in the church. The true Christians experienced persecution under both regimes.

True Christians throughout the following centuries vigorously resisted the adulterous state–church marriage. Every century saw blood shed for this resistance. When the Reformation began, a segment of the population had already been resisting the state church idea, at least mentally. This segment welcomed the Reformation with open arms and immediately identified themselves with outspoken leaders such as Luther and Zwingli. Soon, however, many of them were disappointed. The Reformers did not completely, Biblically reform the false church system. They simply set up another state church system in place of the old.

---

[11] There were fanatic fringes among the Donatists who held some strange doctrines. These fringes gave rise to the charges many historians lay at their feet.

[12] A quote from Augustine makes it clear that the nature of the church was the real issue between the Donatists and the Catholics. "The issue between us and the Donatists is about the question where this body is to be located, that is, what and where is the church?" From *Ad Catholicos Epistula II*. Cited in Leonard Verduin, *The Reformers and Their Stepchildren*, 33.

The Catholic and Protestant leaders of the 1500s understood that the state church was the heart of medieval culture. They saw that to destroy that concept would loosen their grip on society. They thought that this would mean the end of orderly society. So instead of completely following the New Testament, the Protestant Reformers resorted to establishing a new, "purified" state church.

Initially the mainline Reformation leaders *wanted* a church free from civil control. They *wanted* a church that comprised only the regenerated instead of the whole population. But they refused to pay the price to identify with such a church. Consequently, there was an exodus from their ranks. Those who would follow only New Testament doctrine organized a church that left the state out of the picture.

It is no wonder, then, that the Anabaptists were sometimes called Donatists. They followed a tradition of over a thousand years of resistance against the state church, and so they were considered both national and religious traitors.

Stäbler. We noticed that when the state entered the church, it brought its carnal weapons along. To please its new consort, the fallen church invented a few hollow "Scriptural" reasons why the sword could stay.[13] It not only stayed, but it became the badge of the church,

---

[13] Once again, Augustine convinced himself and others that this departure from the New Testament pattern was valid. When the Donatists insisted on separating themselves from the mainstream church, that church attacked them with the sword. The Donatists pointed out that this action was not in line with Jesus' teaching. He had not forced anyone to follow Him; in fact, when many were leaving Him, He asked the disciples, "Will ye also go away?" (John 6:67). Augustine rejoined, "I hear that you are quoting that which is recorded in the Gospel, that when the seventy followers went back from the Lord they were left to their own choice in this wicked and impious desertion and that He said to the twelve remaining 'Do you not also want to go?' But what you fail to say is that at that time the Church was only just beginning to burst forth from the newly planted seed and that the saying

obscuring the cross that had once held that honor.

True Christians in medieval times held to Biblical non-resistance. Instead of carrying swords as men of the world did, they often carried wooden staffs or canes. The harmless staff symbolized their reliance on God instead of the sword. Many of these nonresistant people became known as *Stäbler,* that is, *staff carriers.*

The Donatists carried canes to declare their convictions. The Scotch-Irish in northwest Europe, who resisted state church encroachment for many years, carried staffs to distinguish themselves from the Catholic priests. The Waldensians believed that one should not confess his sins to Catholic priests, but to cane-carrying preachers. The Bohemian Brethren, who organized in 1457, carried canes or wooden swords to show that the steel sword does not belong in the Christian's hand. Staff carrying also marked the Anabaptists. In the Reformation especially, staff carrying was a sure sign of a "heretic."

Nonresistance, then, was not an idea the Anabaptists originated. The early church and many medieval Christians had taught it before them.

Cathar. The name *Cathar* was also applied to the Anabaptists. The word *cathar* means "cleansed" or "pure." The original Cathars lived around the 1100s. According to their accusers, they held the false belief of dualism, which taught that all matter is evil and everything spiritual is good.[14]

---

had not as yet been fulfilled in her "All kings shall fall down before Him, all nations shall serve him." It is in proportion to the more enlarged fulfillment of this prophecy that the Church now wields greater power—so that she may now not only invite but also compel men to embrace that which is good." (*Letter to Donatus,* No. 173. Cited in Leonard Verduin, *The Reformers and Their Stepchildren,* 65, 66.)

[14] This accusation was commonly levied against heretics by the Catholics and comes from the early Gnostic beliefs. In some cases, however, it seems that the "heretics" simply taught against the sins of the flesh and believed in Christian victory over them. This was interpreted as dualism by Catholic historians and theologians.

The Cathars also believed that one should advance toward becoming perfect.[15] Some of them believed that a person could become completely perfect in this life, and all of them believed that the Catholic Church needed much purifying. When "heretics" questioned the sin that the mainstream church sheltered, the church often branded them as Cathars. *Cathar* became so synonymous with heretics that both the High and Low German words for *heretic* were derived from *cathar,* though it originally meant the opposite of *heretic.*

Some of the Cathars held false beliefs.[16] Others, however, believed much like the Anabaptists in areas such as loving their enemies, not swearing oaths, caring for the sick and poor, and trusting that God would overcome evil without His people resorting to physical force. They strongly criticized the Catholic Church; and for this, their blood was shed.

To the Catholics, the term *Cathar* came to mean "someone who believed in living a perfect or nearly perfect life." It represented a belief that a Christian should live a regenerate life—that he should be a different man after conversion. Since the Catholic Church was far from this condition and belief, the Cathars represented an intolerable challenge to them. That the Cathars held some unbiblical beliefs did not really concern the Catholics, for they held quite a few unscriptural positions themselves.[17] The

---

[15] They emphasized moral purity especially, to the point that some of them felt that marriage was a step away from perfection.

[16] In general, these were the result of carrying Biblical teachings to unscriptural extremes.

[17] Examples of Catholic disregard for the Scriptures can be found all through history. Here is a modern example from a Catholic encyclopedia. "From the very beginning the Church has administered the Sacrament of Baptism to infants. Not only was this practice considered lawful, but it was also taught to be absolutely necessary for salvation. . . . It makes little difference whether Scripture has any actual references to the practice of infant Baptism or not. Probably it can be conceded that no explicit references are to be found there." (*New Catholic Encyclopedia,* 1967, article "Baptism of Infants.")

real problem was that the Cathars believed that the Catholic Church was not the true church. That divided society, and anything that divided religious loyalties brought down the wrath of the state church.

Holy Christian living was a mark of many "heretics" from Constantine on. When the church married the state, the conduct of the unsaved masses became the conduct of the church. Since conversion and a voluntary commitment to holiness are prerequisite to Christian conduct, consistent Christian conduct cannot exist in a state church setting. In that setting, partaking in the prescribed ceremonies supposedly brings salvation; therefore, Christian conduct is considered unnecessary and even harmful to the religious order because it is out of the ordinary.

Throughout medieval times, anyone with consistent Christian conduct was suspected of heresy. Virtuous women who refused to be immoral with their priests were sometimes suspected of heresy and were burned. The punishment for a priest who had committed some transgression was that he could not attend drunken parties for one year. Good conduct was forced on him as a punishment for wrongdoing. Obviously, the average priest was not expected to have good conduct most of the time.

When the Anabaptist movement arose, they were at once labeled "heaven stormers" and "works saints" by both the Catholics and Reformers. They were blamed for believing that man is justified by works and that the church on earth can be perfect. These were false charges, but they did believe in a Christian walk and in growing in grace. The Reformers and Catholics complained that "heretical" holiness ideas from ancient sects were gaining popularity. The state church sentiment against Christian living became so strong that not even a Reformer or Catholic could live a decent, moral life without being suspected of Anabaptist "heresy." Once again, an ancient characteristic of "heretics" became a distinguishing mark of the Anabaptists.

Sacramentschwarmer. In English, the word is *Sacramentarians,*[18] and it refers to people who do not believe that salvation is received by partaking of Communion and the other Biblical ordinances.[19] Sacramentarians believe that the ordinances are symbols of a spiritual relationship with God, whereas Catholics teach that a right standing with God is achieved by performing rituals.

The state churches did not tolerate such beliefs, because they wanted entire populations to worship at the same shrine. They could not expect people to voluntarily appear at one altar, because not everyone would make the same choice as to whom they would serve. They had to force people to comply with the state cult. Outward ceremonies, such as baptism and Communion, were necessary so that people could give evidence that they were complying. No inner loyalty or change was needed or expected. To not take part in the expected manner brought social rejection and political oppression.

Many medieval "heretics" and the Anabaptists rejected the Catholic view of salvation by ceremony performance. They believed that "faith cometh by hearing, and hearing by the word of God."[20] In 1025, some "heretics" from Italy were arrested because they testified that "there are

---

[18] Those who believe that salvation comes through performance of ceremonies are called sacramentalists, while those who oppose that ideology are known as Sacramentarians. Thus, two words that look almost the same stand for opposite meanings.

[19] *Ordinances* is better than *sacraments* for the Scriptural symbols we observe, such as Communion and Feet Washing. *Sacraments* denotes ordinances or rites that are a means of obtaining salvation. Since this is a false concept, we should not use the term in relation to the New Testament ordinances. We observe them in remembrance of Christ and as symbols of spiritual truths.

[20] Romans 10:17.

no sacraments in the holy Church by which one can attain unto salvation."[21] These believers further testified that they believed in practicing nonresistance, showing charity to others, and working to provide for their own needs. They said that if their lives were right, the work of baptism was nothing,[22] and if their lives were carnal, baptism would not make them right.

About 1045, Berengarius, a Catholic Church leader in France, questioned transubstantiation (the Catholic view that the Communion emblems turn into the body and blood of Christ when the priest mutters the "magic" words of the mass). This view was vital to the Catholics because it placed tremendous importance upon partaking of Communion. The church excommunicated Berengarius for his daring remarks and accused him of resurrecting ancient heresies. Just how old this "heresy" was we do not know, but doubts about Catholic sacramental teaching had evidently risen long before.

In the 1100s, more "heretics," followers of Tanchelm, arose who proclaimed that the Catholic sacraments were of no saving value. They held that the true church of Christ did not dwell in the Catholic Church. According to some sources, Tanchelm's teaching took root in many areas of Europe and continued until the Reformation. It was a grassroots influence that helped the Reformation spread quickly.

Some Waldensians were Sacramentarians. In Flanders, in the 1400s, large, underground Sacramentarian churches held as their central doctrine that the emblems of Communion do not transubstantiate. Some of these

---

[21] Leonard Verduin, *The Reformers and Their Stepchildren,* 143.

[22] In saying this, the "heretics" likely meant that it was not an agent of salvation. In their fight with Catholic theology, "heretics" tended to overstate their points. The Scriptures teach the necessity of believer's baptism as a testimony as an inner experience. See Mark 16:16; Acts 2:41; 8:12, 36–38; and 10:47, 48.

Sacramentarians paid for this belief with their lives. In the minds of the Catholics and Reformers, the Anabaptists fit squarely into this ancient "heresy" of Sacramentarianism.

Winckler. This term referred to people who gathered in corners or secluded places. "Heretics" did not usually gather in public places to worship, for there was usually no public place that tolerated their kind of worship. This gave rise to calling the people *Winckler,* and their assemblies *Winckel preachings.* Religious and political leaders often threw these terms at true believers to condemn their actions as illegal.

Why were leaders so concerned about *Winckel preachings*? As has been indicated, the state church maintained itself by forcing all society to bow to one shrine. Any worship not in the designated pattern was looked upon as civil insurrection. And *Winckel preachings* were not in the designated pattern. Whether they were actually heretical was not always of great concern to the Catholics and Reformers. That these assemblies appeared to be agitations against the prescribed order brought persecution upon them.

Winckler were common for over a thousand years before the Reformation.[23] The early church in Rome faced accusations of insurrection from the pagans because of their secret gatherings. Roman society allowed the worship of many gods, and they allowed everyone to consider his particular god the first among equals. The Romans built places of public worship for each god. If this sounds tolerant, we must consider two other aspects: the Romans allowed no gods whose worship discriminated against

---

[23] Here *Winckler* are referred to as a type of people. The actual German term *Winckler* was used in lands of the German tongue. Other tongues accused Christians of the same thing in their own languages.

other gods, and they allowed no private worship. Worship had to be *to* one of the legal gods and *in* a legal, public cult building.

Thus, Christianity was illegal because the one true God cannot be worshiped as the first among equals. Where He enters, all other gods must leave. To such an intolerant God, the Romans would not construct a place of worship, nor were they asked to. Since the Christian religion does not depend on civil sanction, the Roman Christians did not waste their time in getting approval for their gatherings. Thus they brought upon themselves the persecution that private worship generates in a state church society.

When the Catholic state church formed, it gave private worship the same ill-treatment. The Donatists could not be tolerated because they refused to worship in the legal manner prescribed by the mainstream church. Hilary of Poitiers[24] bemoaned that Christians were gathering in beautiful public edifices. He said, "We do wrong in venerating the Church of God in roofs and structures. Is it doubtful that the Antichrist will sit there? Safer to me the mountains and the woods, the lakes and the caves and the whirlpools; for in these, either hidden by them or sunken in them, did the prophets prophesy."[25]

Weavers' workshops became common places of *Winckel preaching*. In 1157, the mainstream church strictly warned such gatherings to cease. If they would not, the *Winckler* would be banished from the land. History

---

[24] Hilary of Poitiers was a French Catholic bishop who was converted to Christianity about 350, when he was about thirty-five years old. Three years after his conversion, he was appointed bishop. Hilary did not start a back-to-the-Bible movement, but he did have some concerns about the direction of the church. He expressed those concerns strongly enough that he was exiled from his bishopric after three years of service. His attitude toward legalized Christianity is an example of sentiments that continued to surface after the church married the state.

[25] Leonard Verduin, *The Reformers and Their Stepchildren,* 165.

records that during the 1100s believers gathered in subterranean refuges to hold worship services. In 1199, the pope sent this decree to his subjects who were accused of clandestine Bible meetings: "Now it is doubtlessly true that the desire to know the Scriptures and to exhort men to follow these is not reprehensible . . . but what is to be condemned is the holding of secret assemblies."[26]

Unauthorized worship such as this continued to happen up to the Reformation. A group who met in a weavers' building and called themselves "Christian Brethren" existed in St. Gall, Switzerland, in 1522.

When the Anabaptists formed, they were in a private meeting, as the true followers of God had met for nearly fifteen hundred years before them. Because of persecution, Anabaptist secret worship continued, and it brought upon itself the same ill-treatment heaped on private worship all through medieval times.

Wiedertäufer. This word means "Anabaptist," which means "again-baptizer" or "rebaptizer." Rebaptizers had arisen before the Reformation, and this label had become useful in branding "heretics." So when another batch of *Wiedertäufer* arose in 1525, this old "heretical" label was resurrected to denounce the new rebaptizers. Some medieval heretics and the Anabaptists stoutly denied being rebaptizers because they believed that the infant baptism they had received was not baptism.

We can trace the again-baptizers far back into history. During the 300s, as infant baptism was becoming a mark of political and religious unity,[27] faithful Christians refused to have their children baptized, continuing to

---

[26] Ibid., 168.

[27] Infant baptism began earlier than this but was not solidified into its Catholic form and forced upon everyone until the state church system evolved further.

practice apostolic believer's baptism. This brought them under the frown of the church and the emperor. Since infant baptism made every newborn a member of the empire and church, it helped to make and keep everyone the same. Infant baptism became an institution whereby everyone was supposedly poured into one political and religious mold before they could choose something out of the ordinary.

But this did not keep the Spirit of God from working in men. People kept arising who made their own choices regardless of the established decrees. Most of the medieval "heretical" groups rejected infant baptism administered by the state church. Some of them administered infant baptism privately, but many of them rejected it altogether, practicing believer's baptism instead. The *Martyrs Mirror* lists many people who differed with the Roman church on baptism, and records many Catholic edicts against rebaptizers. Numerous such edicts occurred throughout medieval times, proof of the continual dissent over baptism.

Here are a few examples of this dissent. The Donatists said that "no children, even in the extremity of death, should be baptized, but only believing adults who desired it."[28] Hilary of Poitiers taught that men should be baptized upon their personal confession of faith. In 606, a certain bishop Adrian refused to administer infant baptism, while evidently trying to remain within the Catholic Church. Around 700, it is recorded that some believers in France practiced believer's baptism. A certain man named Haimo wrote in the early 800s, "He, then, that is to be baptized, must previously be

---

[28] Thieleman J. van Braght, *Martyrs Mirror,* 154. The other medieval "heretics" listed here are also named in *Martyrs Mirror,* on the following pages: Hilary of Poitiers, 157; Adrian, 214; believers around 700, 220, 221; Haimo, 233; Hincmar, 238; Berengarius and Bruno, 262; Rupert Tuiciensis, 272; and Petrobrusians, 273.

instructed, that he may first learn faith, which he shall afterwards receive in baptism."[29] Other Catholic leaders also rose against infant baptism, among whom was a bishop named Hincmar, around 860, and Berengarius and Bruno, who were deacon and bishop of Angiers, France, around 1050.

Around 1124, a certain Rupert Tuiciensis wrote against the Catholic view of baptism, saying, "Everyone that is to be baptized, must first believe and confess, and not until then be baptized." The Petrobrusians, followers of Peter de Bruys, an outspoken critic of the Catholic Church, taught against infant baptism in the 1100s. All the Waldensians rejected the Catholic infant baptism, but some of them practiced a Waldensian form of it.[30] These remnants wanted to take away the false hope such baptism gave, as well as to clear the church of the unsaved souls that such baptism brought in.

So when the Anabaptists began practicing believer's baptism, they were not concocting a new practice. Even the mainline Reformers supported believer's baptism, to some degree, until they switched to a state-sanctioned reform. At that point, they needed to include every citizen in the church. To do that they were forced to practice infant baptism.

---

[29] Note that Haimo's teaching is tainted by the baptismal regeneration theory. The Catholics strongly teach baptismal regeneration because they see baptism as an act required to redeem the soul. Although many medieval "heretics" cast aside the infant baptism as false, many of them held to baptismal regeneration, in varying degrees. Reading the accounts of baptism teaching through the centuries in the *Martyrs Mirror* will demonstrate this. The Anabaptists were more sound on this point than many previous "heretics," but even a few of them used some terminology that we would consider inappropriate in describing the nature of baptism.

[30] According to some historical sources, some of the Waldensians baptized their own children as infants but gave new converts adult baptism. To these Waldensians, Catholic baptism in any form was evidently not valid. There is also good evidence that a large portion of the Waldenses rejected infant baptism altogether.

The Contribution of the Mainline Reformers to Anabaptism

We have noticed that resistance against the Roman church was present all through medieval times. Most medieval people were exposed to this influence, to some degree. When Luther sounded his trumpet, part of that segment of truth-conditioned people flocked to him. The "medieval protest" elements already present in society helped Reformation ideas spread like wildfire across Europe.

A Catholic historian wrote, "To Luther came others who, before his activity, had already abandoned the doctrine of the official Church, men who were encouraged by his activity to give expression to their ideas and to organize them into systems."[31]

Zwingli testified of the same thing when he wrote to Luther, "There have been men, not a few, who have known the sum and substance of the evangelical religion quite as well as you; however, out of all Israel no one took the chances involved in stepping forth to do battle, for all feared yon mighty Goliath, standing there in the fearful weight of his weapons and in challenging stance."[32]

To Luther and Zwingli's credit, they originally had a strong desire for reestablishing a Biblical church. This drew the "heretics" to their side. In 1523, Luther said his future intention was to give Communion only to those who had a clear testimony of personal faith. In 1526, he wrote that those who sincerely want to be Christians ought to meet together privately and worship and practice the ordinances. However, he said that he did not have the people to put together such a church yet, but if he

---

[31] *Cornelius*, 2:7. Cited in Leonard Verduin, *The Reformers and Their Stepchildren*, 145.

[32] Ulrich Zwingli, *Freundliche Auslegung of 1527*. Cited in Leonard Verduin, *The Reformers and Their Stepchildren*, 146.

ever had the opportunity, he would be ready to do it.[33] Zwingli also, in his early reform years, believed in a voluntary church and church discipline. He taught some aspects of Biblical nonresistance and theologically rejected infant baptism.

The Reformers largely understood the New Testament church pattern. They made a good beginning in the truth, according to the Anabaptists. But they soon realized that a Biblical church was unacceptable to the civil authorities.[34] The *Hutterian Chronicle* records, "These two, Luther and Zwingli, exposed all the deception and villainy of the pope and brought it to the light of day as if they would strike everything to the ground with thunderbolts. But they put nothing better in its place. As soon as they began to cling to worldly power and put their trust in human help, they were just as bad—like someone mending an old kettle and only making a bigger hole. They left behind a shameless people, whom they had taught to sin. To speak in a parable, they struck the jug from the pope's hand but kept the broken pieces in their own."[35]

---

[33] During this time, people who were putting just such a church together were leaving Luther's camp all the time. Why then did he say he did not have the people to put together such a group? It seems that his real hindrance was that the civil authorities would not give him a peaceful opportunity to start this church.

[34] The civil authorities thought that religious factions would cause havoc in society. Luther and Zwingli also clung to this notion. Fear of civil disorder, loss of political power, and personal persecution all played a role in their refusal to establish a voluntary church.

Even at their most Biblical moments, when the Reformers boldly declared their desire for a pure church, they never quite let go of the idea that somehow there could also be a lower-level church for the "Christian" masses. They felt that a society composed of Christians and non-Christians was unworkable. Against their better knowledge, the Reformers resorted to the "safe" way; but in doing so, they left the supposedly cardinal Protestant principle of following *sola Scriptura* (Scripture only). Luther grudgingly admitted that he had left that principle. Sometimes in his fight with the Anabaptists, he did not even attempt to prove them wrong with Scripture, knowing it was on their side. And yet he fought them bitterly because he was unwilling to let go of the idea of a Christian population.

[35] *The Chronicle of the Hutterian Brethren,* 41.

Thus the Reformers abandoned many of their Scriptural convictions. But the truly committed believers refused to take that route. When the mainline Reformers decided that the price of a pure church was too high, that the time was not yet ripe for such an endeavor, a portion of their followers went ahead on their own. Those followers established just such a church and fully realized the persecution that Luther and Zwingli had avoided.

Many Protestant historians and scholars today believe in voluntary church membership and reject the opinions of their Reformation predecessors. They excuse the Reformers for making the decision to revert to the state church system, agreeing that the time was not ripe,[36] and that there was no workable alternative. They feel that the only way for Protestantism to have begun was to establish a state church with military might to rival the papacy. But there *was* an alternative. Luther and Zwingli could have taken that alternative, but they backed down. True, it was a cruelly hard alternative, and history had a wealth of examples of that alternative being crushed in blood. But it was the only route that fully committed believers could take to maintain peace with God.

Those believers—who became known as Anabaptists—often pointed out that they had learned much Bible doctrine back when they followed the mainline Reformers. "Some things we have received from you the preachers," the Swiss Anabaptists told Protestant church leaders in 1538, "but not everything."[37] Some of the

---

[36] Some Protestants assert that at that point the voluntary church idea had not been developed enough to implement. They see the voluntary church idea as evolving since the Reformation. The New Testament clearly refutes this, as did the medieval "heretics" and the Anabaptists.

[37] Martin Haas, *Quellen zur Geschichte der Taufer in der Schweiz: IV. Band: Drei Taufergesprache.* Cited in Walter Klaassen, ed., *Anabaptism in Outline,* 111

Anabaptists-to-be had waited with patience even after they had misgivings about the Reformers' direction, to see whether things would turn around. But when the mainline Reformers headed back into the old state church system and espoused most of its ancient flaws, the "radicals" became disillusioned with them.

Since Anabaptism was partially rooted in medieval protest movements, it may have arisen even without the Protestant Reformation. As things stand, however, the Protestant Reformers made a definite contribution to the rise of Anabaptism. For several years, they provided a gathering place for those studying the truth and and becoming alienated from the Roman church. In the providence of God, the Protestant and Catholic conflict provided a brief period in which Anabaptism grew rapidly before the death penalty was placed on it. By the time the other faiths attempted to silence the Anabaptists in blood, the movement was too large and vigorous to be wiped out quickly.[38]

Putting the Pieces Together

Anabaptism as a movement began in Zurich, Switzerland, in 1525. That movement was born out of many medieval influences. Those influences already existed in the minds of many common people but were lying dormant under the surface.[39] Anabaptist meetings became gathering points for those who had questions and

---

[38] When Protestantism began, the Catholics wanted to crush it. But at the moment, Catholic military power was being poured into other wars, and they were not able to respond in time to the Protestant threat. Thus Protestantism grew into a formidable machine before the Catholics concentrated on throttling it. This provided a background in which the Anabaptist movement could gain a foothold as well. Certainly, the hearts of the kings are in the hand of the Lord (Proverbs 21:1).

[39] See Delbert L. Gratz, *Bernese Anabaptists,* 1–7. The theory which this book applies to Bern also applies to the rise of Anabaptism in other Swiss areas and in the Netherlands as well.

concerns about the Roman and Protestant churches. The movement helped people to identify with a group that held similar convictions. Banding together gave people courage to live out their once-dormant convictions.

Medieval religious protest had taken many forms, not all of which were Biblical, even though they were usually closer to the Bible on any given issue than the Catholics were. The men who later became Anabaptists learned, partly from Luther and Zwingli, the principle of testing beliefs and practices by the Bible. When they carried that principle to its natural end, it resulted in the rise of Anabaptism.

Faithful Anabaptists borrowed heavily from medieval and Protestant influences, measured those things according to the Bible, kept only those doctrines that stood up to the scrutiny of the New Testament, and added additional truths as they found them in the New Testament. With the blessing of God, they built a church that probably resembled the apostolic church more closely than any of the medieval protest movements.

Anabaptism spread quickly from Zurich. In many areas, people identified themselves with the movement as soon as they heard about it. Scattered by persecution and driven by evangelistic zeal, disciples of the movement spread the word of a believer's church across Europe in a short time.

According to some theories, Anabaptism was like a match suddenly struck after a thousand years of darkness and total deception. Although this may have been the case for isolated areas in Europe, it was not the normal situation. This theory makes the Anabaptists appear as heroic rediscoverers of lost truth and fails to recognize that they stood on the shoulders of those who went before them. It also disregards the Bible truth that the true Christian church has existed ever since Pentecost.[40]

On the other hand, some believe that Anabaptism began back around the time that the church married the state, in the 300s. *Martyrs Mirror* seems to give this idea at first glance. This theory proposes that through the medieval protest movements, Anabaptism can be traced physically right back to the apostolic church. This theory makes modern Mennonites and Amish feel good about their Anabaptist roots, but it lacks historical proof.

Some of the "proof" for this theory is taken from Reformation writings against the Anabaptists. Protestants and Catholics both poured their hatred for Anabaptism into the press. They linked the Anabaptists to many historical "heretics," trying to prove to the population that these people were terrible deceivers. They concocted many horrible lies about Anabaptism, trying to link the group to some of the most reprobate behavior imaginable. Anabaptist teachings did resemble some ancient "heretical" doctrine, and there was justification for linking Anabaptist thought to previous ideology. But these men wrote with a vengeance that contained little regard for the facts. Their writings cannot serve as a credible basis for establishing that Anabaptism can be physically traced to the 300s. Even if one takes their writings at face value, he gains nothing more than a comparison of Anabaptist and medieval "heretic" ideology. These works do not contain proof of *physical links* between the

---

[40] Some of the Swiss Anabaptists felt that the true church had not existed during some of medieval history. In 1538, some of them stated, "We are not convinced when you say that the holy Christian church has continued from its beginning. . . . All that was hidden under the papacy; there were no Christians. Everybody walked in darkness. Therefore the true church came to an end at some time, and we have made a new beginning upon the rule from which others had departed." Martin Haas, *Quellen zur Geschichte der Taufer in der Schweiz: IV. Band: Drei Taufergesprache.* Cited in Walter Klaassen, ed., *Anabaptism in Outline,* 111.

Reformation Anabaptists and previous "heretics."

Van Braght, the compiler and writer of *Martyrs Mirror*, often described medieval "heretics" as Anabaptists. However, his reference to medieval "Anabaptists" seems to refer to the fact that many of the medieval "heretics" were rebaptizers, not that they were connected with the Anabaptists of the Reformation. Van Braght does note that various Catholic critics said that Anabaptism went back to the time of the apostles,[41] but as far as we are aware, he nowhere endeavors to prove from this anything more than an ideological link between various "heretics." He only used anti-Anabaptist Reformation writings to show that there were people *like* the Reformation Anabaptists in previous centuries. In reference to some rebaptizers in the 400s, he says:

> But lest any one should think that the people who, under the name of Anabaptists, were threatened with death by the Emperor Theodosius, held . . . views different from those maintained by the Baptists of the present day, who are likewise called Anabaptists, it is expedient to mention what was said about their views by the inquisitor of Leeuwaerden, in opposition to one of our latest martyrs, namely, Jagues d' Auchi. . . . "It is now 1200 or 1300 years since the Emperor Theodosius issued an edict, that the heretics should be put to death, namely, those who were rebaptized *like* your sect." . . .
>
> When, therefore, the inquisitor says that they "were rebaptized *like* your sect," he certainly indicates thereby, that they were people *like* Jagues d' Auchi was, and, consequently, *like* the Anabaptists.[42]

Van Braght often used the various names of the medieval movements, showing us that he did not consider

---

[41] Thieleman van Braght, *Martyrs Mirror*, 154.

[42] Ibid., 190, emphasis mine.

the Anabaptist movement *per se* to have begun before the 1500s.[43] Here are more quotations showing that he did not try to prove physical continuity. Rather, he recognized that even consistent ideological continuity cannot be proved.

(A.D. 418) It appears therefore, that at that time many people separated from the Roman church, on account of [rejecting] this view respecting original sin and infant baptism. However, we would not defend the views of Pelagius and Celestius, concerning some other points; it suffices us, that there were people in those times, who, notwithstanding the excommunication of the pope, . . . still opposed the Roman church, especially through the rejection of infant baptism, and even, some of them, sacrificed their lives.[44]

(About A.D. 525) From this it can be seen in what detestation, yea, abhorrence, the so-called Anabaptists in the time past, were held by the Romanists. . . .

We will not investigate minutely, whether the so-called Anabaptists of that time held the same views, in regard to every article, with those who, at the present day, are designated by that name; nor will we, if perhaps in some points they did not teach aright, or were not fully enlightened, defend, much less, praise them; it suffices us, that they, besides other good and wholesome articles, mentioned by us in another place, held this in common with the Anabaptists of the present day, namely: *That they did not approve of the*

---

[43] On page 154 of *Martyrs Mirror*, he says, "It is stated that already in the time of Sylvester, there was taught and maintained the same doctrine which was afterwards maintained by countless numbers of the baptistic Waldenses, yea, that those churches which in the 11th, 12th, 13th, and in subsequent centuries were styled Waldenses, Albigenses, and lastly, Mennonites, or Anabaptists, had existed already at that time, and indeed, long before." Here van Braght was referring to anti-Anabaptist Catholic writings. He cites the various movements by their different names, even though he evidently agrees with the critic that there were doctrinal comparisons between the groups.

[44] Thieleman van Braght, *Martyrs Mirror,* 191.

baptism which by the Romanists is administered to infants.[45]

Here it is expressly stated that the Waldenses, from ancient times were designated by the papists by the name of Anabaptists; doubtless, because they baptized those who had been baptized in their infancy again. . . .

. . . the Waldenses were anabaptists, as the ungodly now call the Christian baptists (the Baptists), who did not believe in infant baptism.

It is certainly clearly and plainly said, that the Waldenses were anabaptists, or, at least, that they were called by that name; the reason why is also shown, namely, because they, like the Baptists of the present day, did not believe in infant baptism.[46]

The Word and Spirit of God

God's Word and Spirit worked all through medieval and Reformation times to bring forth a people unto Himself. This was the root of the Anabaptist movement. This was why it succeeded in spite of the powerful men who tried to destroy it.

When the falling church married the Roman state, the whole church was affected. Nothing in the doctrine or organization of the church escaped the taints that this change brought. Basically, the entire "church" eventually became arrayed against the Lord of the church. After generations of such existence, men were so tainted with deception, that without the Spirit of God at work and the New Testament being available in a few precious copies, the medieval protest movements would have never developed. There would have been very little to tell men that the church was wrong.

---

[45] Ibid., 205.

[46] Ibid., 278, 279.

We often think of the medieval times as destitute of the Scriptures for the common people. In many areas, that seemed to be the case, but the Catholics did publish a number of edicts against "heretics" who had translated and made copies of the Scriptures in their everyday tongue. Before the printing press began to rapidly produce copies of the Bible, an inquisitor who spent his life tracking down "heretics" said this of his prey:

> They know the apostles creed excellently in the vulgar tongue; they learn by heart the Gospels and the New Testament, in the vernacular and repeat them aloud to one another. . . . I have seen a youthful cowherd who had lived but one year in the home of a Waldensian heretic who had attended so diligently to all that he heard that he had memorized within that year forty Sunday Gospels not counting those of the feast days. . . . I have seen some lay-folk so steeped in their doctrine that they could repeat by heart great portions of the Evangelists, such as Matthew and Luke, especially all that is said in them of Christ's teaching and sayings, so that they could repeat them without a halt and with hardly a word wrong here or there.[47]

The centuries of darkness were dotted with stars of light. God was at work, and truth would prevail. The pattern for the New Testament church had not changed, and God saw to it that untarnished copies of that plan remained available for the children of men who turned to Him.

---

[47] George Gordon Coulton, *Inquisition and Liberty.* Cited in Leonard Verduin, *The Reformers and Their Stepchildren,* 152.

Appendix II

The Schleitheim
Confession of Faith

February 24, 1527

Brotherly Union of a Number of Children of God Concerning Seven Articles[1]

The Cover Letter

May joy, peace, mercy from our Father, through the atonement of the blood of Christ Jesus, together with the gifts of the Spirit—who is sent by the Father to all believers to [give] strength and consolation and constance in all tribulation until the end, Amen, be with all who love God and all children of light, who are scattered everywhere, wherever they might have been placed by God our Father, wherever they might be gathered in unity of spirit

---

[1] This translation of the *Brotherly Union* is quoted from John H. Yoder, ed., *The Legacy of Michael Sattler*, 34–43. Used by permission.

in one God and Father of us all; grace and peace of heart be with you all. Amen.

Beloved brothers and sisters in the Lord; first and primordially we are always concerned for your consolation and the assurance of your conscience (which was sometime confused), so that you might not always be separated from us as aliens and by right almost completely excluded,[2] but that you might turn to the true implanted members of Christ, who have been armed through patience and the knowledge of self, and thus be again united with us in the power of a godly Christian spirit and zeal for God.

It is manifest with what manifold cunning the devil has turned us aside, so that he might destroy and cast down the work of God, which in us mercifully and graciously has been partially begun. But the true Shepherd of our souls, Christ, who has begun such in us, will direct and teach the same unto the end, to His glory and our salvation, Amen.

Dear brothers and sisters, we who have been assembled in the Lord at Schleitheim on the Randen[3] make known, in points and articles, unto all that love God, that as far as we are concerned, we have been united to stand fast in the Lord as obedient children of God, sons and daughters, who have been and shall be separated from the world in all that we do and leave undone, and (the praise and glory be to God alone) uncontradicted by all the brothers, completely at peace. Herein we have sensed the unity of the Father and of our common Christ as present with us in their Spirit. For the Lord is a Lord of peace and not of quarreling, as Paul indicates.[4] So that you

---

[2] This is likely a reference to Ephesians 2:12, 19. Sattler was speaking of the reconciliating work of Christ toward those who were alienated by their unbelief.

[3] The Randen are hills overlooking Schleitheim.

[4] See 1 Corinthians 14:33.

understand at what points this occurred, you should observe and understand [what follows]:

A very great offense has been introduced by some false brothers among us, whereby several have turned away from the faith, thinking to practice and observe the freedom of the Spirit and of Christ. But such have fallen short of the truth and (to their own condemnation) are given over to the lasciviousness and license of the flesh. They have esteemed that faith and love may do and permit everything and that nothing can harm nor condemn them, since they are "believers."

Note well, you members of God in Christ Jesus, that faith in the heavenly Father through Jesus Christ is not thus formed; it produces and brings forth no such things as these false brothers and sisters practice and teach. Guard yourselves and be warned of such people, for they do not serve our Father, but their father, the devil.

But for you it is not so; for they who are Christ's have crucified their flesh with all its lusts and desires.[5] You understand me well, and [know] the brothers whom we mean. Separate yourselves from them, for they are perverted. Pray the Lord that they may have knowledge unto repentance, and for us that we may have constance to persevere along the path we have entered upon, unto the glory of God and of Christ His Son. Amen.

The Seven Articles

The articles we have dealt with, and in which we have been united, are these: baptism, ban, the breaking of bread, separation from abomination, shepherds in the congregation, the sword, the oath.

---

[5] See Galatians 5:24.

I. Notice concerning baptism. Baptism shall be given to all those who have been taught repentance and the amendment of life and [who] believe truly that their sins are taken away through Christ, and to all those who desire to walk in the resurrection of Jesus Christ and be buried with Him in death, so that they might rise with Him; to all those who with such an understanding themselves desire and request it from us; hereby is excluded all infant baptism, the greatest and first abomination of the Pope. For this you have the reasons and the testimony of the writings and the practice of the apostles. We wish simply yet resolutely and with assurance to hold to the same.

II. We have been united as follows concerning the ban. The ban shall be employed with all those who have given themselves over to the Lord, to walk after [Him] in His commandments; those who have been baptized into the one body of Christ, and let themselves be called brothers or sisters, and still somehow slip and fall into error and sin, being inadvertently overtaken. The same [shall] be warned twice privately and the third time be publicly admonished before the entire congregation according to the command of Christ (Mt. 18). But this shall be done according to the ordering of the Spirit of God before the breaking of bread, so that we may all in one spirit and in one love break and eat from one bread and drink from one cup.

III. Concerning the breaking of bread, we have become one and agree thus: all those who desire to break the one bread in remembrance of the broken body of Christ and all those who wish to drink of one drink in remembrance of the shed blood of Christ, they must beforehand be united in the one body of Christ, that is the congregation of God, whose head is Christ, and that by baptism. For as Paul indicates, we cannot be partakers at the same time of the table of the Lord and the table of devils. Nor can we at the same time partake and drink of the cup of the Lord and the cup of devils.[6] That is: all those who have fellowship with the dead works of darkness have no part in the light. Thus all who follow the devil and the world, have no part with those who have been called out of the world unto God. All those who lie in evil have no part in the good.

So it shall and must be, that whoever does not share the calling of the one God to one faith, to one baptism, to one spirit, to one body together with all the children of God, may not be made one loaf together with them, as must be true if one wishes truly to break bread according to the command of Christ.

IV. We have been united concerning the separation that shall take place from the evil and the wickedness which the devil has planted in the world, simply in this; that we have no fellowship with them, and do not run with them in the confusion of their abominations. So it is; since all who have not entered into the obedience of faith and have not united themselves with God so that they will to do His will, are a great abomination before God, therefore nothing else can or really will grow or spring forth from them than abominable things. Now there is nothing else in the world and all creation than good or evil, believing and unbelieving, darkness and light, the world and those who are [come] out of the world, God's temple and idols, Christ and Belial, and none will have part with the other.

To us, then, the commandment of the Lord is also obvious, whereby He orders us to be and to become separated

---

[6] See 1 Corinthians 10:21.

from the evil one, and thus He will be our God and we shall be His sons and daughters.[7]

Further, He admonishes us therefore to go out from Babylon and from the earthly Egypt, that we may not be partakers in their torment and suffering, which the Lord will bring upon them.

From all this we should learn that everything which has not been united with our God in Christ is nothing but an abomination which we should shun. By this are meant all popish and repopish[8] works and idolatry, gatherings, church attendance, winehouses, guarantees and commitments of unbelief,[9] and other things of the kind, which the world regards highly, and yet which are carnal or flatly counter to the command of God, after the pattern of all the iniquity which is in the world. From all this we shall be separated and have no part with such, for they are nothing but abominations, which cause us to be hated before our Christ Jesus, who has freed us from the servitude of the flesh and fitted us for the service of God and the Spirit whom He has given us.

Thereby shall also fall away from us the diabolical weapons of violence—such as sword, armor, and the like, and all of their use to protect friends or against enemies—by virtue of the word of Christ: "you shall not resist evil."[10]

V. We have been united as follows concerning shepherds in the church of God. The shepherd in the church

---

[7] See 2 Corinthians 6:17, 18.

[8] *Repopish* refers to the Protestant practice of retaining certain characteristics of Catholicism that the Bible does not support or teaches directly against.

[9] This likely refers to economic or business ties with the worldly. One of these ties was the guild, or trade association. All craftsmen were expected to be a part of the respective guild of his craft. The guild set prices and quality standards and formed an economic bloc that made business difficult for those who were not a part of it. The faithful Anabaptists refused involvement with this unequal yoke.

[10] See Matthew 5:39.

shall be a person according to the rule of Paul,[11] fully and completely, who has a good report of those who are outside the faith. The office of such a person shall be to read and exhort and teach, warn, admonish, or ban in the congregation, and properly to preside among the sisters and brothers in prayer, and in the breaking of bread, and in all things to take care of the body of Christ, that it may be built up and developed, so that the name of God might be praised and honored through us, and the mouth of the mocker might be stopped.

He shall be supported, wherein he has need, by the congregation which has chosen him, so that he who serves the gospel can also live therefrom, as the Lord has ordered.[12] But should a shepherd do something worthy of reprimand, nothing shall be done with him without the voice of two or three witnesses. If they sin they shall be publicly reprimanded, so that others might fear.[13]

But if the shepherd should be driven away or led to the Lord by the cross, at the same hour another shall be ordained to his place, so that the little folk and the little flock of God may not be destroyed, but be preserved by warning and be consoled.

VI. We have been united as follows concerning the sword. The sword is an ordering of God outside the perfection of Christ. It punishes and kills the wicked, and guards and protects the good. In the law the sword is established over the wicked for punishment and for death, and the secular rulers are established to wield the same.

But within the perfection of Christ only the ban is used

---

[11] See 1 Timothy 3.

[12] See 1 Corinthians 9:14.

[13] See 1 Timothy 5:20.

for the admonition and exclusion of the one who has sinned, without the death of the flesh, simply the warning and the command to sin no more.

Now many, who do not understand Christ's will for us, will ask: whether a Christian may or should use the sword against the wicked for the protection and defense of the good, or for the sake of love.

The answer is unanimously revealed: Christ teaches and commands us to learn from Him, for He is meek and lowly of heart and thus we shall find rest for our souls.[14] Now Christ says to the woman who was taken in adultery not that she should be stoned according to the law of His Father (and yet He says, "what the Father commandeth me, that I do") but with mercy and forgiveness and the warning to sin no more, says: "Go, sin no more."[15] Exactly thus should we also proceed, according to the rule of the ban.

Second, is asked concerning the sword: whether a Christian shall pass sentence in disputes and strife about worldly matters, such as the unbelievers have with one another. The answer: Christ did not wish to decide or pass judgment between brother and brother concerning inheritance, but refused to do so.[16] So should we also do.

Third, is asked concerning the sword: whether the Christian should be a magistrate if he is chosen thereto. This is answered thus: Christ was to be made king, but He fled and did not discern the ordinance of His Father.[17] Thus we should also do as He did and follow after Him, and we shall not walk in darkness. For He Himself says:

---

[14] See Matthew 11:29.

[15] See John 8.

[16] See Luke 12:13, 14.

[17] This means that Christ did not believe that the people's desire to make Him a king was in accord with His Father's will.

"Whoever would come after me, let him deny himself and take up his cross and follow me."[18] He Himself further forbids the violence of the sword when He says; "The princes of this world lord it over them, etc., but among you it shall not be so."[19] Further Paul says, "Whom God has foreknown, the same he has also predestined to be conformed to the image of his Son," etc.[20] Peter also says: "Christ has suffered (not ruled) and has left us an example, that you should follow after in his steps."[21]

Lastly one can see in the following points that it does not befit a Christian to be a magistrate: the rule of the government is according to the flesh, that of the Christians according to the spirit. Their houses and dwelling remain in this world, that of the Christians is in heaven.[22] Their citizenship is in this world, that of the Christians is in heaven. The weapons of their battle and warfare are carnal and only against the flesh, but the weapons of Christians are spiritual, against the fortification of the devil. The worldly are armed with steel and iron, but Christians are armed with the armor of God, with truth, righteousness, peace, faith, salvation, and with the Word of God. In sum: as Christ our Head is minded, so also must be minded the members of the body of Christ through Him, so that there be no division in the body, through which it would be destroyed. Since then Christ is as is written of Him, so must His members also be the same, so that His body may remain whole and unified for its own advancement and upbuilding. For any kingdom which is divided within itself will be destroyed.[23]

---

[18] Matthew 16:24.

[19] Matthew 20:25, 26.

[20] Romans 8:29.

[21] First Peter 2:21.

[22] See Philippians 3:20.

[23] See Matthew 12:25.

VII. We have been united as follows concerning the oath. The oath is a confirmation among those who are quarreling or making promises. In the law it is commanded that it should be done only in the name of God, truthfully and not falsely. Christ, who teaches the perfection of the law, forbids His [followers] all swearing, whether true nor false; neither by heaven nor by earth, neither by Jerusalem nor by our head; and that for the reason which He goes on to give: "For you cannot make one hair white or black." You see, thereby all swearing is forbidden. We cannot perform what is promised in swearing, for we are not able to change the smallest part of ourselves.[24]

Now there are some who do not believe the simple commandment of God and who say, "But God swore by Himself to Abraham, because He was God (as He promised him that He would do good to him and would be his God if he kept His commandments). Why then should I not swear if I promise something to someone?" The answer: hear what Scripture says: "God, since he wished to prove overabundantly to the heirs of His promise that His will did not change, inserted an oath so that by two immutable things we might have a stronger consolation (for it is impossible that God should lie)".[25] Notice the meaning of the passage: God has the power to do what He forbids you, for everything is possible to Him. God swore an oath to Abraham, Scripture says, in order to prove that His counsel is immutable. That means: no one can withstand and thwart His will; thus He can keep His oath. But we cannot, as Christ said above, hold or perform our oath, therefore we should not swear.

Others say that swearing cannot be forbidden by God

---

[24] See Matthew 5:34–37.

[25] Hebrews 6:13–20.

in the New Testament when it was commanded in the Old, but that it is forbidden only to swear by heaven, earth, Jerusalem, and our head. Answer: hear the Scripture. He who swears by heaven, swears by God's throne and by Him who sits thereon.[26] Observe: swearing by heaven is forbidden, which is only God's throne; how much more is it forbidden to swear by God himself. You blind fools, what is greater, the throne or He who sits upon it?

Others say, if it is then wrong to use God for truth, then the apostles Peter and Paul also swore. Answer: Peter and Paul only testify to that which God promised Abraham, whom we long after have received. But when one testifies, one testifies concerning that which is present, whether it be good or evil. Thus Simeon spoke of Christ to Mary and testified: "Behold: this one is ordained for the falling and rising of many in Israel and to be a sign which will be spoken against."[27]

Christ taught us similarly when He says: Your speech shall be yea, yea; and nay, nay; for what is more than that comes of evil.[28] He says, your speech or your word shall be yes and no, so that no one might understand that He had permitted it. Christ is simply yea and nay, and all those who seek Him simply will understand His Word. Amen.

The Cover Letter

Dear Brothers and Sisters in the Lord; these are the articles which some brothers previously had understood wrongly and in a way not conformed to the true meaning. Thereby many weak consciences were confused,

---

[26] See Matthew 23:22.

[27] Luke 2:34.

[28] See Matthew 5:37.

whereby the name of God has been grossly slandered, for which reason it was needful that we should be brought to agreement in the Lord, which has come to pass. To God be praise and glory!

Now that you have abundantly understood the will of God as revealed through us at this time, you must fulfill this will, now known, persistently and unswervingly. For you know well what is the reward of the servant who knowingly sins.

Everything which you have done unknowingly and now confess to have done wrongly, is forgiven you, through that believing prayer, which is offered among us in our meeting for all our shortcomings and guilt, through the gracious forgiveness of God and through the blood of Jesus Christ. Amen.

Watch out for all who do not walk in simplicity of divine truth, which has been stated by us in this letter in our meeting, so that everyone might be governed among us by the rule of the ban, and that henceforth the entry of false brothers and sisters among us might be prevented.

Put away from you that which is evil, and the Lord will be your God, and you will be His sons and daughters.[29]

Dear brothers, keep in mind what Paul admonished Titus. He says: "The saving grace of God has appeared to all, and disciplines us, that we should deny ungodliness and worldly lusts, and live circumspect righteous and godly lives in this world; awaiting the same hope and the appearing of the glory of the great God and of our Savior Jesus Christ, who gave himself for us, to redeem us from all unrighteousness and to purify unto himself a people of his own, that would be zealous of good

---

[29] See 2 Corinthians 6:17, 18.

works."[30] Think on this, and exercise yourselves therein, and the Lord of peace will be with you.

May the name of God be forever blessed and greatly praised, Amen. May the Lord give you His peace, Amen.

Done at Schleitheim, St. Matthew's Day,
Anno MDXXVII

---

[30] Titus 2:11–14.

Appendix III

Congregational Order[1]

The original document, in the State Archive of Bern, Switzerland, has no title. The title given here is the label attached to it at the archive.

The handwriting of the document appears to be in the same hand as the Brotherly Union, *and it circulated among the brethren, with the seven articles. Quite likely, Michael Sattler penned this copy, although he may not have been the orginal author.*

Words in brackets were added by the translator to aid the sentence flow.

Since the almighty eternal and merciful God has made His wonderful light break forth in this world and [in this] most dangerous time, we recognize the mystery of the divine will, that the Word is preached to us according to the proper ordering of the Lord, whereby

---

[1] This translation of *Congregational Order* is quoted from John H. Yoder, ed., *The Legacy of Michael Sattler,* 44, 45. Used by permission.

we have been called into His fellowship. Therefore, according to the command of the Lord and the teachings of His apostles, in Christian order, we should observe the new commandment[2] in love one toward another, so that love and unity may be maintained, which all brothers and sisters of the entire congregation should agree to hold to as follows:

1. The brothers and sisters should meet at least three or four times a week, to exercise themselves[3] in the teaching of Christ and His apostles and heartily to exhort one another to remain faithful to the Lord as they have pledged.

2. When the brothers and sisters are together, they shall take up something to read together.[4] The one to whom God has given the best understanding shall explain it, the others should be still and listen, so that there are not two or three carrying on a private conversation, bothering the others. The Psalter shall be read daily at home.[5]

3. Let none be frivolous in the church of God, neither in words nor in actions. Good conduct shall be maintained by them all also before the heathen.

4. When a brother sees his brother erring, he shall warn him according to the command of Christ, and shall

---

[2] John 13:34.

[3] "Exercising themselves" likely included Bible memorization, since literacy and Bibles were rare.

[4] "To read together" included exposition. "Readings" was one of the names given to the early Bible study meetings held in Zurich and St. Gall.

[5] "Reading the Psalter . . . at home" is one of the rare Anabaptist references to worship outside of the congregational setting. The Psalter refers to the Psalms.

admonish him in a Christian and brotherly way, as everyone is bound and obliged to do out of love.

5. Of all the brothers and sisters of this congregation none shall have anything of his own, but rather, as the Christians in the time of the apostles held all in common, and especially stored up a common fund, from which aid can be given to the poor, according as each will have need, and as in the apostles' time permit no brother to be in need.[6]

6. All gluttony shall be avoided among the brothers who are gathered in the congregation; serve a soup or a minimum of vegetable and meat, for eating and drinking are not the kingdom of heaven.[7]

7. The Lord's Supper shall be held, as often as the brothers are together, thereby proclaiming the death of the Lord, and thereby warning each one to commemorate, how Christ gave His life for us, and shed His blood for us, that we might also be willing to give our body and life for Christ's sake, which means for the sake of all the brothers.

---

[6] "The common fund" here is not referring to a complete community of goods such as was practiced later in Moravia. It simply reflects the Bible principle that each was ready to give all that he had for his brethren, and that a fund was laid by in store against emergency needs. (See Acts 11:29 and Ephesians 4:28.) Although the Swiss Anabaptists did not practice complete community of goods, they still considered themselves to be following the economic example of the early church. (See Acts 4:34, 35.)

[7] See Romans 14:17.

Appendix IV

The Discipline Adopted by the Strasbourg Conference of 1568[1]

Brackets indicate omissions in some copies of the discipline. Parentheses indicate words not found in the German original.

Agreement of the ministers and bishops of many localities in conference at Strasbourg in the year 1568, and reaffirmed at the Strasbourg conference in 1607.

1. It was decided to warn against leaving the meeting,

---

[1] Quoted from "The Discipline Adopted by the Strasbourg Conference of 1568," The *Mennonite Quarterly Review,* January 1927. This translation was made from several copies of the discipline that found their way to America. It appears that the line of descent was through Swiss Brethren who attended the 1568 conference, and then through Amish groups who migrated from Switzerland into other areas of Europe. The same Amish groups subsequently migrated to America, bringing the manuscripts with them through Somerset County, Pennsylvania; Holmes County, Ohio; and finally to Indiana and Iowa. Several copies are currently held by the Goshen College Mennonite Historical Society.

to earnestly admonish those who leave the meeting without godly causes, and not to permit it.

2. The ministers shall visit the neighboring congregations, and supply their needs, and comfort the brethren with wholesome teaching; with these shall travel ordained bishops by whom the oncoming bishops may be instructed in pastoral care.

3. The ministers and bishops shall visit, provide for, and comfort the wives and children of those ministers who travel in danger or are in prison, so that the ministers may be comforted and gladdened by the assurance of brotherly love and care, whether he be in prison or absent for other reason.

4. All those who are sent out for this purpose shall be provided and furnished with all necessities.

5. Orphans shall be remembered and taken in before other servants, and shall be disciplined as children.

6. The poor, undeveloped children and orphans of brethren and bishops shall be brought up as opportunity affords from the common property; the rich orphans, however, shall be brought up from their own property for a reasonable allowance.

7. Such bishops as are ordained shall visit the congregations, fill all offices, and where there is a vacancy, they shall ordain ministers and bishops by laying on of hands.

8. In the Communion there shall be no fixed rule observed as to whether the minister shall break and give or each one break. But each one shall be admonished so that in blameless heart and conscience and in unity with Christ there may be one bread and one manner of breaking. Yet no one shall be forced to accept another usage, and each one shall commune in the congregation in which he is.

9. The kneeling and self-humbling of those who have

sinned and return with penitent hearts shall take place in the heart before God, but the actual kneeling in posture shall not be done away with by this.

10. The avoidance[2] shall be practiced toward those who forsake the truth of the Gospel and the brotherhood, causing reproach to the Name of God and the brotherhood; therefore we desire that the brethren in all temperance and lowliness withdraw from those who have fallen away, according to the teaching of the apostles.

11. The brethren and sisters, each to each, shall greet each other with a holy kiss; those who have not been received into fellowship shall not be greeted with a kiss, but with the words, "The Lord help you."

12. Those who wish to enter the state of matrimony shall do so with the knowledge and counsel of the ministers and bishops, and it shall be undertaken in the fear of God; and since it is fitting they should inform and report to their parents.

13. If believers are persecuted and driven from their homes by unbelieving husband or wife, they shall be encouraged to continue in earnest prayer to the Lord for patience until He shall show a way out; in order to avoid this danger believers shall marry only in the Lord, and not in unbelief, whether they be maidens, youths, or widows (or widowers).

14. As regards the incarnation of Christ, one should abide by the Scriptures according as Paul testifies concerning Him, a Son of God after the Spirit, and a Son of David after the flesh, and according as Peter

---

[2] Though the Swiss and South German Anabaptists used the words *avoidance* and *ban,* they did not practice the strict avoidance advocated by some Dutch Anabaptists. Their practice of avoidance was basically limited to exclusion from Communion and church membership. See J. C. Wenger, *Glimpses of Mennonite History and Doctrine,* page 42. Not until after the Amish division in 1693 did strict avoidance come into use in Swiss Anabaptist areas, and then it was only established in the Amish churches.

confesses Him, a Son of the living God; and as far as possible all disputing should be avoided and omitted.

15. All those who wish to unite themselves with us, but have been baptized by others, shall be diligently examined, whether they have repented, and have believed on Christ, and have been baptized thereupon; such shall not be baptized again.

16. No brother shall engage in buying or building or other large, [unnecessary] business dealing without the counsel, knowledge, and consent of the brethren and bishops.

17. If one or more brethren assert themselves to cause trouble by attacking or withstanding the ministers or bishops, such an one shall be warned and censured in a Gospel manner, and such gossip and backbiting shall not be allowed to anyone, nor shall such slander be accepted by any brother or sister, whether from strangers or from home people, but such matters shall be dealt with according to the regulation.

18. Also, if a member of a congregation shall withstand the ministers and bishops, he shall be silenced and admonished privately by the bishops lest they be discouraged.

19. Those among the brethren who catch or shoot game shall be warned according to the order of the Lord, and if they are disobedient, they shall [be punished] with the ban [and] expelled, unless it is done in free territory.[3]

20. Tailors and seamstresses shall hold to the plain and simple style and shall make nothing at all for pride's sake.[4]

---

[3] This ruling was against hunting in areas where hunting was not legally permitted.

[4] There is some variation in the wording of this article in the preserved copies of the discipline. Some copies say that tailors and seamstresses shall abide by the plain and simple "custom of the land" (*Brauch des Landes*) in their clothing patterns.

Brethren and sisters shall stay by the present form of our regulation concerning apparel and make nothing for pride's sake.[5]

21. If a brother or sister has money or valuables and wishes to entrust them to someone, they shall entrust them to brethren and sisters, and not to the world.

22. If a brother or sister has debts from the world, he may let the authorities demand it, and let them set a date (for payment) but thereafter not let anything be mortgaged.

23. If a brother is to watch or guard in village, field, wood, or forest, he may hire someone, if it is for the best or he himself may guard but not to anyone's harm, and he may not carry any weapon such as spear and the like.

Another Discipline (1630)[6]

Agreement: On the 10th day of October, anno 1630, the Swiss Brethren of Switzerland were together near Hoffingen in the dark valleys and discussed, counseled, and agreed with one another to hold closer to the order

---

[5] The second paragraph of this article, regarding the regulations on clothing, is apparently a later addition and not part of the original discipline. Whether it was added by the copyist or from a later ministers' meeting is not known. Perhaps it was added as the dress patterns of the world became increasingly vain and as more clothing styles became available that were not suitable for Christians. J. C. Wenger, in *Separated Unto God,* page 81 (Scottdale, Pa.: Herald Press, 1955), states that "while the Anabaptists did not have any distinctive garb, yet it was not long until they became more or less recognizable at sight from the fact that they carried no weapons and because they shunned everything which they felt was worn to display wealth or vanity." While this was true for at least the first hundred years of Anabaptism, a more or less distinctive, regulated dress was adopted by later Anabaptists, especially for the sisters.

[6] This discipline was usually circulated with the Strasbourg discipline.

of the Gospel in the church of God according to the statement and deposition of the old brethren, to hold fast to them, and take care where something might have been neglected.

1. If a brother or sister has committed a public transgression, may God forbid, such shall be publicly punished.

2. If someone should wish to move away on account of tribulation, it shall not be allowed them without godly cause.

3. No one shall let himself be brought before the government court, or shall cause anyone else to be brought before such court on account of money debts.

4. Anyone who has been appointed, who has a good testimony, and is in the confidence of the people, such an one may take charge of Communion, baptism, marrying, punishing, and expelling, if no ordained bishop should be on hand, who might have been hindered for cause.

Selected Bibliography

Anabaptism in Outline. Edited by Walter Klaassen. Scottdale, Pa.: Herald Press, 1981.

Bender, Harold S. and Horsch, John. *Menno Simons' Life and Writings.* Scottdale, Pa.: Herald Press, 1936.

Bender, Harold S. and Smith, C. Henry. *Mennonites and Their Heritage.* Scottdale, Pa.: Herald Press, 1964.

Braght, Thieleman J. van. *Martyrs Mirror.* Translated by Joseph F. Sohm. 5th English ed. 1950. Reprint, Scottdale, Pa.: Herald Press, 1994.

Chronicle of the Hutterian Brethren, The. Translated and edited by the Hutterian Brethren. 2 vols. Rifton, N.Y.: Plough Publishing House, 1987.

Complete Writings of Menno Simons, The. Translated by Leonard Verduin. Edited by J. C. Wenger. Scottdale, Pa.: Herald Press, 1956.

Dyck, Cornelius J. *An Introduction to Mennonite History.* 3rd ed. Scottdale, Pa.: Herald Press, 1993.

Estep, William R. *The Anabaptist Story.* Rev. ed. 1963. Reprint, Grand Rapids: William B. Eerdmans Publishing Company, 1975.

Friedmann, Robert. *Mennonite Piety Through the Centuries.* Goshen, Ind.: Mennonite Historical Society, 1949.

———. *The Theology of Anabaptism.* Scottdale, Pa.: Herald Press, 1973.

Gratz, Delbert L. *Bernese Anabaptists.* Scottdale, Pa.: Herald Press, 1953.

Hartzler, J. S. and Kauffman, Daniel. *Mennonite Church History.* Scottdale, Pa.: Mennonite Book and Tract Society, 1905.

Horsch, John. *The Hutterian Brethren.* 1931. Reprint, New York: Garland Publishing, Inc., 1971.

———. *Mennonites in Europe.* Crockett, Ky.: Rod and Staff Publishers, Inc., 1995. Originally published at Scottdale, Pa.: Mennonite Publishing House, 1942.

Horst, Isaac R. *Close Ups of the Great Awakening.* Mount Forest, Ont.: Amish Publishing Service, 1985.

Hostetler, John A. *Hutterite Society.* Baltimore: The Johns Hopkins University Press, 1974.

Israel, Jonathan. *The Dutch Republic: Its Rise, Greatness, and Fall, 1477–1806.* Oxford: Clarendon Press, 1995.

Krahn, Cornelius. *Dutch Anabaptism.* Scottdale, Pa.: Herald Press, 1981.

Kuiper, B. K. *The Church in History.* Grand Rapids: Christian Schools International, 1964.

Legacy of Michael Sattler, The. Translated and edited by John H. Yoder. Scottdale, Pa.: Herald Press, 1973.

Letters of the Amish Division: A Sourcebook. Translated and edited by John D. Roth. Goshen, Ind.: Mennonite Historical Society, 1993.

Littell, Franklin Hamlin. *The Anabaptist View of the Church.* 2nd ed. 1952. Reprint, Boston: Starr King Press, 1958.

McGrath, William R. *The Mystery of Jacob Amman.* Carrollton, Ohio: A-M Publications, 1989.

Mennonite Encyclopedia, The. Edited by Harold S. Bender and C. Henry Smith. 5 vols. Scottdale, Pa.: Mennonite Publishing House, 1955–1990.

Moore, John Allen. *Anabaptist Portraits.* Scottdale, Pa.: Herald Press, 1984.

Philip, Dietrich. *Enchiridion or Hand Book of the Christian Doctrine and Religion.* Translated by A. B. Kolb. 1910. Reprint, Aylmer, Ont.: Pathway Publishing Corporation, 1978.

Ruth, John L. *Conrad Grebel, Son of Zurich.* Scottdale, Pa.: Herald Press, 1975.

Schaff, Philip. *History of the Christian Church.* 8 vols. 1910. Reprint, Grand Rapids: Eerdmans Printing Company, 1995.

Snyder, C. Arnold. *The Life and Thought of Michael Sattler.* Scottdale, Pa.: Herald Press, 1984.

Sources of Swiss Anabaptism, The. Edited by Leland Harder. Scottdale, Pa.: Herald Press, 1985.

Verduin, Leonard. *The Anatomy of a Hybrid.* 1976. Reprint, Sarasota, Fla.: The Christian Hymnary Publishers, 1992.

———. *The Reformers and Their Stepchildren.* 1964. Reprint, Sarasota, Fla.: The Christian Hymnary Publishers, 1991.

Verheyden, A. L. E. *Anabaptism in Flanders, 1530–1650.* Scottdale, Pa.: Herald Press, 1961.

Weaver, Clair R. *The Swiss Anabaptists.* Ephrata, Pa.: Eastern Mennonite Publications, 1990.

Wenger, John Christian. *Glimpses of Mennonite History and Doctrine.* 3rd ed. 1947. Reprint, Scottdale, Pa.: Herald Press, 1959.

Writings of Pilgram Marpeck, The. Translated and edited by William Klassen and Walter Klaassen. Scottdale, Pa.: Herald Press, 1978.

Index

Bold numbers indicate a map location.